Writing Your Self

Writing Your Self

Transforming personal material

Myra Schneider
and
John Killick

continuum

Continuum International Publishing Group

The Tower Building 80 Maiden Lane
11 York Road Suite 704
London SE1 7NX New York, NY 10038

www.continuumbooks.com

© Myra Schneider and John Killick 2010

Myra Schneider and John Killick have asserted their right under the
Copyright, Designs and Patents Act, 1988, to be identified as the
Authors of this work.

British Library Cataloguing-in-Publication Data
A catalogue record for this book is available from the British Library.

ISBN: 978-1-8470-6251-2 (hardback)
    978-1-8470-6252-9 (paperback)

Library of Congress Cataloging-in-Publication Data
A catalog record for this book is available from the Library of Congress.

Typeset by Newgen Imaging Systems Pvt Ltd, Chennai, India
Printed and bound in Great Britain by CPI Antony Rowe, Chippenham, Wiltshire

Contents

Notes on the authors

Myra Schneider taught severely disabled adults for many years, has been a writing tutor since 1988 and currently works for the Poetry School. She is consultant to the Second Light Network of women poets and has co-edited anthologies of work by contemporary women poets. Her first book publications were novels for children and teenagers. Since the 1980s her main writing has been poetry. She has had ten collections published and her work has appeared in many journals and anthologies.

John Killick was a teacher for thirty years before becoming a full-time writer in 1989. For ten years he ran a small press. For the last fifteen years he has worked with people with dementia, first as a writer in residence and later as a research fellow in communication at the University of Stirling. He has published and spoken widely in this field. His other poems, articles and reviews have appeared in a variety of magazines.

Both authors have long been interested in the field of personal writing and previously co-wrote the popular handbook *Writing for Self-Discovery* (Element Books 1997, now out of print).

Recent publications: Myra Schneider

Insisting on Yellow: New and Selected Poems (Enitharmon Press 2000)
Writing My Way Through Cancer (a fleshed out diary with poems and writing suggestions) (Jessica Kingsley 2003)
Multiplying the Moon (Enitharmon Press 2004)
Becoming (Second Light Publications 2007)
Circling the Core (Enitharmon Press 2008)

Recent publications: John Killick

Openings: Poems and Photographs (Hawker 2000)
Communication and the Care of People with Dementia (with Kate Allan) (Open University Press 2001)

The Arts and Dementia Care (with Anne Basting) (National Center for Creative Ageing 2003)

Over the Land: Poems and Paintings (with Alison McGill) (Fisherrow 2007)

Dementia Diary (Hawker 2008)

Myra Schneider: www.esch.dircon.co.uk
John Killick: www.johnkillick.co.uk

Acknowledgements

The authors are very grateful to the following people for their contributions which are central to this book: Linda Chase, June English, Vicki Feaver, Kate Foley, Katherine Gallagher, Miriam Hastings, Wendy Lawson, Lance Lee, Grevel Lindop, Hilary Llewellyn-Williams, John Lyons, John Mackay, Mary MacRae, Chris McCully, Pascale Petit, Maggie Sawkins, Clare Shaw, Penelope Shuttle, Matt Simpson, Duncan Tolmie, Dilys Wood.

We would like to thank Dilys Wood for all her help with the manuscript.

We are indebted to Erwin Schneider for formatting the text and for preparing the index.

Introduction

We begin with a poem by Sybil Ruth:

The Autobiography Class

He died you see,
says the lady. My son.
That's the reason I came.

There's a silk scarf tied at her throat.
She says We just stopped talking about him.
It seemed a good way to cope.

A room put to different use, repainted.

It works, she says.
She is wearing a lambswool sweater
pinned with a gold brooch.

Half-smiling she says
you start forgetting.
He began to disappear quite fast.

Black-and-white photos on a high shelf.

I may be remembering things wrong
she says slowly.
Then shrugs inside her camel hair coat.

Talk comes to a narrow place, backs away.

Her pale hair is beautifully set.
I want to write about him, she says.
But only the facts. Nothing creative.

Chairs spaced more widely round a table.

She says, I buried him.
I buried him inside me.

(from My Mother Threw Knives)

We wrote this book because of our conviction that everyone has people, events, thoughts, feelings 'buried inside' and that there are ways of bringing these to the surface so that they can be examined, shaped and perhaps offered to others. In *Writing Your Self* we explore this concept in depth with a wide variety of examples from known and unknown writers illustrating the achievements possible in this area. Our text also incorporates a number of frank and insightful accounts by writers of what personal writing means to them.

We believe that some of the most powerful literature is derived directly from experience. We have designed the book to be at the same time a resource book for personal use, and a convincing demonstration of the potency of therapeutic writing as a tool for self-development.

Part 1 examines how writers have explored a very wide range of experiences. These include broad areas: childhood, identity, adult relationships, loss, facing death and spirituality. We also cover more specific topics: displacement and disability, abuse, physical and mental illness, and caring for and coping. At every point examples are given from raw and finished writing, by well and little known authors and ourselves. Most of the in-depth contributions from individuals are in this part of the book.

Part 2 opens with chapters offering a number of different techniques with exercises and examples to help people tackle their own subject matter. This is followed by a discussion of the distinction between raw and finished work, with illustrations of both. Of course no book of this length can be comprehensive in its choice of themes, or exhaustive in its provision of techniques, but we have tried to provide as rich and balanced a diet as possible.

The book can be approached in a number of ways. One is obviously that of the order in which the material is presented. Another is by working through the exercises first and coming to the thematic chapters later. It is also a book that can be dipped into. Whichever approach is adopted, we need at the outset to say we deal at times with sensitive material, and it is also the case that those of our readers who attempt to develop their writing by making use of the practical section of the book may uncover unexpected and distressing episodes from their lives and feelings which are difficult for a person to come to terms with on their own. We would urge anyone in this situation to seek support. There is no shame in doing so when working through difficult material.

That said, we are excited by the possibilities opened up by self-discovery through writing. We believe we have found an extraordinary range of texts and approaches, and have often been moved by the honesty and insightfulness of the writers. We wish you well on your exploration of the subject-matter covered by this text, and on your own personal journeys.

Myra Schneider and John Killick

Note: where we have not referenced quoted work it is unpublished.

Part 1

Childhood and relationships with parents

It seems appropriate to begin with the place from which we all start, though that does not mean, of course, that we all begin with the same set of advantages and disadvantages. Without entering the nature vs nurture debate, it is clear that there are many 'givens' and each one of us has to come to terms with the story spelled out by our genes while we are still in the womb. That narrative is hindered or helped by the social conditions we are heir to, and this is also something which, at first at any rate, is beyond our control. As we grow, develop and mature the desire is manifested, in as many ways as possible, to take over our lives, write the book ourselves. But we can never escape our childhood influences. That is the time in life when we are most impressionable, everything seems vivid and memorable, and custom has not begun to dull our senses. We form our world-view early, and the conclusions we come to at this stage, and the attitudes formed, will inevitably colour our later experiences. In this chapter we also include relationships with parents that affect later life.

Here is a poem, 'Seeing that Woman', by Anne Cluysenaar from her book *Water to Breathe*:

Seeing that woman walk across a field,
I remembered your blue wool coat,
the warm smell of it the day you left.

Blue-coatèd, she walks diagonally, alone.
Behind her, rows of blank windows.
I don't have the feeling anyone's waiting.

The train I'm in gathers speed and something
in the light has changed, so that now I see
myself out there too, sliding along beside her.

Of course, she doesn't look up: only I
can see my ghost, so weirdly seated,
floating over the grass, but gazing away

from her towards the woman in the train.
It's comic. Except that now I'm crying,
as if I could reach out to hold the coat

and see again the double seams yours had
on the shoulder, see small hands gripping
the blue, bunching it, hear myself crying.

What we have here is an amalgam of two experiences – an observation of the present moment and the memory that it conjures up. Because of the emotional charge created, the two are almost fused: the writer hardly knows which is the present reality. This poem has the authenticity of all good personal writing, the sense that the poet is in the presence of a moment of illumination which she is trying to make clear for herself and for the reader.

Childhood is not a subject that will be kept in its box. Like a Jack it will keep springing out all over the place, so expect it to make its presence felt in other chapters too. Both of us have felt impelled to explore areas of our childhoods in writing so we begin by looking at the different ways we have gone about this, before going on to consider material by four other writers.

Me and my parents: Myra

Whenever I think of my childhood my immediate memories are happy ones of the various imaginative games I played with my sister and friends in our nursery and in the garden where we transformed the sandpit and climbing frame into boats, magic carpets, or whatever else we chose. I think of walking on the moors behind our house which was high above the town of Gourock on the Firth of Clyde. I think of making up plays which we acted, sometimes to our parents. I've recorded this sense of happiness in poems but behind the bright images are prickly uncertainties and memories of being in disgrace. I remember my adolescence as a time of constant anxiety, guilt and conflict with my parents, a time when there was often a tense atmosphere of friction between my parents, whole days when everything felt unbearable – as if a huge weight would crush me. I remember too moments of almost intolerable joy and longings which I couldn't imagine had any chance of being realized.

When I married at the age of twenty-seven my husband commented on the way my parents criticized me. We had many discussions about my childhood and I began to gain insights about the way I'd been repressed and undermined, the great stress laid on success and the demand that I should be a dutiful daughter. Until then my view of my parents was overridden by a sense of guilt and I only recognized a sense of anger from time to time. Years later, when I had already had two collections of poetry published, I felt a strong urge to write about them and how they had affected my early life. However, I knew their intentions had never been malicious, knew they intended to be, and believed they were, very good parents and I didn't want to hurt them. This made me hold back. Instead I sent a letter to a well-known poet who had written about the much more destructive behaviour of both her parents. She replied with only one suggestion that I plunged into writing at once but I didn't feel I could. In fact it was only after each of my parents died that I felt able to write about them. I realized then that one can only write about any subject when and if one feels psychologically ready.

I didn't often feel in tune with my mother's attitudes but when she talked about her childhood and her mother's life, which she enjoyed doing, I felt a closeness to her. About a year before she died something prompted me to make notes about her early life and the life of my grandmother who had died before I was born. I liked the thought of recording family history but I had a sense too that I was going to write something even more important using the material I was noting down. I told my mother I was thinking of writing about her childhood and she was pleased.

I was distressed by what I learnt about my grandmother, Leah. In her late teens she was in love with a young man but his family shipped him out of the country because she had no dowry and she had to be her invalid mother's nursemaid. At twenty-eight she married my grandfather, who was ten years younger than herself, because she saw it as her last chance. She had four children but this capable woman, an excellent pianist who often entertained family and had relatives new to England to stay, had to put up with her husband openly keeping a mistress for most of her marriage. There were years of resentment. I thought of my grandmother as 'the loser' and felt sorry for her. I was shocked, though, to learn that she never kissed or cuddled my mother when she was a child. When my mother fell in love she was warned that men used women as their lavatories. Eventually she escaped from home and being a dutiful daughter and went to live in London.

After my mother died I wanted to write about the ways in which she and her mother had been undermined partly because it related to myself, also because these were graphic examples of the treatment of women in the late nineteenth and early twentieth centuries. I read and re-read my notes trying to think how to use them. I didn't know enough to write a memoir or a novel but when I read an anthology of poem sequences it hit me that the sequence was the mode to use. Excited, I fleshed out key incidents in my grandmother's life and as I imagined her feelings it was as if I was my grandmother. When I moved on to writing about my mother, Louie, exactly the same thing happened.

I found writing this sequence, 'Mother and Daughter', which appeared in my book *Crossing Point*, illuminating. Because I had felt empathy with each woman I understood the problems which limited their relationship. My insight into my mother made me feel a new sympathy for her and I saw how her upbringing had influenced her behaviour as a mother. Writing the poems had another effect. It gave me the permission I felt I needed to write about my own feelings of being insufficiently mothered and how this had affected me. When I was adult I knew my mother had tried to redress the shortcomings of her own childhood but as a child I had no idea why she was often suddenly angry or why her favour and love were withdrawn for what seemed like a long time.

I depicted her behaviour in another sequence, 'Willows', which I wrote about two years after 'Mother and Daughter'. The willow trees in the park behind the house I live in now presented themselves as a metaphor for security. In the first section they provide a frame for a recurring childhood incident:

> I walk in the stillness beneath the twine
> of finger leaves, feel a certainty
> I couldn't find when I was a child,
> and the tea table was a white field
> stiff with woven flowers.
> Instructions thistled my head: 'Sit up . . .
> remember your manners . . . the visitors.'
>
> I remember the china petals on the jampot,
> talk spreading ease like butter,
> my hands peeling paper frills
> from a fairycake, anger flaring
> in my mother's eyes, ready
> to strike when the guests had gone.
> Had I forgotten a 'please', a 'thankyou'?
>
> The day cracked; its brightness ran.
> No way to save myself. Words
> fell. Then a fortress face.
> For hours I was chained to disgrace
> that rubbed me raw while the voice
> that lulled with song, the mouth that smiled
> stories, held back forgiveness . . .
>
> The snow-capped cakes, the words
> that cut, the white tablecloth, the wound,
> shiver into fragments, dissolve . . .
> In the green quiet I'm peering

at pale water that doubles
the dark arch of the bridge to make
a mottled egg I long to hold.

(from *Insisting on Yellow*)

The second section sketches the difficulties, fears and conflicts I experienced as a new mother, wanting to be 'all-enfolding' but unable to cope with the 'always-on-demand' needs of a baby. At one point it shows how unsupported I felt by my mother:

On the phone my mother's voice
was clipped, mine needy.
No cord between us . . .

The third section describes postnatal depression but it also suggests the beginnings of recovery. The fourth records the 'the love/I've slowly learnt to take in'. These were difficult poems to write as the feelings from my childhood were still painful but the willow trees seemed to support me and they carry some of the emotional weight of the poem.

Around the time I was working on 'Willows' I wrote other poems which recalled the bright side of my childhood but they all had references to parental anger. About three years later I was looking at a reproduction of Egon Schiele's *Mother and Daughter*. In this painting a naked daughter is embracing a mother clad in a red dress. The tenderness between the two cut through me as I thought: 'I never ever felt such closeness, such unconditional love'. I began to cry. The painting stayed with me and became the trigger for a new poem, 'Need'. I think it's significant that a painting, smell, sound, piece of music, words in an unexpected context, can lead back to profound emotional experience and offer a way of expressing it.

'Need' didn't find itself as a poem until I managed to look beyond my initial reaction to the painting and remember again the lives of my mother and grandmother. This brought me face to face with the way emotional problems are handed down the generations. Finally, I returned to the present and breaking the pattern which had been set up. I see the poem as one of reconciliation with my mother and in this sense it goes further than 'Willows'. Here is most of it:

The tenderness stops my breath
with a blade of pain that splits me
apart. In the gape is my mother's face
closed to mine, the silence
dividing us cold as glass.

And down a passage I make out
a dark-haired child – not me
but her. Blanks for eyes she shrinks
from the woman whose pecking mouth
never sweetens with kisses.

In pale outline behind
the bitter woman is a girl
whose fingers flutter music. Duty
chains her to sickroom, kitchen,
rubs salt into her feelings . . .

So it goes back, must not go on.
I sift feathers of kindness, find
illuminating words, fill myself;
mark the place in my book
with the clasped mother and daughter.

(from *Insisting on Yellow*)

My father was a brilliant scientist. The child of Jewish immigrants from Lithuania, he grew up in poverty in London and in adult life he was motivated by a strong sense of responsibility. He was emotionally childish, expected everyone to fit in with him and was often a bully. When he was in a good mood he had a great sense of humour and he could be kind, charming even. He was also imaginative. When I was small I loved his imaginary games and I looked up to him but from pubescence he seemed a huge critical presence, a frightening person who had no sympathy with my ideas and feelings. In my adult life after my marriage his hold over me lessened to some extent and I could see other sides of him. I also managed to stand up to him once or twice but the feelings I'd experienced in adolescence continued to be very strong.

About two months before my father died, at a time when his behaviour was upsetting me, I did some connected pieces of flow-writing in my notebook. I saw later that these were a new and metaphorical way for me to write about the feelings I'd experienced when I was young. Here are two extracts:

That moment when the ground, the floor, the chair, the cushion – buildings, roads, my stomach, my body lose their substance. Stones crack, roads break up; beneath me only shifting vapoury layers. My voice, my whole being carries no weight. There is nowhere safe. I am fragmented. I cannot hold onto my core and the Critical Voice is shouting: 'You ought to be able to cope. You're not a child, you are nearly an old woman.'

Terror that the huge voice outside will swallow me whole, that I will be torn into shreds of paper, dust, that I will be nothing in my own right . . . And yet if I hold tight, summon up even a smattering of courage, turn a few degrees the huge figures begin to shrink and I begin to gain weight . . . and although I am afraid I can look the panic bird in its terrible eye and although my voice trembles I answer it back and it begins to let go of its hold on my neck.

I don't know where the 'panic bird' image came from but it seems to be a symbol both of the bullying I received and the fear I felt. My confrontation of the monstrous creature is at the heart of 'The Panic Bird', a poem that draws on both pieces of flow-writing and ends with some lines from later on in the first piece in which the bird is transformed into a waterbird on a calm lake. The material went through many drafts before I saw I must discard the opening verses which were a rather bald record of therapy. In the end I turned the poem fully into a mythic form and found a rhythm to carry it:

The Panic Bird

That moment
when the mattress splits
and seeps its stuffing
when floors crack, roads
break up, ground gapes

that moment
when the breathstream
dries, the belly ceases
to exist and the self
can no longer hold on

that moment
when reason bolts
and six obsessive words
pound pound on the shell
of the emptied brain

is the moment
the wingspan spreads.
The predator descends,
traps hair, neck –
I am eclipsed.

I try to yell
for someone to put out
the rock-blue eyes,
smash the razor beak,
crush the claws.

Only a child
looms. Weightless as a leaf
she's crouched on a mountain ledge
whimpering: 'I can't bear
blood, illness, change.'

I want to
take her in my arms, struggle
to a safe place, outstare
the bird, seize it by the neck,
pull the gaudy feathers.

I want to
call out, voice belled
by fierce red joy, to alight,
toes touching waterbird
rings on lake calm.

(from *The Panic Bird/Insisting on Yellow*)

Parents die but their voices remain in their children's heads. Sometimes these voices are difficult to separate from other inner voices but I was very much aware of 'hearing' my father speaking in characteristically forcible language a few years after he died. It was at a time when I began making soup regularly for a very elderly neighbour and his wife and I had to fight against the shame 'my father' wanted me to feel. Hearing his anger, and remembering that he had often told us in his last few years to send him telegrams with news of the world after his death, were triggers for a very different poem, 'Soup and Slavery' which is in my book, *Insisting on Yellow*.

I took a liberty with the telegram idea and turned it into telephoning because the poem suggested itself as a telephone call. It was fun and enormously satisfying to write because for the first time ever I had total control of a conversation with him. I say conversation but the poem is largely a monologue delivered by me. When he raged at me for helping a stranger and failing to look after him he received a long answer which he had to listen to. When he tried to answer back I told him that in spite of the fact that I knew he could be kind I couldn't forgive him for his behaviour to my mother when she was dying. When he lost his temper I simply cut him off and then at the time of my choosing I re-connected with him to offer an appreciation of a piece of research he'd done in World War Two which helped bring the war to an end sooner. Not surprisingly the poem had an extraordinarily empowering effect.

I didn't expect to write about my father again but in 2002 I saw the 1901 census details for 87 Nelson Street in Stepney, London, the house where he was born. I discovered facts about his family I didn't know and I was shocked by the graphic evidence of the poverty he'd grown up in. The census recorded that two families, which included five children and also a lodger, all lived in a house which only had three rooms.

Soon afterwards I wrote a sequence called 'Finding My Father'. As with 'Mother and Daughter' I felt a new sympathy with him when I wrote the first two poems about his family and childhood. I was struck too by how far removed I'd always been from the experience of poverty and the third poem in the sequence is about the one example of it I saw at close quarters. This was at the beginning of the 1960s when I lived in the threadbare attic of a house whose owner resided in grandeur on the ground floor rooms while her Irish housekeeper lived with her family in squalor in the damp basement. The final poem draws on my father telling Bible stories to me and my sister when we were children. It focuses in particular on Joseph and the forgiving of his brothers. This story showed me where the poem, 'The Old Testament', wanted to go and that it was a poem of reconciliation:

> I remember that forgiveness, how its waters
> soothed, wish it was possible to take your hand,
> say I forgive you your obsessions, angers,
> your need to dominate – all your shortcomings,
> as I ask forgiveness for mine.

> (from *Multiplying the Moon*)

I've twice used another technique to write about my parents: fictionalizing. In each case this was after a small incident triggered overwhelming feelings. The mode allowed me to deal technically and emotionally with a welter of subject matter relating to my past. The first incident was triggered by seeing a charity poster on an Underground platform which said that continual criticism and silent disapproval of children were severe forms of cruelty. When I read these words I felt as if they were addressed to me, a confirmation that I had been unkindly treated. For years I'd harboured guilt that I had exaggerated the way my parents had behaved. As I re-read the words I shed tears of relief. I wanted to write about this episode but it seemed quite impossible. A few years later it occurred to me that the incident and my reaction would be very appropriate to Rebecca, a character in 'The Waving Woman', a long narrative poem I was writing. This explored some contemporary social problems and the ongoing relationships of four people. Rebecca had certain traits in common with myself and I had indicated that she'd had a repressive upbringing. Most importantly I saw the incident would make its mark in the context of the poem and not need complicated explanatory detail. I found writing about it in this mode very releasing:

. . . Rebecca leans
against brown and dirty white tiles
until a poster across the rails
arrests her:

'Constant criticism,
continual silent disapproval
are as cruel as beating a child.'

The words are written for her, spoken
to her. As if an arrow of light
had slanted through tall windows
her darkness is slit in two.

She sees her parents' stern shapes
magnified on the tunnel walls, hears
the whip in their voices, withholdings,
recognizes at last the wrongness
she's borne as long as she can remember.

Hundredweights shift, lift.
. . . and as the train rushes in
with silvers and ambers, distances open out.

(from *The Panic Bird*)

The second incident which prompted me to fictionalize was a phone conversation with my father at a time when I had already had some books published. My guard down, I was talking about my writing career when he interrupted and said: 'You are secondary'. This meant, as he made clear, that I was secondary to my husband and son. Of course I was fully aware of his attitude to the place of women as I, my mother and sister had been on the receiving end of it ever since I could remember. His remark sounded ridiculous in the mid 1980s but the words still wounded. Nearly twenty years later I wrote a long narrative poem, 'Becoming', in which the central character's experience in a completely different setting is an equivalent of mine. The poem also features other women finding or not finding themselves. It was important to me, though, that the poem wasn't a rant against men and one of the key characters, Bob, is a sympathetic person with problems of his own. I found it hard to manage the main character and her emotions because her story was such a close parallel to my own but after many drafts I felt satisfied that the poem would speak to others and it was published as a book.

In total, writing about my parents in these different ways has allowed me to release painful feelings left over from childhood and adolescence, to see them in a new perspective and, in the main, lay them to rest. The process has also helped me to perceive more clearly the nature of my childhood. It has also enabled me to understand each of my parents more fully in the context of their lives as well as mine and to feel a sense of reconciliation. Drawing on my experience to create finished poems has been affirming and a way of creating something positive from relationships which were often painful. This has been crucial to my life.

In writing about his childhood John has made more use of prose than Myra did.

An only childhood: John

The situation of the only child is a fascinating though uncomfortable theme for those who have experienced it. It perhaps provides the individual with the opportunity to feel the extreme loneliness of the human in an acute form, and the pain of adaptation to social environments which those brought up with siblings can barely understand. It conditions responses to a greater or lesser extent throughout adulthood, and it is hardly an exaggeration to say that it provides a perspective from which it is impossible ever wholly to escape.

I began writing personal poetry and prose when I was in my teens, and there has never been a period of my life when I haven't turned to it. At first I did not deal with what I call 'onlyness' specifically. It was after I suffered a minor breakdown in my early twenties that I perceived that writing had provided me with a tool for confronting my stresses directly, and that most of these stemmed from my early sense of isolation and the ways I had attempted to adapt to the social worlds of school and work.

I wrote about my parents and the unhealthily inward-turned nature of their relationship, sometimes including and sometimes excluding me. I also wrote about the environment in which we lived, a very large Victorian house set in its own grounds, and part of an upper middle-class suburb. The wooden gate seemed to symbolize for me the enclosed nature of our world; it both kept me safe, and prevented me from taking part in the universe that surrounded us:

> Over the course of time the gate rotted and began to fall apart. Instead of mending it my parents decided to await the inevitable. I was bigger and heavier by this time and was warned to treat the gate with consideration: in other words, no more climbing on it. One day it was carted away, and a gap existed where it had been, much wider, it seemed to me, than that which the gate had filled. I was horrified by this degree of exposure. I could see everything I wanted to, but there was nothing to offer me even partial protection. Dogs wandered in from the street and messed on our lawns and borders. People who stood on the corner outside seemed to spend their time peering into the garden and at the house in ways they would never have thought of before. Even when I was in another part of the grounds I felt my privacy had been invaded.

Eventually the gate was replaced, but this was by a modern cast-iron structure, hideously inappropriate, with its curlicues and crosspieces. It didn't seem to offer any real security. And what is more, when it shut, instead of a neat click there was a metallic clang. When I went in the garden now it was to mow the lawn or dig the vegetable patch. People-watching became an activity exclusively to be practised behind net-curtains.

I kept a journal around this time and this is an extract from it. But I also wrote poems, sometimes on the same subject, and these acted as pared-down versions of the prose entries.

I have continued to wrestle with these subjects throughout my life, simply because they would not go away. The image of having my face pressed to the glass of a window in the big house was just as potent as that of the gate. This is from a poem, 'The Big House', written about forty years later:

Face pressed to the glass –
so little before the eyes
so much behind the eyes –

to be held within
the confines of that room
afraid ever to leave . . . .

Once that face was mine.
Until I picked up a stone
and hurled it through the pane.

Sometimes even now
the slivers surge in reverse
and I'm back inside again.

It is difficult to exaggerate the sense of isolation that I felt as a child. I was indulged by my parents and discouraged from mixing with other children or adults. Thus the gate and the glass are powerful images for me because they were actual as well as metaphorical.

I was sent to boarding school, and this was traumatic. From being on my own most of the time I found myself thrust into an environment where others, and conforming to what was expected of me in company, made incessant demands on me. I stayed the course for six terms before running away. During those months I can remember only one brief period of happiness, and not unexpectedly it was the time when I was temporarily released from the pressures. I wrote about it in my early twenties:

Lying in the school sanatorium extension in the dark of winter, with the fire in the grate and shadows flickering on the walls, with only one companion . . . we grew close in complicity, ourselves against the universe. We talked of everything, subjects never thought about before by either of us, nor broached since; there was a freedom to articulate, a hunger to share, no fear of ridicule or offence. We played games of chance, devised and known, filled all that warm cocoon with the mind's curiosity and precocity.

Thus by circumstance and invention we wholly managed to shut out that place of prefects, servitude, inkpots, impossible expectations, masters in black gowns lunging with caustic barbs, manhood's manoeuvres in battledress, the hamper-room with its homesick cargoes . . .

There was only ourselves, and the almost graspable entities of friendship and privacy. We never wanted the nights to end, and each time dawn crept through the curtains, stretching our world into the semblance of normality, we moaned for the loss of our intimacies, our timeless time shattered by the clock-watchings of others. When breakfasts appeared on trays we fell back into our separate selves . . . and resumed our roles of being ill.

I find myself constantly revisiting childhood events and relationships as part of a process of coming to terms with who I am. It may be objected that one is just indulging oneself, wallowing in self-regard, in writing personally in this way, but I do not believe that that is the case. I never emerge without some fresh insight which assists me with that re-evaluation, that taking stock, which forms part of a growth process which lasts as long as life.

I have said that for me childhood is a subject-matter I can never exhaust. Consciously I regularly make imaginative forays into that country. But even if I did not do so my dreams would accomplish those retrospective forays for me. Sometimes these take on a nightmarish quality: particular incidents or individuals return to give me a temporary haunting. I have unfinished business with both my mother and my father. Here is part of a poem, 'Dreams of My Father', which I wrote after two particularly unsettling encounters with my father who was long dead at the time:

In this scene my father stands
holding out his empty hands.

With the impetuosity of a boy
I run towards him spilling joy.

Ignorant of my intent
he turns away indifferent.

Another time his anguished calls
echo around unfriendly walls.

I shout and shout for him to appear.
There's no reply. He cannot hear?

Or won't appear? *Or can't I see?*
O father, father, come to me!

Although the onlyness of my childhood caused me many problems there were many happy times to report, and one dream I had was particularly memorable for its unsullied nature. The image which I find so affecting in the following piece was, of course, inherent in the dream. My task in writing it down was to attempt to be as precise as possible in recording the details, so that I could look at it and evaluate its meaning:

I am walking along the riverbank in a place I used to know well. It is a hot summer's day and the river is flashing as it travels over the stones. The grass is springy to my tread.

Suddenly there they are – mother and father sitting on a rug on the grass. There is a picnic laid out on the rug. They gesture for me to join them. It is a perfect place and a perfect time – how can I refuse?

I am a small boy again. I can feel the rough surface of the rug against my knees as I crawl onto it. My mother smiles one of her all-enfolding smiles and hands me a sandwich and a cup of tea. My father is at his most relaxed – in his shirt-sleeves; for once his tie is undone. My mother is humming a song that is a favourite with her. My father indicates a dragonfly skimming the stream. Nothing disturbs us. A car passing over a bridge in the distance could be in another reality.

The meal finished, and the remains of it packed up in the picnic-basket, I lie in the middle of the rug staring up at the wisps of cloud suspended in the blue. Gently, very gently, my parents take the ends of the rug and roll me tightly in it. When I am completely enclosed they lift me off the ground and begin steadily to swing me round. Faster and faster I travel. I experience the exhilaration of flight whilst remaining protected within my warm wrapping. I am fully alive and alert in the world right down to my toes and fingertips. I am in darkness but I can clearly see through the material to everything around me.

Gradually the motion lessens and I travel closer to the ground. Eventually I make contact with the grass again. The rug unrolls and I spill out. I am elated and unhurt. I am aware that no-one is now holding the rug. When I have picked myself up even the rug has vanished. Without even a backward glance I resume my walk along the riverbank.

This dream was not a recall of an actual event or a telescoping of a number of such occasions; in fact picnics with my parents were a rarity. Rather it appears to be an idealization of all that was most loving and secure in my childhood, a significant corrective for me of the view that all was dark and distressing during that period of my life.

My childhood came to an abrupt end when I met someone who was preparing to be a psychoanalyst. He regarded me as 'fair game' and proceeded to attempt a dissection of my onlyness which left me aware but highly vulnerable. It took a year or two before I had the confidence to move on and carve out for myself a place in adult life.

Nearly fifty years later I was involved in running a writing course in Normandie, France. We paid a visit to a beach where seafood was being commercially harvested. Immediately I saw a way of writing about the whole of my childhood experience in a new way. 'In Noirmortier' was the poem that came out of it:

the baby mussel brood is born
spat is settled on ropes
hung horizontally between the poles

      I think of my parents
      both of them stitching
      a small tent of endearments
      from which the flap is closed against me

in June spat is brought ashore
and laid on wooden frames
where it remains until the spring

      school is like being shaken
      in one of those small globes
      in perpetual blizzard conditions
      trapped yet out in the cold

to stop them being swept away
lengths of mesh are wound around
the buchots to hold them in place

      I run away
      back to the big house
      its walls like a second skin
      much harder, impermeable
      holding the world at bay

eider ducks and tingle bore holes
in the shells, and seaweed snarls
the poles, hence the precautions

      comes a wellmeaning friend
      sees me there on the shelf
      like some neglected vase

takes me down and apart
but is quite unable
to put the pieces back together

after a year on the poles
they are harvested, cleared
from the nets, sold around the world

What seems to be happening here is that I unconsciously perceived a parallel between the process of mussel cultivation and my own development. By placing them side by side I could examine similarities and differences, gain a whole new perspective by juxtaposing the objective and the personal. Sometimes following an unexpected lead can result in fresh light being shed on very familiar subject-matter.

We move on to the only childhood of a writer from a very different social background. Whereas John's parents had money and property and lived the life of suburbia, James Kirkup was brought up in a poor street in the working-class town of South Shields. He was born in 1923, so his childhood encompassed those very lean years of the1930s. His father was a joiner and work was often hard to come by. Cockburn Street was, in Kirkup's own words, 'a near-slum'. Yet his parents had standards, the house was kept spotless, and the boy was treated with unfailing kindness and offered as many stimulations as a limited environment afforded.

Kirkup's two volumes of autobiography, republished together in 1996 as *A Child of the Tyne*, constitute one of the clearest and most affectionate portraits of such an upbringing that we have. They are an astonishing feat of memory: the first book, packed with circumstantial detail, only deals with the first six years of his life, and the second with the years up to his eighteenth birthday. This was an almost idyllic childhood (the downside of that period of his life referred to in the title of the second of the original volumes applies almost exclusively to his primary and secondary school experiences; these proved stultifying to a curious and imaginative child). Kirkup takes us almost systematically through a variety of enthralling areas: street-games, parks, sweets, early friendships, reading and writing among them. Throughout he adopts the descriptive mode and his descriptions are unfailingly vivid and exact. Here he is writing about a snowflake:

I would often try to follow the course of one turning, shivering, drifting flake as it fell and fell, but could never be sure if my eyes had lost it and seized on another before it reached the ground. I loved the snow's absolute quietness. It was a stillness I knew well, and that I sympathized with. I would fasten pieces of cotton-wool to long lengths of white thread and hang them inside the white lace curtains, against the window-panes, like an arrested snowstorm in the house, and then I would gaze and gaze through the artificial snowflakes at the real snowflakes falling outside, falling so densely, so silently, so steadily, that a kind of hallucination would gradually come upon me, my eyes would stare and stare until they went out of focus, and I would slowly begin to feel that the veils of snow were no longer falling: they were still, and I was rising, and the window, and the table I sat on, and the whole heavy house were rising weightlessly with me. (Kirkup 1996, pp. 99–100)

Unlike John, Kirkup is not an introspective writer about his childhood. Indeed, his strengths throughout his extensive output are those of an observer: that is why his most famous poem 'A Correct Compassion', which describes a surgeon's work, and his poems about the sights and sounds of Japan, are so effective: he does not let himself get in the way of his subjects. Nevertheless in passages such as the above the personal does leak through: the sentence 'It was a stillness I knew well, and that I sympathized with' says more than it would if it was surrounded by other insightful remarks.

Here is another revealing example:

It was natural that, a Taurean, I should really love the earth itself: I would often play with it like sand, and stretch full-length upon it, burying my face in its warm, crumbling darkness. The manure heap had a broad, jolly stink, like a wink from Nellie Wallace: it was the smell of life. What is strange is that I should also have such a strong affinity with water – not only with the sea, the ancestral element, but also with rivers, streams, springs, rainwater and common tap-water. The rain-water tubs in our backyard were to me sources of mystery and power: their dark, soot-flighted water had an elemental smell, an unforgettable mineral tang with a "snatch" of tar: their depths had often held the reflected outline of my head and thrown back a deepened, gloomy echo of my lonely talks with myself. (Ibid., p. 185)

What is so remarkable about this passage is that, while dealing with outward things, particularly sights and smells, it is also self-revealing. It is not only the phrase 'my lonely talks with myself' which lets us in under the writer's guard. It is also the case that Kirkup imagines the real with such intensity that he sometimes takes off into a creative realm, as in the sentence here about the manure heap.

This is the pattern throughout *A Child of the Tyne*: the judiciously placed personal observations have a cumulative effect, so that the reader builds up a picture of a personality, his tastes, his strengths and weaknesses, and projects them forward into the developing adult. But more than this, the almost overwhelming immediacy of person and place in the book are filtered through the sensibility of a unique individual, and the reader quite subconsciously absorbs a way of looking at the world. Paradoxically, the consistently outward-going nature of the narrative conveys a series of messages about the interior processes of the author. We appreciate his hypersensitivity, his timidity, his sensuality, his sense of propriety, his inquisitiveness. We feel we know James Kirkup just as well as if he had provided us with an interior monologue to absorb. We learn from him that it is not always necessary to wear one's heart on one's sleeve to explore one's inner self.

New-Zealand writer, Janet Frame, partly owes her fame to her three volumes of autobiography. Unlike John and James Kirkup she was one of a large close-knit family. In *To the Is-Land* she re-creates a childhood in which language, poetry and 'the world' were important to her from a very early age: '. . . the world being My Place by the fallen birch log, with the grass, the insects in the grass, the sky, the sheep and cows and rabbits, the wax-eyes and the hawks – everything Outside' (Frame 1987, p. 18). She had three sisters and a brother who was an epileptic. Her father had uncompromising ideas, worked on the railways and was often hard on his children although he clearly cared about them. Everything was held together by an endlessly loving mother who coped uncomplainingly with poverty, tried for years to find a cure for her son's illness, wrote poetry and passed on to her children her enthusiasm for life.

When Frame was very small her father's work led to several moves but eventually the family ended up at Oamaru. In this small town, in spite of their straitened circumstances she records:

> I was now vividly aware of myself as a person on earth, feeling a kinship with other creatures and full of joy at the sights and sounds about me and drunk with the anticipation of play, where playing seemed endless, on and on after school until dark, when even then there were games to play in bed – physical games like 'trolley works' and 'fitting in,' where each body curled into the other and all turned on command, or guessing games or imagining games, interpreting the masses of shape and colour in the bedroom curtains, or codes, hiding messages in the brass bed knobs. There were arguments and fights and plans for the future and impossible dreams of fame as dancers, violinists, pianists, artists. (Ibid., p. 41)

This passage summons up a childhood in which closeness with siblings diminishes the world of other people. The five children were united in their resentment of their maternal grandmother who they'd been told was a special mother but when she came on a visit she kept finding fault with both her daughter and grandchildren. Once she'd gone home Frame realized that the special mother was their own: '. . . who was soft and went on about nature and God but who would never be cruel to anything or anyone' (ibid., p. 73). The strength of the family and Frame's growing love of books carried her through the tragic time when the eldest sister, who had a serious heart condition, died in a swimming pool. Poetry became even more important to her during adolescence when lack of money and her own awkwardness made her acutely aware that she was different. This is how she reacted to her teacher's reading of 'The Ancient Mariner':

> I listened, only half-understanding, to the story of the grim journey; and all else vanishing, I, too, was alone on the sea, living the living death, feeling the nearness of a seascape that was part of Oamaru . . .
>
> I did not comprehend the curse and the blessing of the mariner, only the journey and the suffering, and when in the last stanza Miss Gibson adopted her familiar preaching tone to read, 'He prayeth best who loveth best,' I resented her intrusion and the intrusion of the land and the landscape and the reduction of the mariner, seen through land-focusing eyes, from a man of mysterious grandeur even in guilt to a 'greybeard loon'. (Ibid., p. 127)

This first volume of autobiography is graphic, intimate, poetic and humorous as Frame records her childhood and then her searches as a teenager for ways to express herself imaginatively and become adult. This memorable book carries the sense of a profound need to write about the evolving self.

Colin Rowbotham was a poet who died in 2000 but whose work is unaccountably little known. He was deeply committed to honesty of expression, and probably relates to the 'confessional' school of poets rather than any other. Much of his work consists of a coming-to-terms with pain and loss. His dedication to the craft of writing, and his consequent mastery of forms, means that his moods and observations are articulated with precision. 'The Christening Gifts', in his collection, *Lost Connections*, is a poem which illustrates these characteristics well:

> Who'll give him the smile?
> I, said the Grandad.
> To wise eyes and easy mouth
> I'll add a glad hand
> that seems without guile.

Mine the will to endure
and the way to hurt, stated
the Grandmother. Sure-
cutting tongue, iron spine
are all mine.

My touch like the sun
on his shoulders, a mesh
to hold others
when older
said Mother.

The tunnels of mind,
muttered Father,
my patience
and anger to light them, the rhythm
of words to delight him.

I'll be the peg, cried self: a
small but constant something else
beneath these cloaks you hang on me,
I'll take
the strain until I break.

This is a remarkable balance-sheet of a poem: by allocating a verse to each of his relatives and totting up the sum of characteristics in the last he imparts a structure to what might otherwise have been a vague catalogue of traits. He is also echoing a childhood nursery rhyme form but giving it a contemporary feel. At the same time he brings an adult's understanding to bear on a childhood situation. Another poem in the same book, 'Flowers and Thorns', is told from a child's point of view with affecting simplicity:

When Dad and Mother went away
to talk out whether they should stay
together, friends took John and me
off somewhere for the day.

Was it the summer of the year
that I turned ten? A Saturday
or Sunday? Strange that details blur
when feelings stay so clear.

Beneath the hot blue day: a heath
yellow with gorse. Between us both:
untold anxiety – instead
we played at hide-and-seek

all afternoon. I learned that gorse
is good to hide inside; the thorns
won't hurt if they're ignored. Of course,
I won the game. I knew

(as kids do) that to win would save
the day somehow. My parents stayed
together. Gain and loss were too
entangled to undo.

Here the rhymes impart a kind of sing-song quality to the verse which belies the serious emotional content. The image of the gorse and the concluding sentence have a devastating authenticity which universalizes the experience.

We end this chapter by looking at *I Know Why the Caged Bird Sings*. In this first volume of autobiography Maya Angelou, singer, dancer, civil rights activist and writer, brings alive her complex childhood. She was born in St. Louis, Missouri in 1928 but her parents' marriage broke up when she was three and she and her brother, Bailey, were sent off by train with tags on their wrists that stated their names, the name of their grandmother, Mrs. Annie Henderson, and their destination, Stamps, Arkansas. Their tickets were pinned inside Bailey's coat.

Annie Henderson, whom the children were soon calling Momma, took the role of mother in Angelou's childhood. She was a dominant personality in her community. In Stamps, as elsewhere in the South, the black population lived totally separate lives in their own areas of town and almost all of them were poor but Momma was a determined and ingenious woman who opened a store. During the depression in the 1930s she worked out a method which helped negroes and also kept the store going. How Momma ran the store, her strict standards, her determination and the huge strength she found in the church and religion, feature in the early chapters of *I Know Why the Caged Bird Sings*. And it is striking that Angelou, in the process of writing about herself, fleshes out the life of a whole community. Some of the incidents read like short stories.

An early episode shows the emotional influence Momma had on her granddaughter and the stability she offered. Sometimes a troop of girls from poor white families, 'powhitetrash', visited the store. They showed Momma no respect and on one particular occasion they began aping her as they came into the yard. What ensued is seen through the child's eyes as a terrible drama. She felt the girls were a huge threat and saw their behaviour as an appalling insult to her grandmother. Aware Maya was very upset Momma told her to go inside but she herself stayed outside and, apparently calm and unmoved, began singing a hymn. Furious and frightened, Maya watched from inside as the taunts increased and went on and on. But the singing continued and eventually the girls gave up and called out goodbyes to Annie. It was rude not to address her by full name but each was quietly answered. This is what happened after they had gone:

> She stood another whole song through and then opened the screen door to look down on me crying in rage. She looked until I looked up. Her face was a brown moon that shone on me. She was beautiful. Something had happened out there, which I couldn't completely understand, but I could see that she was happy. Then she bent down and touched me as mothers of the church 'lay hands on the sick and afflicted' and I quieted.
>
> 'Go wash your face, Sister.' And she went behind the candy counter and hummed, 'Glory, Glory, hallelujah, when I lay my burden down.'
>
> I threw the well water on my face and used the weekday handkerchief to blow my nose. Whatever the contest had been out front, I knew Momma had won.
>
> I took the rake back to the front yard. The smudged footprints were easy to erase. I worked for a long time on my new design . . . When I came back in the Store, I took Momma's hand and we both walked outside to look at the pattern.
>
> It was a large heart with lots of hearts growing smaller inside, and piercing from the outside rim in the smallest heart was an arrow. Momma said, 'Sister, that's right pretty.' Then she turned back to the Store and resumed, 'Glory, glory, Hallelujah, when I lay my burden down.' (Angelou 1984, p. 32)

There are other stories which are funny, ironic or angry and many of them, like the one just described, involve the position of black people. Indeed, in her adult voice, Angelou comments about the way black people are treated throughout the book.

When the children were eight and nine they went to live in St. Louis with their beautiful and loving mother, whom they had mythologized. They found the environment strange and often uncomfortable. The narrative about the months here is an amazing mixture of the characterization of Angelou's powerful maternal Grandmother Baxter, impressions of life in the city including its glamorous nightlife and life at home with her mother's lover, Freeman, who seduced and later raped the little girl. The rape led to a court case and the children being sent back to Momma. Emotionally damaged and confused about herself and her sexuality, Angelou hardly spoke for the next few years but the security of living with Momma helped her to return to ordinary life.

Regaining her confidence, her happiness in life at school, finding herself sexually, are central themes in the second half of this book.

The other all-important and supportive relationship in Angelou's childhood was that of her brother, Bailey. At the beginning of the autobiography she describes him as 'the greatest person in my world' (Angelou 1984, p. 21). He seemed to her perfect in every way and he always stood up for her. When Freeman raped her he made terrible threats about what would happen if she told. In the end though she did confide in her brother and during the years Angelou was more or less mute she spoke to him.

The need to express her adult reactions is a driving force behind this autobiography and the way Angelou moves from immersion in her childhood to adult comment without interrupting the flow is a remarkable achievement.

2 Identity

How we form, maintain and develop a sense of self is one of the most complex and mysterious aspects of the human personality. Personal uniqueness is especially prized in Western nations, and a highly developed sense of identity is judged one of the signs of maturity. It is affected by a wide range of factors, including age, gender, ethnicity, sexuality, social class, health status and appearance. In a sense, self can be regarded as a multi-layered phenomenon, and exploring it can be one of the most rewarding (and sometimes risky) challenges a writer can set him or herself. Just as the proliferation of self can be lifelong, so can the process of identification and evaluation. The poet Matt Simpson has described for us what this aspect of personal writing means to him:

> Hindsight allows me to understand that in a sense I am writing to find out what selves I can lay claim to. A consequence of this is that most of my poems have a habit of feeding into one another – they create imaginative links with each other and imply an ongoing between-the-lines narrative. What I realise I'm doing is piecing together the story of myself in the way James Joyce in *A Portrait of the Artist as a Young Man* found his vocation and therefore himself by patterning significant memories.
>
> When I say 'the story of myself' I mean exploring what it means to be part of a network of relationships, how one relates to a particular place or places and to the history of those places, its language and culture. In my case the place is Liverpool and my history involves seafaring, something brought into relief by the fact that I never followed family footsteps but ended up teaching. In other words, I'm trying to fill out a context in which to see myself – ideally and, in the words of Joyce, 'as wholly as I can'. I am content when I have produced something that is honest, truthful and that also, hopefully, energises the language.

We shall be examining how Matt Simpson achieves this in Chapter 3. Here, we begin with childhood, and the recognition of the self as separate, and this forms a link with the previous chapter. We then move onto ancestry and race, and in one of the pieces we discuss we look at the profound effects of poverty. Religion is identified as a significant factor for many, as are gender, sexuality and an overriding passion or interest. We also deal with self-knowledge – the coming to terms with and systematic exploration of the self. We end with an example of the possible transcending of the individual consciousness.

The discovery in childhood that one is a separate being, that one exists independently of parents or anyone else can be a potent experience. Poet Lance Lee begins his book, *Becoming Human*, with its title poem. In it a dream allows him to re-create this recognition from a moment when he was two years old, a moment which melts into his adult experience:

> The dog's tail pounds the crib's bars,
> black and ominous, waking me—
> or the moans do from the nearby bed
> where my parents couple. Slowly
> my eyes move up the wall,
> but where the ceiling should enfold,
> star beyond star pulls me deeply
> into the night. Fear swells,
> and my heart throbs – I gulp the
> breathless vacuum, and thrash –
> then wake, swallowing
> great gulfs of air like milk.
> Slowly night spins down
> and topples over. . . I see the terror
> that fills my heart so suddenly, so often,
> is just the memory dreamed here
> of how I learned I was alone
> and became human. That terror lies
> at the root, nutriment and gnawing tooth:
> it is the life I must not wake from, now.

Lee has commented that the poem begins:

> as a dream of identity recalling an age when there are no sure memories. I am two, in my parents room, 'remembering' when in fact all we have for that root time is metaphor to link known and unknown. The image of waking, of my eyes scanning up the wall and seeing the brilliant but largely empty universe resonates with what I think made me, *me*. Even if this recall of my parents' love moans and

my awakening and awareness of being alone is a memory of what cannot be remembered, that realization of isolation rings true and is central. The parental love-making was not the interest but itself the wall cutting me off from those nearest. Perceiving oneself as a separate being is frightening. The poem drives past the dream to a present perception of my essential reality. Being human means to be an individual, however linked to others, isolated in his own consciousness: fear and separation and self-consciousness are our condition. There are no enfolding arms to keep us from our individual journeys.

Elizabeth Bishop wrote in prose and poetry about the moment, just before her seventh birthday, when she was struck by her awareness of her self as a separate entity. She ends her short memoir of childhood, 'The Country Mouse', which is in her *Collected Prose*, with a description of going to the dentist with her aunt Jenny and being left in the waiting room with a copy of the *National Geographic Magazine*. This is what happened when she looked round the room at the people and a big yellow lamp and then back at the magazine:

A feeling of absolute and utter desolation came over me. I felt . . . *myself*. In a few days it would be my seventh birthday. I felt I, I, I, and looked at the three strangers in panic. I was *one* of them too, inside my scabby body and wheezing lungs. 'You're in for it now,' something said. How had I got tricked into such a false position? . . . The awful sensation passed, then it came back again. 'You are you,' something said. 'How strange you are, inside looking out. You are not Beppo, or the chestnut tree, or Emma, you are *you* and you are going to be *you* forever.' It was like coasting downhill, this thought, only much worse, and it quickly smashed into a tree. *Why* was I a human being? (Bishop 1994, pp. 32–3)

Bishop's precise recall of a seven-year-old's thoughts makes this feel like a diary entry. The shock is expressed in staccato sentences, questions and the striking image of the thought smashing into the tree. It is the same sense of shock and fear which Lee expresses, the same dislocation and feeling of 'utter desolation'. Lee also uses broken up sentences in the first two-thirds of his poem and this, combined with his use of the present tense, creates a sense of immediacy.

Bishop's extraordinary poem, 'In the Waiting Room', is her other account of this moment of self-recognition. It is differently focused from the prose memoir and more sophisticated. She begins by setting the scene and then builds up her sense of dislocation and fear by describing the frightening photographs in the *National Geographic Magazine* of naked black women with wire wound round and round their necks as if they were the necks of light bulbs. The moment of recognition is dramatic – at the point when her aunt (whose name has been changed to Consuelo) cries out in pain in the next room. The poem ends with an image of sliding under black waves before it shifts back to the reality of the room, the War being on, the cold outside and that the date is February 1918. The telling of these apparently simple details is poignant and powerful. They both anchor the writer and underline how total her disorientation has been.

∙∙

We return to Lance Lee for consideration of the next aspect of identity – that of the origin of the individual in the family. He shows that his own ancestry was mixed, but claims, perhaps more controversially, that we all have more than one identity:

Ancestral roots: Lance Lee

German, English, Welsh, Polish/Lithuanian, and Russian war in my roots – sometimes I explain my moods to my family as a genetic inheritance from traditional enemies . . . Being an American brings a Whitmanesque perception to bear, a feeling of being someone who encapsulates a long line of forbears in something new and unique. This is both a virtue that makes everything seem possible, and a vice that leads to a sense of being free of history. Just how a long line of ancestors leads to anyone's very particular shaping is not well understood beyond a generation or two but that shaping rides on the iron rails of the genetic inheritance of character as well as on family conditioning. I have always had an atypical sense of history, in part because of the deep divisions in my family, and the peculiarity of never bearing my father's name, Levy, or sharing his religion, Judaism. History has been an anchor for my constant probing of self. Here is the opening of 'Bats':

> I have been troubled by bad dreams,
> so when twilight floods out of things
> into darkness, and my face appears
> in the window when I turn on the light,
> I study its broad, high cheekbones
> that make the flesh photograph heavier
> than it is, the straight Gentile nose,
> brown eyes that stare straight out, head
> held high: brown hair the sun burns blonde
> from the Celt and German in my blood;
> the familiar, ironic twist of lips.

> Not much suggests the ghettos of Kiev
> or Polish Vilna my father's fathers left,
> or why any from those left behind
> should crowd into my dreams
> with my face, my pipe, book, beercan,
> wallet photos, loose change in their hands
> from the mass graves and lime
> they must have gone into, holding air . . .
> Their history is divorced from mine.
> They never came here. They are divorced
> by my father's family's rush
> from Gumbinski to Levy, now Lee,
> divorced once my father let my mother
> raise me Anglican, not Jewish.

(from *Becoming Human*)

My father quietly maintained his Jewishness in our Anglican midst, the Hebrew prayers for the dead on his bureau when his father died. Late in life almost all his friends and connections were Jewish as he left behind the life of assimilation he chose with my mother. But I identify with her side of the family, although my creative roots are more obviously on his. Her side has a mythologic underpinning of a larger than life, lost maternal grandfather, Daddy Wilds, who would have made everything right if he had only lived longer, the head of a family of WASPs, sure of themselves and their primacy in the world. Yet I imagine in '*Bats*' a newer version of the Hebrew prayers for the dead:

> . . . Remember
>
> those who were lovely in their lives
> whether they were killed, slain, slaughtered
> burned, drowned, or strangled:
> ask for their names in your blood:
> 'blood remembers' I say, now,
> though words never saved anyone,
> though I cannot imagine being led out
> to a hot dissolving dark . . .
>
> and in a dream:
>
> I look in the mirror – I am twenty
> years older than I thought. I stand up,
> stretch my legs, strange from the coma
> that held me. I walk down a street

and push a Jew into the gutter:
he bobs, he cringes, he snaps one look
at my well-dressed pitiless shape —.

This is a way of imagining the price paid by disconnecting from my father's side of the family, of rejecting his inheritance, of adopting my mother's maiden name, Wilds, as my middle name: Lance Wilds Lee, wild poet, self-created, fatherless, my own father, runs a stream of fantasy. In the dream my renunciation takes a dark turn: I become an oppressor. That too is metaphor, a way to express the dark turn taken within the recesses of the psyche by someone who walks my path, alienating a key part of himself, an act for which the poem by simply *being* constitutes an exorcism, a healing, if with no easy ending:

We always think we'll do the right thing.
Outside bats hunt down the helpless
with their sharp, black wefts of song.
I slide downwind with them, violent and small.

We instinctively think of ourselves as good, prepared to do the right thing, but it is people like ourselves who throughout history have done terrible things to one another, never realizing we had such a capacity until we acted. Even then, for the most part, we think we are in the right, but in my experience, moving between different possible identifications, it is possible to see that belief for the illusion it is, and to see some of the inner twisting that lets such acts be part of our capacity. Identity proves to be a prism; in the right light, a full spectrum of behaviors emerges for the same 'I'.

Religion was a strong factor in Lance Lee's ancestry and upbringing. So it was in Patricia McFarland's. In the following piece she expresses well the bewilderment of a child being brought up in Northern Ireland in a community divided along sectarian lines:

Beyond the Pale

I was seven when I found out what a Huguenot was. I was sitting on a mossy bank looking down into the Pig's Hollow. There the oaks spread their branches over a carpet of bluebell and wild garlic. Beneath the flowers, down in the damp earth, below the sinewy roots and thread-like veins lay the bones of the Huguenots.

I knew the story, how they had escaped from Catholic France and landed on our beach. I knew how they had been herded into the hollow and horribly butchered, all of them, even the babies, and I knew that on a dark night, when the wind blew in from the sea, you could still hear the sound of the French women weeping and see them searching for the souls of their little ones, but I did not know what a Huguenot was. Mary Redmond told me.

'Don't worry', she said. 'We don't do that to Irish Protestants, my Dad says you will just roast alive in Hell.' It was then the black dreams came and they have never quite left me.

I was born into a land of weeping women, of long Catholic candles and mortal sins, but we were not part of it. We had our own God and we prayed to him in cold, silent churches with brass plaques commemorating those that had fallen in Sebastopol. I knew what our Christ looked like; there was a picture of him over the piano in Sunday School. He stood there, under the text, 'Suffer Little Children', in his white flowing robes surrounded by blonde, blue-eyed children holding buttercups, cowslips and forget-me-nots. It was a far cry from the suffering, pain and purgatory of Catholic Ireland.

I cannot forget their Christ. He was thin, white, and naked and nailed to the Cross. I can still see the gaping holes where the nails ripped the skin. On His head this Christ had a Crown of Thorns like three rows of barbed wire. I cannot remember His face for it is His heart that I see in my dreams. Their Christ had an external heart, a heavy, crimson piece of raw flesh ripped open with deep gouges. From these scars blood spurted, deep red sacrificial blood, falling on that pale translucent body. It was a pagan, deeply religious bloodletting, horrifying, but strangely beautiful and although it was alien, I felt its power.

It was a long time before I realised it was the same God. Then I grew up and left the land of the concrete Madonnas, the Holy Pictures and the bleeding hearts but I can not forget it. It is there, in the dark towers of my childhood among the fears and the suspicions and the Huguenot bones. Once, when I stood looking down on one of the great rivers of Africa, heavy and swollen with red dust, I heard, from a tin hut, a bell ring the Angelus and then an Irish voice leading the Latin Mass. The dark towers crumbled and fell at my feet and there, in the heart of Africa, I heard the sound of the French women weeping and smelt the wild garlic.

But religion does not exist in a vacuum. It is often impossible to separate its demands from other needs such as sexuality and pressures like class solidarity. Jeanette Winterson's first novel, *Oranges are Not the Only Fruit*, is a heady mix of religion, sex and social mores, and for that reason difficult to talk about purely in a spiritual context. Nevertheless we feel the book should be featured here because it describes in sympathetic terms a growing child's exposure to a fundamentalist form of Christianity and wholehearted embracing of a world of proselytizing. Yet it does so also with the benefit of hindsight and with full awareness of the comedic possibilities of the process. This is made all the more ironical by knowledge of the lesbian tendencies which the heroine will display. Here is an example:

> 'Now for the sermon' shouted Pastor Finch, and we all settled back to enjoy our-
> selves. He told us about the doings of his tour, how many souls had been saved,
> how many good souls, oppressed by the demon, had found peace once again.
>
> 'I'm not one to boast', he reminded us, 'but the Lord has given me a mighty
> gift.' We murmured our agreement. Then we were shocked as he described the
> epidemic of demons, even now spreading through the north west. Lancashire
> and Cheshire had been particularly blighted; only the day before he had cleansed
> a whole family in Cheadle Hulme.
>
> 'Ridden they were.' His eyes roamed the hushed congregation. 'Yes, ridden,
> and do you know why?' He took a step back. We didn't make a sound. 'Unnatural
> Passions.' (Winterson 2001, p. 83)

One of the most liberating ways in which one might come to terms with major experiences and aspects of one's life which have a dominant influence on one's moral outlook such as religious belief is to laugh at them. That way one can sometimes attain a perspective which is otherwise difficult to come by. Large expanses of Winterson's book are couched in this vein. And yet it is a strength of the narrative that it can also modulate into serious reflection. These words occur as part of a summation passage on one of the novel's last pages:

> I miss God. I miss the company of someone utterly loyal. I still don't think of God
> as my betrayer. The servants of God, yes, but servants by their very nature betray.
> I miss God who was my friend. I don't even know if God exists, but I do know that
> if God is your emotional role model, very few human relationships will match up
> to it. (Ibid., pp. 164–5)

We now move on to look at religious belief in a mature personality. R.S. Thomas is a particularly interesting writer for us to consider in this context because, although he was a clergyman and a prolific poet, he cannot be called a religious poet in a conventional sense. There are poems of his in which faith is proclaimed in a convincing manner, such as 'In a Country Church', (*Collected Poems*) but more often, where God's presence is a given, he is beseeched for a reassurance that his values are ones to which the supplicant can give assent.

As he grew older, Thomas's message to the reader becomes bleaker. Sometimes his belief completely deserts him. At others hints are vouchsafed but they are insufficient to found a faith upon. Perhaps Thomas's finest poem of longing for a sign is 'The Absence'; here it is complete:

> It is this great absence
> that is like a presence, that compels
> me to address it without hope
> of a reply. It is a room I enter
>
> from which someone has just
> gone, the vestibule for the arrival
> of one who has not yet come.
> I modernise the anachronism
>
> of my language, but he is no more here
> than before. Genes and molecules
> have no more power to call
> him up than the incense of Hebrews
>
> at their altars. My equations fail
> as my words do. What resource have I
> other than the emptiness without him of my whole
> being, a vacuum he may not abhor?

(from *Collected Poems*)

This short poem says so much in so little. The whole of science and mathematics are dismissed, as well as traditional religious sources. The poet's longing is conveyed by the powerful images with which it begins and ends, the first so touchingly domestic, the second so interior. The context widens out in the middle of the poem and then contracts again. The intensity of his lack is such that he almost succeeds in turning a negative into a positive. The directness of Thomas's language is an object-lesson in plain speaking. Even when he is self-communing the reader feels immediately drawn into empathizing with his predicament, even into dialogue with him. His honesty is unflinching.

Thomas is not a poet one would go to for variety of tone or technical innovation, but he is deeply interested in ideas and following where trains of thought may take him. He is one of those writers who can be relied upon to provoke us into exploring our own responses to faith issues, and to asking some of the most profound questions we can put to ourselves. In this sense he is an exemplar for anyone wanting to explore their own faith issues through writing. Of one thing he constantly reminds us: that how we respond at this level of enquiry constitutes an essential element of any consideration of our identity as persons.

Race and poverty also exercise crucial influences on the development of the self. Maya Angelou's *I Know Why the Caged Bird Sings*, which we wrote about in Chapter 1, shows in graphic detail what it felt like to grow up in a segregated society. We look now at a remarkable book brought out by a community publisher as part of a series called *People's History of Yorkshire*. This is *To Live it is to Know it* by Alfred Williams. Ray Brown is credited as co-author because Williams was only semi-literate and could not have completed it without help from his neighbour, a professional writer.

The book is a first-person account of Williams's childhood in Jamaica, his early work experiences there, and his subsequent emigration to England, and attempts to make a life for himself in the mother country. It is a no-holds-barred account of grinding poverty, exploitation and prejudice, and as such is a significant social and human document. Here is Williams describing work conditions in his part of the West Indies in the 1930s:

> Imagine, you out of work and you hear canepiece might take on a man. And you go and there is a line of men crushed maybe over a hundred yard and broad as a road. You keep on going and you keep on hoping that you might reach the front. Slowly you advance, the land is dry, no rain, the machine is running; they take fifty men. Now molasses start to flow from machine; take on a hundred. The machine get lively we hear, and they take on a hundred and fifty! Then come day when you go and hear your name call out. Oh, you are the one. It like somebody call you a goldmine! When they call you, they inspect you, the only thing left was to search mouth for your age on your teeth . . . semi-slavery. 'You come here! And you, come here!' This is red face who going to pick if you work or not. When I find myself in the batch of the selected one, I start to snap my finger, and my heart feel like a piece of paper screwed up tight and the screw of the paper start to open. (Williams 1987, p. 14–15)

A great strength of this text is the way the prose remains that of the speaking voice. You do not for a moment doubt the authenticity of the account you are reading. There is a great temptation in transcribing a text to tidy it up in accordance with the demands of polite or orthodox English. This has been resisted. Consequently the language retains its liveliness, and it is not without subtlety: the extended metaphor of the scrap of paper, for instance. And here is Williams encountering prejudice in the North of England a decade or so later:

> Man come to Leeds from Ashton under Lyne, say there is plenty of work there, good work. So I get myself to Ashton, and I get this work in the factory. But can I get somewhere to live? No, I cannot. It seem I the wrong colour for Ashton!

> I tell you, I walk up every house door in that town, half the time they look through window and see it a coloured and don't even answer when I did knock. And them that answer, they say 'Sorry we have no room for you today.' And I *know* they have room. They have no room for *me* because I am coloured. I am black.
>
> The day goes by and I walking and walking, knock this door, knock that door, walking, walking. I near wear out my boots. Every time I am turned away I feel a little bit smaller. In the end I no bigger than an insect . . . and I'm still knocking on them doors. But there was no room even for an insect because he was black. (Ibid., pp. 39–40)

Again we have a figure of speech, the insect this time, which is just as effective as the scrap of paper. It is important that we have such accounts to give us insights into how those lacking education or opportunity manage to survive, and that they put out into the world their views of how the world is organized as a contribution to the debate. Their identities have been formed in the crucible of hardship, and there is a sense in which they have been denied the choice to develop in different ways, to be other than who they are. But that can be a strength rather than a weakness: the urge to communicate in Alfred Williams is so strong that he easily overcomes any lack of sophistication.

. . . .

Male and female roles, whether the result of biology or cultural models, exercise pressures upon us all. Here is the poet Vicki Feaver outlining their profound influence upon her as a child and a woman:

War baby: Vicki Feaver

'If anything happens to me, promise you'll look after mother' Uncle Jack said when he got called up in 1942. In fact Grandma left the pub she ran in Wigan and came to live with my parents in Nottingham while he was still sending cheerful letters from India. He was still alive when I was born, on the 14 November 1943, commiserating with my mother that I wasn't a boy. Then, about six months later, an official letter came from Burma to say that he'd been wounded. Although my father wrote letter after letter to the authorities, it wasn't until much later that they discovered that the hospital to which he had been sent was overrun by the Japanese.

I don't consciously remember the war: the blackout or victory celebrations. But babies are not oblivious to feelings. The grief in the house, the helplessness and guilt of my father (he'd been rejected for military service because of his poor eye-sight) cast a huge shadow over my childhood. Later Grandma showed me photos of Jack: one of them 'in a striped Rugby shirt holding a silver cup'. He was held up for me as a hero, as opposed to my father: 'gentle, nervous, "not a man"' as I wrote in my poem 'Hemingway's Hat'. I resented him: felt jealous of all the space he took up. I wished his boxing gloves weren't kept in the cupboard in my bedroom. I hated Remembrance Day when the curtains were closed and my mother and grandmother sat in the dark crying. There was also a sense in which I felt I should be him, describing in the same poem how my mother:

> . . . wanted a son to replace her brother
> lost in the last months of the war in Burma.
> I tried – when I started to bleed,
> getting my hair cut short as a boy's.
>
> Then . . . I changed myself
> into a girl – stilettos, stiff
> nylon petticoats, a perm.

(from The Book of Blood)

The grief in the house is described in another poem, a kind of autobiography of my growing up, 'Girl in Red':

> I was born to a mother in mourning.
>
> The mood in our house was black
> as soft tar at the edges of pavements
> I stirred with a stick.
>
> Red was my favourite colour:
> scarlet, vermilion, ruby.
>
> At school, I painted a red girl in a red wood.
>
> 'Trees are green,' the teacher said.
> So I painted them green,
> and she said, 'Red and green clash.'
>
> But I wanted them to clash.
> I wanted cymbals, trumpets,
> all the noises of rowdy colour
> to drown the silence of black.
>
> I got my mother to make me a scarlet dress.
> (I didn't care that Grandma said
> it made me look like a tart).

I stole a lipstick –
the sizzling vermilion
that made boys and old men look.

I squeezed into ruby high heels
that on hot days filled with blood.

I drank tumblers of pink gin
and told my sister (sent to spy on me)
it was Cherryade.

I dreamed in red: scarlet, vermilion, ruby.

And now I dream in black.

(from *The Book of Blood*)

Of course the first line is a half-lie. The mourning didn't begin until six months after I was born. But the line came into my head one morning and I couldn't let it go. It seemed to explain the war in my head: the war between the ecstatic, exuberant, colour-loving child who was always being put down – told to be quiet, that she was a show-off – and the child who was so miserable and fearful that she wished not to have to get out of bed.

My sister and I were always dressed in identical clothes, in the drab grey or pastel colours of the Forties and early Fifties. So the first dress I chose for myself – with an 'A'-line pattern and brilliant poppy-red material – was enormously significant for me. It shrank at the first wash (as if my misery wasn't enough I was blamed for choosing such unsuitable material!) and the dress in the poem is a later scarlet strapless dance dress.

There was another war: the war between my mother and her mother. United in grief they very soon began to hate each other. It must have been a battle for dominance in the house. It was also a battle for me. When I was six weeks old my mother went back to teaching full-time and Grandma looked after me. I became her child. Two years and three months later my mother had her own child. She stopped teaching and breast fed my sister. When the rows in the house started my loyalty was torn between mother and grandmother. I went between them, trying to make peace. My sister was always loyal to mother.

At every turn I angered and disappointed my mother: not siding with her against my grandmother, not doing as well as my friend Patricia in Grade II Piano, not getting a scholarship to the High School, starting my periods at eleven. She had been sixteen. I was a freak: a daughter to be ashamed of. And all the time, the rows between my mother and grandmother were growing worse. I was genuinely afraid that there would be violence in the house, as I describe in my poem 'Woman's Blood':

> Burn the soiled ones in the boiler,
> my mother told me, showing me how to hook
> the loops of gauze-covered wadding pads
> onto an elastic belt, remembering
> how my grandmother had given her
> strips of rag she'd had to wash out
> every month for herself: the grandmother
> who had her chair by the boiler,
> who I loved but was plotting to murder
> before she murdered my mother, or my mother –
> shaking, sobbing, hurling plates and cups,
> screaming she wished she'd never been born,
> screeching 'Devil!' and 'Witch!' –
> murdered her. I piled up the pads
> until the smell satisfied me
> it was the smell of a corpse.
> 'How could you do such a thing?'
> my mother asked, finding them
> at the bottom of the wardrobe
> where the year before she'd found
> a cache of navy-blue knickers
> stained with the black jelly clots
> I thought were my wickedness
> oozing out of me.

(from *The Handless Maiden*)

At the time I didn't understand what was going on. I just felt an enormous misery and confusion and responsibility for trying to put things right. I was always searching for an alternative mother to put her arms round me, to say 'It's all right.' Even now I still feel the blackness: the terror and rage. I am still the child who loved red.

In her memoir, *Desert Flower*, Waris Dirie is deeply concerned with the issue of gender, how deeply embedded it was in her culture and how profoundly it affected her life. She grew up as a desert nomad in Somalia. Existence was hard and at a young age she was responsible for taking the family's sheep and goats out to graze but she loved being a child in the wilderness and running about with giraffes, zebras and foxes. She was still a little girl when she underwent the ceremony of circumcision which all female children went through to make them *clean* and allow them to become women. Like all the others Dirie looked forward to this important occasion but she nearly died when the Killer Woman performed this horrific operation:

> My legs were completely numb, but the pain between them was so intense that I wished I would die. I felt myself floating up, away from the ground, leaving my pain behind, and I hovered some feet above the scene looking down, watching this woman sew my body back together while my poor mother held me in her arms. (Dirie 2001, p. 46)

At the age of thirteen she rebelled against her role as a woman when her father decided to marry her to an old man who was willing to give five camels for her. With her mother's blessing she ran away and made her way to Mogadishu where she lived for a while with various relatives of her mother's. Then an uncle, who was the Somalian ambassador to the UK, agreed to take her as a servant to England. For some years she worked very hard in his house but when he and his family returned to Somalia she determined to stay in London even though she had only had the chance to learn a few words of English and was not literate in any language. Someone had already expressed an interest in photographing her and rather nervously she began modelling. It was at this point that Dirie became conscious of her feelings about female circumcision and sexuality:

> I can't imagine what my life would be like if I hadn't been circumcised. I like men and I'm a very emotional, loving person. At that time, it had been six years since I ran away from my father, and the loneliness had been hard for me; I missed my family. And someday I hoped to have a husband and family of my own. But as long as I was sewn up, I was very much closed to the idea of a relationship, shut away into myself. It was as if the stitches prevented any man from entering me – physically or emotionally.
>
> The other problem that prevented me from having a relationship with a man came up when I realized I was different from other women, particularly English-women . . . (Ibid., pp. 149–50)

Dirie plucked up courage to have an operation and afterwards did have relationships and eventually a baby. Over a period of time she developed a strong sense of her own identity and became a famous model. She was already very well known when, with some trepidation, she allowed herself to be interviewed for the journal *Marie Claire* about her experience of circumcision.

It was a relief to talk about the truth which she'd bottled up for so long. The need to write about what had happened to her is taken much further in her straightforward, immediate and very frank book:

> Besides the health problems that I still struggle with, I will never know the pleasures of sex that have been denied me. I feel incomplete, crippled and knowing that there's nothing I can do to change that is the most hopeless feeling of all. (Ibid., p. 227)

Because she wrote openly and with concern about the circumcising of women Dirie was asked to be a special ambassador to the United Nations for women's rights in Africa. Touchingly, she remained completely sympathetic to her parents whom she sees as victims of their culture. In *Desert Flower* she shares her courageous journey and highlights a problem which many women still have to face.

The birth of a child meant fulfilment for Waris Dirie: 'From the day he was born, my life changed. The happiness I get from him is everything to me now' (ibid., p. 223). Becoming a mother profoundly affects a sense of identity. In her taut rhyming poem, 'The Victory', Anne Stevenson sees childbirth as a fierce battle which the baby wins.

The Victory

I thought you were my victory
though you cut me like a knife
when I brought you out of my body
into your life.

Tiny antagonist, gory,
blue as a bruise. The stains
of your cloud of glory
bled from my veins.

How can you dare, blind thing,
blank insect eyes?
You barb the air. You sting
with bladed cries.

Snail. Scary knot of desires.
Hungry snarl. Small son.
Why do I have to love you?
How have you won?

Fatherhood, of course, also has its effect and in Chapter 8, *Caring and Coping*, we include a poem by Charlie Druce in which he shows the profound influence of his baby on his viewpoint.

· ·

In his memoir, *Firebird*, Mark Doty is as frank as Dirie. The thinking and language though are more complex as he traces his growing awareness of being different, his recognition early in his teens that he was gay and how he coped with his sexual identity. Born in 1953, he grew up in a middle-class family in America in a culture where homosexuality was rarely admitted. Indeed it was still illegal.

At the age of ten the young Doty had the idea of dressing up as Judy Garland and while his friend Werner played the bongos he threw himself into singing one of her songs. Suddenly his mother appeared and said, horrified: 'Son, you're a boy' (Doty 2001, p. 101). These words told him he'd failed and he understood he'd been 'warned . . . instructed to conceal my longing' (ibid., 102). When he reached adolescence he thought he 'existed in a special zone, no one felt what I did' (ibid., p. 106). He hated finding the signs of puberty on his body, was desperately worried about getting an erection when he changed for PE and secretly idolized a boy called Rudi. A little later though he was one of a group of friends who called themselves freaks, a label which denoted:

> a stylish, desirable otherness. Heaven only knows how many of us . . . were young homosexual men and women; that aspect of ourselves simply did not come under examination, was not made visible in our new category. (Ibid., p. 139)

Family circumstances were far from easy. His father's work meant frequent moves and though Doty was close to his artistic mother as a child she was drinking heavily and behaving unpredictably by the time he reached his teens. She decided he must have his long hair cut and finally his father agreed, possibly to placate her. He bullied his son into the car and took him to the barbershop where he was 'shorn bare'. Afterwards, in utter misery, Doty took an overdose of sleeping pills. While he was recovering in hospital the male nurse in charge of him asked him if he was a homosexual and in an attempt to be supportive arranged for another nurse, who was gay, to talk to him. Unfortunately, this nurse had no idea how to broach the subject and simply asked Doty how he was. The lad said he was all right and there was virtually no conversation:

I have no questions; my sense of anything my life might be is tiny, inchoate, buried beneath a great weight. Where would I start to talk to this man, the first gay person I've ever met who actually says he's a gay person? *Does* he say it – to me I mean? I don't even remember. (Ibid., p. 147)

After the attempted suicide episode Doty's parents left him more or less alone. His mother became increasingly alcoholic and he avoided her by shutting himself in his room, going out and even staying away from home. Not surprisingly, he tried drugs. However, a teacher at school was impressed by his poems and introduced him to a poet who took an interest in his writing, invited him to his house and suggested poets to read.

The most poignant sentence in this book is: 'My mother taught me to love the things that would save me, and then, when I was sixteen, she taught me that I wasn't worth saving' (ibid., p. 171). What she did was to try and fire a pistol at him but she was so drunk she could not get the safety catch off. The scene is written, like the rest of the book, in the present tense and the reader re-lives the trauma which Doty suffered.

At seventeen he escaped from home and attempted to escape from his sexuality by marrying. In *Heaven's Coast*, which is about a later period in his life, he records the end of his marriage ten years later. It was then that he began to be himself and he describes the life he lived openly with his partner, Wally. At the end of *Firebird* Doty writes about his father's acceptance of him as a homosexual years later – his mother was dead by this time.

Many people discover a calling in themselves which provides a strong sense of identity. This is not restricted to the arts and could apply to research scientists, leaders of causes, athletes and so on. Mark Doty affirms in *Firebird* that art saved his life and he identifies himself as a writer. 'How is it that making sustains?' (ibid., p. 188) he asks and then lists the creative people who supported him, beginning with his mother and ending with poet, Charles Simic. He adds:

The gift was a faith in the life of art, or, more precisely, a sense that there was a life which was not mine, but to which I was welcome to join myself. A life which was larger than any single person's, and thus not one to be claimed, but to apprentice oneself to. (Ibid., p. 188)

Van Gogh's remarkable letters to his brother, Theo, reflect his growing sense of himself as a serious artist. This shows itself in the amount of detail about the drawings and paintings he is working on, his vision of his work, his responses to the work of other artists and also the frequent references to the money he needs to buy materials for painting or pay models. In a letter written in Arles in September 1888 he suddenly stops describing and speaks directly and emotionally about how he sees himself:

> Oh, my dear boy, sometimes I know so well what I want. I can very well do without God both in my life and in my painting, but I cannot, ill as I am, do without something which is greater than I, which is my life – the power to create.
>
> And if, defrauded of the power to create physically, a man tries to create thoughts in place of children, he is still very much part of humanity.
>
> And in a picture I want to say something comforting as music is comforting. I want to paint men and women with that something of the eternal which the halo used to symbolize, and which we seek to confer by the actual radiance and vibration of our colourings. (Ed. Roskill 1983, p. 286)

Sometimes the attainment of a sense of personhood is more of a baptism of fire than a conventional rite of passage. *A Lie About My Father* by John Burnside is many things: an insightful examination of a relationship with an inadequate, alcoholic and abusive father, a memoir of a working-class upbringing in a Catholic family which documents with sympathetic understanding the lives of men who have no direct way to express their feelings, an account of alienation in adolescence and early adult life which led to heavy drug-taking. It also records hauntingly the search for personal identity and the self-knowledge gained by the time the writer became a father.

Burnside has structured the book to juxtapose and make connections between himself and his father. In the prologue he lies to a stranger about the kind of person his father had been because it was too difficult to tell him the truth. Lying is a keynote in this memoir. We learn that his father, an illegitimate child who was abandoned on a doorstep, had a huge inferiority complex. He spent his adult life inventing lies about his successes and for a long time fantasized about making new starts. Such changes as he did make did not improve the family's life so he escaped reality by drinking heavily with friends who believed the stories he made up. At first his young son believed the fantasies he heard and he was excited by the make-believe of starting a wonderful new life in Canada.

The child was often humiliated by his father. For example, a sister, Elizabeth, had died before John was born and his father frequently told him he might have died and his sister lived. He understood that this outcome would have been better. He soon became afraid of his father. He describes the way his presence in a room created a sense of threat that some force might break loose at any moment and make something terrible happen. The bright child, whose reading and education were strongly encouraged by his mother, was being exploited by his father before he was ten years old. After an evening at the pub Burnside senior would bring his friends home and wake John up so that he could wait on them with drinks and show off his education.

From an early age the child searched for an otherness, for something more. He found it in the woods some distance from home:

> a dangerous realm of spent bonfires and burnt fur, the half-decomposed bodies of unclaimed dogs, farmers with shotguns, stark displays of rats and crows . . . I went there as often as I could. This was the place where I learned the deep pleasure of being alone, of being out in the open with an angel-haunted sky over my head, and the damp earth, packed tight with tubers and seeds and the bodies of the dead, under my feet. All that time, I was engaged in that search a childhood sometimes becomes, a search for the perfect instrument, for some compass point, some line of cold steel, some buried filament of copper and smoked glass . . . Once found, it might turn boys into something more interesting and much stranger than the handful of men I knew . . . (Burnside 2006, p. 40–1)

This extract exemplifies Burnside's need for a place where he could be himself, his sense of closeness to the energy of the natural and spirit world and his awareness of the brutal existing side by side with the beautiful, life and death being inextricable. It also shows his imaginative powers.

Around the age of nine Burnside heard his mother say to his father in a quarrel – there were many – that she should have married George Grant, a man she'd known before she met her husband. The child began to daydream that his father went away and George Grant replaced him. The Catholic religion was instilled in him by his mother and sometimes he had visions – one was of Christ in the garden. Very unhappy when his father moved the family from Cowdenbeath in Fifeshire to Corby, he began inventing companions, in particular a ghost brother who originated in Andrew, a brother who had died at birth several years previously.

> In one form or another, I would keep him by me all my life: my brother, my soul-friend, my other self. He would continue where I left off, and I would live for him, tuned into the rhythm of an other-world nobody else could hear. (Ibid., p. 133)

During this period his father became openly violent towards both his son and his own friends and after a while Burnside stopped doing well at school and started hanging around with misfits, building fires and destroying things. He writes potently about the excitement he had felt since childhood in watching things burn, the noise and beauty of fire, the sense that making a fire was a work of art, a piece of theatre, making something beautiful happen. For a while when he was in his mid teens there was something of a truce, a pretence of friendship and he went off to the pub with his father who considered these outings as a kind of education. Nevertheless Burnside stopped trying to see the good side of his father and was unable to feel anything but contempt for him. It is significant that he interrupts his narrative to say he is saddened by this now and he records incidents which show this parent in a very positive light before going on to write about his growing hatred for him.

At the age of sixteen Burnside started taking drugs which he found offered an awareness, a grace he had not found in communion or anywhere else. He continued his education but when he left college he drifted and kept away from home until his mother was dying. After her funeral he had a row with his father and left, feeling it was for good. Friends helped him but he continued with heavy drug-taking and went through a period of 'falling' which he saw as a way of keeping his 'private wildness', of experimenting and searching. He takes the reader fully into this experience – its amazements and possibilities but notes his failure to see his paranoia. He had two stays in mental hospital; each was part of the process of becoming something new.

By the time he left the hospital the second time Burnside was tired of 'falling' and excess and went to work in a retirement village as a dogsbody. Although he'd cut himself off from his father he was always in some way present in his mind. One of his jobs was to clear out the garages of residents who had died and he writes that among their belongings:

> I half hoped I would find a clue to the keepsake or talisman he [his father] would have held on to for half a century, had he lived as these people had . . . I had lost my father – whatever I thought my father had been – and the only way I could bring him back was by this process of sorting and honouring and bagging up somebody else's junk. If I couldn't have my own father, I could, perhaps, distil from the possessions of these many fathers a kind of essence . . . (Ibid., p. 291)

This search for his father, for fatherness, the deep need it expresses, is very poignant and the way Burnside harnessed his imaginative powers as a resource to cope with the terrible damages is profoundly moving. This disturbing and insightful book is remarkable for its honest self-examination, sympathetic understanding and the sense of reconciliation he finally achieved with his father. The writing is both trenchant and poetic. *A Lie About My Father* is work of literature.

Self-knowledge leads to acceptance of oneself, of one's past. Here is a poem by Mark Roper which expresses this very poignantly:

Unbecoming

For too long he has stood at your door,
this small bewildered boy, fringe hung
over national-health specked eyes,
timbertongued boy, unworthy of mention.

For too long in his only mirror,
your eye, he has seen himself
othered, ambered, pupilled, only meal
in that eye's desert his own tears.

It is time to let him in. Time
to sit him down and serve him.
Take off your arms. Take out your eyes.
Enter his mouth. Loosen his tongue.

Listen. All his life he has loved you.
Take his word. Onto his heart graft your heart.

(from *Even So: New & Selected Poems*)

The nature of identity is a subject that has fascinated thinkers down the ages. In the twentieth century one of the most extended and intensive but unacademic explorations of her own self-consciousness was undertaken by Marion Milner (pen-name: Joanna Field). Milner was a psychologist, later a psychiatrist, and began her pursuit in 1926. She published a series of books as progress reports over a period of nearly sixty years. Milner's approach is direct and involving. She turns self-knowledge into an adventure story, using as little jargon as possible, and quotes from her diaries at every turn. She comes back from the frontier with straightforward techniques of universal application. One of these is automatic writing (what we call flow-writing), and this results in her making a number of surprising discoveries about herself.

One of Milner's objectives in her journey is to be able to control her moods. One day she goes on a holiday in the Black Forest. The conditions are unpropitious: the weather is poor, and her companion is not well. But she goes for a walk in the woods and repeats a mantra to herself, 'I see a white house with red geraniums and I hear a child crooning'. Suddenly she is carried on a wave of ecstasy. She puts down some of the details afterwards in her diary, and quotes them in *A Life of One's Own*. She analyses what happened in the following passage:

> I sat motionless, draining sensation to its depths, wave after wave of delight flowing through every cell in my body. My attention flickered from one delight to the next like a butterfly, effortless, following its pleasure; sometimes it rested on a thought, a verbal comment, but these no longer made a chattering barrier between me and what I saw, they were woven into the texture of my seeing. I no longer strove to be doing something. I was deeply content with what was. At other times my different senses had often been in conflict, so that I could either look or listen but not both at once. Now hearing and sight and sense of space were all fused into one whole. (Milner 1986, p. 79)

She also says:

> I had never suspected that the key to my private reality might lie in so apparently simple a skill as the ability to let the senses roam unfettered by purposes. I began to wonder whether eyes and ears might not have a wisdom of their own. (Ibid., p. 80)

Milner gives herself the difficult task of not just conveying to the reader the quality of the new experiences she was having, but also theorizing from them in such a way as to provide precepts that might prove useful to others. Anybody who is attempting to explore the nature of their own individuality would find her example invaluable.

· ·

In our final example of an aspect of self-awareness we return to Lance Lee who shows us his vision of reaching beyond a sense of individual consciousness to connect with others and the wider world.

Transcending identity: Lance Lee

Identity and individuality are our burden as well as essential core: it has been so since the first 'man' down the evolutionary tree looked in the water and recognized himself as a separate being, or raised his eyes from some chore, looked over his surroundings and fellows, and with a sharp pang realized he existed apart from them, that he was alone. Consciousness is not part of the subject matter here but identity and individuality are inseparable from our consciousness of self. Everyone is an 'I' to himself: 'you' is everyone else.

But this most natural and assumed sense of ourselves comes at the cost of our unthinking, unreflective sense of being at one with nature, of being caught up in a stream of experience, of wholeness, not 'apartness'. In such wholeness is an end to the sense of alienation that has haunted modern society, driven by the ongoing industrial/technological revolution transforming our lives at an ever greater pace. Many an anguished soul searches for such wholeness with a desperate hunger.

We do not live less living without our narrow sense of identity: we live more, opening ourselves to the wider self and stream of experience from which ego self-consciousness alienates us. Religion tries to return us to this state of wholeness by oneness with God. That means debasing, humiliating, or ridding oneself of the troublesome individual sense of self, in religion the fallen self. By contrast Zen Buddhism seeks an immediacy of reaction unpremeditated and unconditioned by that intrusive sense of identity that weighs all experience with reference to its use or danger to the self.

Animals serve me metaphorically as my way out of this divided sense of reality built into a self-aware identity. In 'Opossum's Death And What Comes After' I am a privileged viewer who knows omnisciently what that animal is feeling as he moves into a meadow, hunting:

> (he) smells how wetly fear threads in the air
> he rolls on his tongue until drunk
> and full enough of courage he goes
> after the mouse or rat that unspools fear
> like that.

> (from *Wrestling with the Angel*)

But in 'Ravens', published in *Becoming Human*, the sense of identity moves towards a union with another's. As ravens 'glide through winter trees':

> I glide with them as the white world unscrolls below
> in words so familiar they go unread
> until a soft breast turning hard
> sets a cold and carrion joy clicking in my head . . .
> There's something savage in my heart . . .

What is savage is the sense of the *animal's* pleasure in an experience I would normally find repulsive, sighting carrion lying in the woods to eat. But in the 'red world' there is 'something twofold',

> the muscles, imbued, enfold; the enigma
> as old as spirit versus flesh,
> the trapped incandescence
> shining beyond the gore
> that sets me free from the gathering wings
> swooping to their prey in the cold . . .

If identity is a burden, it is also a freedom, because at its outer edges we sense ourselves as spirit, something that exceeds the mere life of flesh. It is an intuition more hope than not, growing stronger as we age and feel our body betraying an 'I' that does not otherwise age. In another era we would have been certain we possessed and knew our soul, that ultimate essence of self, the imperishable core of our identity. We don't hold that view commonly any longer, but we certainly have that common experience of a growing disjunction between body and inner flame.

But sometimes I realize that defining as our sense of identity may be it is more conventional than thought, and that a less absolute gulf exists between you and me than believed. In fact we leap beyond our narrow sense of identity every time we identify with a hero or heroine in a film or play, lose ourselves in a character in a novel, or feel a companion's pain as our own. In 'Totem' malleability of identity takes the form of first perceiving how:

> A great bear dwells in himself
> a bee sinking in his own honey.
> He's white as I am under his fur,
> a greater man made bearable by disguise.
> He's my familiar stranger, shadowing my dreams . . .

Then by fusing entirely with the bear, with nature, all self-divisions are overcome:

> How loose this heavy hide, how delicious
> 　　this heat burning inward,
> refining my mind to an undivided whole
> still and focused as a brilliant coal . . .

(*Becoming Human*)

I believe we are always more and less than we think we are. Our 'I' is rock-solid and a shadow on the wall we watch entranced until we get up and leave the cave of the self for the wider world.

3 Adult relationships

The relationships we have as adults are central to our emotional lives. They affect our sense of well-being, our attitudes and the way our minds develop. They are, of course, hugely various, involve feelings which are often complex, and they change over a period of time. In this chapter we have focused on ways people have found to write about relationships between lovers, partners, siblings and friends. Some are loving and supportive, some ambivalent, others are difficult and have destructive elements.

We have found that quiet, deep love relationships are rarely written about during the partners' lifetimes perhaps because they seem so natural, so much part of everyday life that there is nothing to remark upon. However, R. V. Bailey captures this kind of love in 'With You', an apparently low-key poem. The everyday details and the statement in the last verse carry the emotional weight.

With You

I stand with you in the garden
The birds' surprising madrigals
Rise through the roar of bees.

I stand with you in the kitchen
Dear damaged long-loved over-used
Pans and pots protect us.

I stand with you in the hallway
With the deep oak tick of the clock
And the turning stair.

We sit by books in the lamplight
Importunate nondescript dog and cat
Surround us warmly.

We lie in the lofty bedroom
The church clock through the window
Quartering Gloucestershire silences.

Without you, no garden.
Sunshine withers on the plum tree
House shrinks derelict into dust.

(from *Marking Time*)

Katherine Gallagher's first experience of love was a very difficult one. We move on to her in-depth exploration of it.

Losing game: Katherine Gallagher

'Better to have loved and lost than never to have loved at all . . . ' If for some reason, one partner opts out of a relationship commitment, the other may heroically, even foolishly, refuse to accept the situation and continue to love. I feel such unrequited love, such obsessive hankering after the loved one is a necessary part of a grieving process which, given time, leads to healing: this healing is like a return from exile, exile from the self.

In my own case, my relationship with J was my first deeply-felt, passionate love-affair (I was twenty-six) and when it ran into difficulties, I could neither believe nor accept that it was over. Of course, I was a bit of an innocent and not used to such rejections. But the latent writer in me was in saving-mode and, even at this early stage of my writing career, to jot down my feelings became freeing, a solace – and a 'way of seeing' – a habit that's continued throughout my life.

The background to my situation was that after a relationship lasting over a year, my partner returned to a former girlfriend, and much to my chagrin, married her. At the time it seemed perverse. Eighteen months later he contacted me, claiming he'd made a mistake: 'Could he see me'. From both sides now in this new scenario there was a sense of wasted opportunity, of love and joy irrevocably lost. It became the timeless story of romantic angst and doomed love. The picture was further complicated in that now I was booked to travel overseas in a few months – about to become a voluntary exile from my country, family, friends, and from him.

The story of our affair, evoked mostly in poem-notes at the time, became a learning curve for me, a process of discovery and growing personal awareness that informed my life choices. The inherent sadness in all this was to some extent balanced by the discovery of how writing about the situation – in my case, poetry, clarified it and gave me a distancing from the experience which in turn contributed to an increasing sense of liberation from it. The situation was double-edged – in that he was my mentor and the person who introduced me to writing poetry.

My initial reaction to his marrying someone else was a feeling of deep rejection and disbelief. Hence, seeing him clandestinely a couple of years on, though foolhardy and daring – 'as if we believed we could remake/what we had lived' was restorative and provided a kind of balancing. This quote is from '1969' in my book, *Tigers on the Silk Road*.

At the same time, the following excerpt from 'The Affair' suggests the ironies and sadnesses in this situation:

> Still, this was safe,
> they could go on for years –
>
> wait, phone-call, visit.
> Not enough, but it was something.
>
> How little, she realized one day
> when he sent her flowers,
>
> remembering her birth-
> day and she cried.

(from Fish-Rings on Water)

The American poet Theodore Roethke called a poem 'a temporary stay against chaos'. Certainly, writing poems – or sometimes notes, helped assuage the pain as in this poem:

Lines for an ex

> You used to say thousands of people
> have died without water
> but no one ever died without love.
>
> I got the gist – it hurt like hell.
> I longed to prove you wrong
> which you were, with your excuses.
>
> Part of me still loves you –
> a shade . . . For love's sake,
> I would go without water.

(from Fish-Rings on Water)

I see now that many of J's arguments were an intellectual smokescreen designed to 'push me away'. I should have been more adept at reading his signals.

Meanwhile with my obsessive love, I chose to ignore the advice of friends to break the relationship. Many years later, I examined the question of the reciprocity of our relationship in 'Poem for a Shallot'. Initially, I had no idea of turning a vegetable-poem into a love-poem but the tutor, Jo Shapcott, suggested we study our chosen 'légume' – smell it, examine its surfaces, feel it, taste it, listen to it . . . I started to flow-write. Increasingly conscious of the 'otherness' of this small vegetable, its individuality, I found the lines, 'You compartmentalise/I don't know how./ I can peel you back to nothing'.

This latter thought was a turning point, the recognition of a tension – of my power over the shallot but also of its power over me, for my eyes had started to water. And I thought: 'Why am I doing this?' It was like being in a relationship. Tears. Unhappy, negative. The shallot had moved from being an object under scrutiny to a metaphor for a lover – a reluctant lover, one whose heart I couldn't win. And yet I was peeling back, hunting, layer upon layer . . . hunting for what wasn't there. The poem is in my book *Tigers on the Silk Road*.

Poem for a Shallot

I am fooled.
You insist on the secret of skins –
how perfectly each wraps you.

You compartmentalize,
I don't know how.
I can peel you back to nothing.

I hunt for what isn't there –
layer upon layer –
down to your cagey heart.

When I try to get away
you've snuck into my breath, eyes,
making me cry

into my hands.

Working through the experience of the poem further illuminated the nature of the love obsession and helped to break it. Two other poems are important within this cycle – a coda as it were. 'On the Pass from Kathmandu' relates my experience of a Himalayan tourist-bus brake-failure. This near-death experience was a wake-up call: 'my fractured heart, shepherded all the way/from Melbourne, shocks me to sense/' as miraculously, the bus 'rights itself/on a handkerchief-sized plateau'. The poem, which is in my book *Circus-Apprentice*, ends with the thought: 'There's nothing now/but to go on'.

Suddenly, I'm looking forward rather than back. Of course, I still think about J, but see how on this Calcutta–London bus trip, I am moving away from him, psychologically and physically. I pass through Afghanistan, Iran, Turkey to Delphi – scene of this final poem. Here is an extract:

At Delphi

I breathe the scented air, feel the sky's silk,
there for the taking. I can almost unknot
my unhappiness, see how its underside
is the impossible love
I've carried all this way
like spare, necessary baggage.

Can I ungrip it, leave it here
for random gods to give one last blessing?
I hear your voice urging me on
to walk through this
steady fire of butterflies.

(from *Circus-Apprentice*)

Time and distance have settled me – I am freeing myself.

We turn now to marriage and a poem by Colin Rowbotham which is in his book: *Lost Connections*. It is a celebration of love, of partnership:

For Maggie

Five Augusts back we set up house
then married. If that sounds
like a story's opening, it felt then
the happiest of endings; one to halt
the film in its tracks, sealing protagonists
for good in amber sunset.

Suns go under – and what's amber?
A token blink, splitting
go from *stop*; and yet the way in which
you've braced this household on its bed of love
embodies such skill that I expect the walls
to obstruct time's thoroughfare.

No: the flow pulls homes along
with all else. Though their bright
promises look to be fixed; like twin

sunlit glitterings on an iron track,
apparently static, they skim and the lines
soon approach a conclusion.

I daren't trust we'll meet up in some
infinity, yet hope
the light we mirrored in this house shines
on still, when all our hulls have been swept
out into tracklessness; bobbing, bobbinning
till the sea folds them under.

Rowbotham does not go into detail about the relationship but expresses his love and respect for his wife in the image of bracing the house 'on its bed of love'. He inverts the 'happy sunset image' of films into a recognition that their life together cannot last for ever but sets against it a passionate wish that some of the strength of the relationship will survive their deaths. There is an intellectual vigour in the imagery which is reminiscent of the metaphysical poet, John Donne.

The next piece, a prose poem by Mo Gallaccio, is a complete contrast. It is about a marriage which is doomed from the start. Written in the third person, its precise detail and its knowing, ironic humour are apparently detached. Then it shifts. The conclusion is very poignant.

Wedding List

for George William

On the day of their wedding the king of Noroway came to fair Edinboro' Toon and the streets were bedecked with flowers, but so many were blocked off the bride couldn't make her hair appointment, and near tears had to resort to stuffing lank locks into a fake fur hat, hastily purchased in Jenners, while the groom was so long going to pick up the rings it was feared the ceremony would take place without him – meanwhile her Jewish relatives boycotted the whole occasion because it was happening in a church, even though it was only Unitarian and the groom's best friend, a Catholic, was barred from being best man by his Bishop – the Unitarian problem again – and her parents were unhappy a) with the wedding and b) at seeing each other but managed to just about keep on the polite side of civility and her future in-laws came down from Up North, bearing Forfar Bridies which they ate in the tiny bed-sitter where the couple were plainly co-habiting – but never a word did they utter – and on that October day the bride, unlucky in green, threw up, genuinely believing she had a bad dose of the flu', but was eternally grateful she never learnt the absolute truth till at least a week after they'd both said 'I do', and the Unitarian Minister, her friend, made them a wedding of poems and Kalil Gibran, but in spite of promising to stand like pillars of the temple separately but together – the marriage caved in.

Now they are truly separate. Once looking through Palgrave's Golden Treasury she found the corsage she wore on her special day pressed in its pages, which sent her to the photos where they were both so young and glaikit-looking it should have been a crime, and she thought although the whole shebang had been so ridiculously laughable, it was also profoundly sad.

The poet Matt Simpson deals with a long-term love and marriage relationship in an unusually rounded way. In his book, *In Deep*, there is no idealizing in the poems he has written about and for Monika. There are differences of language and culture to be reckoned with, and he confronts these honestly, admitting his own failings, and seeing her side of the story as well as his own. This allows him to say things like:

> 'How's your German?' people ask.
> 'She's fine', I answer, ashamed of how
> I twice gave up, afraid of syntax,
> Hitler words that bite.
>
> ('Tongues')

and in presaging her death and burial in her native city Berlin:

> Will they find the cemetery,
> pour your ashes on the numbered plot
> where the first man you ever loved is laid,
> your grandfather? Look at him here, this photograph,
> a silver-tached old man, at ease
> with his pre-war self, a steadfast look offering securities
> you have longed for, I could never absolutely give.
>
> ('The River on a Black Day')

These poems eschew histrionics in favour of a clear-eyed acknowledgement of what is. Simpson himself comments on what he has attempted in the following piece:

In Deep: Matt Simpson

I have explored marriage in what I've called 'an uncompleted sequence' entitled 'November Song', which takes up the last half of my most recent collection *In Deep*. The poems are love poems of a sort (not the one-sided sort which asks you to admire the *writer's* finer feelings or be sorry for him in his grief): what they try to show is a relationship as many-sided and dynamic. A writer's worst enemy is ego. As a reviewer of *In Deep* astutely points out, the 'constant effort of the poems is to ground mutual feeling in the diverse responses of each partner to their common experiences.' Perhaps the following from the sequence entitled 'An Autumn Rose' might give some indication of this:

So much, I know, depends on me.

Let's be positive, you say.
Not always easy when, deprived of choice,
the ability to come and go at will,
I stiffen into glum resentment like a child
kept in and punishing the world with sulks.
When I try it works,
seems such a simple thing to do.

This morning I discover on my desk a rose
fetched from the garden, an October rose,
and by its side a shy lover's letter shaming me,
thanking me for being kind.

Sometimes I am asked what I write about. It's a difficult question and one that only the poems themselves can properly answer. Forced into a corner, I'd probably say, looking back over them, I write about things that make loving each other difficult.

A very different marital relationship is suggested by Penelope Shuttle in her poem, Redgrove's Wife, which is in the book of that title. Shuttle writes wittily about the role of wife. The tone of the poem, a conversation about a marriage, is playful and it conveys that the partners are close.

Redgrove's Wife

Pity Redgrove's Wife?
I think not.

Praise Redgrove's Wife?
Why not?

Kiss n'snog Redgrove's Wife?
I dare not.

Be-jewel Redgrove's Wife?
With topaz and coral?
I will not.

Publish Redgrove's Wife?
I shall not.

(*But I shall*).

Forget Redgrove's Wife?
No, I have not.

Question Redgrove's Wife?
Not yet, not yet.

Confuse Redgrove's Wife?
I need not.

Fear Redgrove's Wife?
Oh fear not.

Dream of Redgrove's Wife?
Yes, night after night.

Translate Redgrove's Wife?
Why not,
she's not made of tin.

Amaze Redgrove's Wife?
Leave that to Redgrove.

'Redgrove's Wife' is a comment about a very grounded marriage. We now look at a relationship which is affected by an earlier marriage. This is the subject of Sibyl Ruth's poem, 'A Crowd'. She comments:

> When I moved in with my partner I thought we'd be a couple. And when his children came to stay, we'd be a family. I hadn't anticipated that my partner's ex would be with us too. Okay, she would never physically cross our threshold. But her ghost was powerful, omnipresent. Though my partner was getting a divorce, I wondered if we would ever – could ever – truly leave her behind. Writing 'A Crowd' was simultaneously an acceptance and an act of exorcism.

Here is the poem:

A Crowd

Your wife is a bird
who flaps by my head.
Pecking phone calls
at eight o'clock in the morning
to squawk about lost socks,
scratching at our plans.

I could gawp round the corner
at her box of a house
– we live that close –
walk past her gate if I wanted.

She's a vulture,
the scary monster at the centre
of your best-loved stories
which could even be true,
the way you tell them.

We are not alone.
In bed my bones get nudged over.
Her name clambering between us again
like a child with a bad dream, only bigger.

There's three of us in the dark.
I stay awake trying
to work out how long,
how wide, how deep is the gap
between separation and leaving.

(from *I Could Become That Woman*)

Some relationships are so complex, and the sensibilities of the protagonists so highly developed, that ecstasy and pain are inextricably mingled. The only development possible is their dissolution. Such was the love of Franz Kafka and Milena Jesonska. It lasted two years, and was carried on largely through letters. Kafka also confided thoughts about its progress to his diaries. At one point he characterizes Milena's approach as: 'You cannot love me, much as you would like; you are unhappily in love with your love for me, but your love for me is not in love with you' (Kafka, ed. Haas 1983, p. 8).

Without letters it is doubtful if this relationship would have lasted as long as it did. There is a sense in which the writing fuelled the passion, but the degree of introspection was its undoing. Early on in their correspondence which was published as *Letters to Milena* Kafka writes:

Sometimes I have the feeling that we're in one room with two opposite doors and each of us holds the handle of one door, one of us flicks an eyelash and the other is already behind his door, and now the first one has but to utter a word and immediately the second one has closed his door behind him and can no longer be seen. He's sure to open the door again for it's a room which perhaps one cannot leave. If only the first one were not precisely like the second, if he were calm, if he would only pretend not to look at the other, if he would slowly set the room in order as though it were a room like any other; but instead he does exactly the same as the other at his door, sometimes even both are behind the doors and the beautiful room is empty. (Ibid., pp. 37–8)

We now look at an unusual and exploitative relationship which had elements both of love and friendship. *After a Funeral* by Diana Athill is, as the title suggests, a text written in memoriam. The relationship explored with acute honesty is that with Didi, an Egyptian man damaged by his childhood experiences, who as an adult becomes a promiscuous alcoholic gambler: he displays personality traits which invite the adjective 'impossible'. Yet Athill, over a period of years, by an almost heroic effort, refuses to accept this, and attempts to love him. At first she is physically attracted but this is not reciprocated; latterly she struggles to tolerate his waywardness, untruthfulness and ingratitude. He lives, and dies (by his own hand), in her flat.

Didi is a depressive, and a hopeless scrounger. He has a talent for writing, but an inability to see any project through, so is forced into economic and emotional dependency. We see events through Athill's eyes, and it is like being given access to a private journal. But Didi also kept a diary to which she gains access at various points of the narrative, and the five volumes of which he bequeaths to her when he takes his overdose. The book contains extensive quotations from these, and the reader gains from the conflicting interpretations often of the same event.

Here is an extract from late on in the story when Athill has come to the realization that she is helpless to offer Didi the support he needs. The extract it includes from Didi's diary reveals some convergence of awareness:

Didi knew that I had given him up, but while the fact was a relief to me, to him it was something different: 'How my life will continue from here it is impossible to visualize. There is no prospect of any money coming in to me at all. Diana, I instinctively know, has given up. Given up in the sense that knowing she is too kind – that it would be against her innermost nature – to put me out of the door, she is resigned to leaving me alone and to paying the expenses which, as I have said before, sap her of all items of luxury which she is entitled to through her work and writing-earnings. Not only is she resigned to my presence – she makes it as agreeable as possible for both of us. She is charming to me – and my heart bleeds for her.' There was hardly a day during this period when Didi seemed so gay and carefree that he didn't wake up to the knowledge that he was soon going to kill himself. It was worse than 'being in a dep'. It was because what he recognized as the symptoms of 'a dep' were absent that it was so bad. Lacking those symptoms, he didn't look at himself and say 'I am ill'; he looked at himself and said 'I am hopeless'. (Athill 2000, pp. 144–5)

After The Funeral is a salutary reminder that some adult relationships are fundamentally flawed, messy and painful, even predestined to end in tragedy. Writing, for individuals caught in such a net of mutual dependency, can have a cathartic urgency.

The love affair which Linda Chase describes in the next piece had its destructive side but it was also very fruitful. She examines its connection with different strands of her life and the effect it had on her writing.

Surrender: Linda Chase

Over a period of 15 years I was involved with a much younger man who became a vital source of creative energy for me. My Buddhist teacher called him a *daka*, a young male figure representing pure inspirational thought-form. He said people on a spiritual path often sought the purer energy of a young devotee. In terms of poetry and the arts, it might be more appropriate to call him a muse. It's really quite common – the older artist with the younger source of inspiration. Ibsen, Picasso, Isherwood, Britten, Fonteyn, Greer are just a few examples. Also spiritual teachers often have younger partners, but I think they'd prefer not to be named. Somehow the *shakti* or pure energy of the younger person acts as a catalyst for the older, more focused artist/teacher.

Well, that's my story and I stuck to it during the first time I was together with my young lover. He was twenty-six and I was exactly twice his age. It was a short lived, erratic and wildly passionate affair. He was two years older than my eldest child and I was two years younger than his mother. The window open to us was very small indeed but I succumbed to the passion and the deliciously powerful love of this young man. He had been my student for many years before we became lovers, so I already knew him well when we slid off the student/teacher map into uncharted zones.

We had, and still have, a deep dedication to one another. Partly this was set by our original, rather traditional relationship. He was my tai chi student. He had great physical ability as well as determination. I was his teacher in the Chinese formal template which demands respect and discipline. He was so eager to learn, not just the outward patterns of tai chi, but also the Taoist philosophy which informed the movements. In fact, he was the kind of student teachers dream of – attentive, talented, spiritual, beautiful and charming. Once, while we were dancing at a party, before we were lovers, he told me that he had dreamed about me the night before. We had been together under a tree in a field, he said. When I asked him what we had been doing he said he wasn't sure but he knew it had been wonderful. His confession of intimacy in a dream fired up the desire for intimacy in me. Our relationship was still spiritually based, but a new undercurrent of eroticism began to pull us together even tighter.

Here are some lines from a villanelle, 'Undressed', written during the first period we were together. Surrender seems to be the main theme, which is also central to most forms of spiritual transformation, as in dying and being reborn or purging and achieving purification.

> You slip this T shirt off so easily.
>
> I let you do it. You're completely free
> to strip me down like this. Who would have guessed
> the image and the feeling could hold me,
>
> a hostage for so long? My mind can see
> you still and feel you. Please, I need a rest
> so slip this T shirt off as easily
>
> as you had done before, a simple plea.
> I have surrendered and I have confessed.
> The image and the feelings have become me.
> The T shirt slips. I'm off so easily.

(from These Goodbyes)

In this next poem, written during our final phase together, I attempt to describe how, through our love, we were surrendering to one another and thereby creating a purification ritual – letting go into the unknown, trusting the Tao, the love and the process. Again, surrender is a key factor, as in many spiritual traditions, especially those which also prescribe disciplined physical practices. Once the mind and body are focused (through yoga, tai chi or meditation), the aim is to release the mind into a spacious awareness of higher consciousness. In this poem, which is in my book, *Extended Family*, sex becomes the disciplined practice.

Purification

> I feed the length of you through me
> like a yogi with an endless rope –
> ecstatic and clean as a whistle.
>
> Threaded through my bones
> you're the wick, sealed in place –
> smouldering, dripping wax.
>
> Are we afraid of blasphemy,
> in this communion with each other –
> binding us, unwinding us, igniting?

Originally I felt guilty about taking the attention of a young man who instead could have been looking for a life partner with whom to have children. However, by the time we got together the last time, he had *had* children, and had recently split up with their mother. So there he was – a single father in his mid-thirties. I could no longer use his childlessness as a reason for talking myself out of falling in love again. In our minds, we had become almost plausible as a couple. We began to go out in public and were up-front about being together. The following poem, also in *Extended Family*, shows us in a restaurant with a group of my friends.

Restaurant

People are eating and passing food across this table
upon which you have immobilised my right hand
against the wood with your own firm left hand.

Everyone can see that you have got me
anchored in place, your hobbled left handed lover
still able to eat, but not to wander off.

There is no struggle whatsoever to be seen.
Not a finger of mine slips through any of yours
as part of a cunning strategy for escape.

Tamed and tethered, I graze contentedly
in front of the very friends who think me wild.
It excites them. In their dreams you pin me down.

I quote this poem in full because it not only demonstrates my total surrender to him, but also how others saw us. We had been out to eat with friends who were staying for the weekend. In the morning, one of them said to me 'I dreamed about you and your lover. He had pinned you down'. I was made very uneasy by this comment and decided to see if I could make it work in a poem in the hope of being able to understand why my friend might have said it. As the image appears in the poem (he, pinning me down) it seems to highlight the way in which I had given in to him – the older strong woman surrendering to the dominant youthful male and how this image seemed to have an erotic effect on this friend, a man of my own age.

The full story of this relationship would be incomplete if I didn't include some lines from the tormented poems written after we finally ended the relationship. At that point, writing poems took on another dimension. They became a lifeline, a focus for the chaos of my broken expectations. Who knows, maybe poetry pulled me through, along with a touch of irony and even humour. I later published a sequence of thirty-nine poems called 'Younger Men Have Birthdays Too'. It is the second part of *Extended Family*. More than half the poems in this sequence were written during and after the relationship collapsed. Here are the first and last stanzas of one of these poems, 'Scuffing.'

> Life has scuffed the varnish off the kitchen floor
> under the chair which is mine,
> so we know whose life did it.
>
> I blame breakfast as well as lunch
> and occasional cups of coffee with friends
> and you for leaving the table without asking.

Throughout the various times he and I were together, I continually harboured the thought that I should have resisted this love or somehow transformed it. Instead, I used it – all of it – the guilt, together with the love and fear, to fuel more and more poems. And, I am happy to say I have even written new poems since.

Whether they are easy or fraught with difficulty, relationships between siblings are often key. In the prologue to her memoir *About My Sisters* Debra Ginsberg writes:

> I can neither remember nor imagine my life without sisters. As the eldest of five children, four of them girls and one of them our only brother, my role as sister will always be an inextricable part of my personal identity. All four of us maintain an exceptionally intimate bond with each other . . . This is not a recent phenomenon. My sisters and I have been close our entire lives. The four of us are hardly ever in unanimous agreement and our very different personalities prevent us ever thinking or speaking with one mind. Yet, in our relationships, our work, the face we present to the world, in every day of our lives, each one of us carries some part of her sisters with her. (Ginsberg 2004, p. 2)

She also says that they are 'each other's harshest critics and strongest supporters' and that 'we define ourselves as women through each other's eyes' (ibid., p. 6). She adds that she needed to have their approval before starting on the journey of writing this book.

The structure Ginsberg has chosen for her memoir is an interesting one. It is framed within a single year – often bringing in the get-togethers of her large, eccentric family which includes her parents and Blaze, her gifted and unusual son. Boyfriends make some appearance too. There is a chapter for every month and in each some focus on what is currently going on in the family. The happenings are a springboard for exploring in depth different aspects of her relationship with each sister. Most of the explorations lead to a delving into the past.

She writes in great detail about Maya, the sister closest to her in age. As children there was never rivalry between the two and Ginsberg comments: 'I needed my sister in order to feel complete' (ibid., p. 38). The family was frequently on the move and the two girls led a self-contained life. They invented a game, the Mariannes, in which they were both grown-ups with the name of Marianna who talked about their husbands and babies. As they grew older the game became more sophisticated and reflected tensions in the family and what they did not understand in the adult world. Ginsberg describes the total and practical support Maya has given her in adult life. Since the time in her mid-twenties when she was pregnant and split up with her boyfriend she has lived with Maya who shared looking after her child, Blaze, and in many ways took on the role of a second parent.

Déja, the youngest sister, was born when Ginsberg was sixteen and she acted as an intermediate mother. At that time she shared her innermost thoughts with the baby and in adult life Déja is the sister she feels emotionally closest to. Her relationship with Lavander, her third sister, is much more tempestuous. The two have serious quarrels although they are very fond of each other. Near the end of the book Ginsberg concludes:

> She will keep challenging me and I will keep questioning my version of reality as long as she's there to call me on it. This is who she is and this is what we do. She doesn't always like me, of this I am certain – just as certain, in fact, that she will always love me. (Ibid., p. 249)

About My Sisters has an easy, almost novel-like style. Its immediacy draws the reader into the life of this extended family. Its light touch is deceptive. What distinguishes the book is Ginsberg's honest recording of the uncomfortable and the painful and her perceptiveness which extends to herself.

Jamaica Kincaid, who grew up in Antigua, had no bond with any of her siblings and in total found her birth family unsupportive. However, she decided to write a book to help her understand her relationship with her brother, Devon, and to try and cope with his dying. His birth, when she was a teenager, made life very difficult for her mother who already had two other small sons. The young girl was angry and upset when her mother removed her from school to help at home. One day when she was fifteen she had to look after this youngest child all day but she read most of the time and did not change his nappy. Her mother, in fury, burnt all her beloved books. The trauma of this incident is returned to several times in *My Brother*. The effect Devon had on the family and herself explains Kincaid's emotional distance from him. She left her home and the island when she was eighteen and made another life for herself as a writer in New England. However, she did keep up some contact with her family. The memoir begins twenty years later when she had a husband and two small children. Worried because Devon was very seriously ill with Aids, she went to see him.

She found her brother in a rundown and dirty hospital which was unable to provide the medical treatment or care he needed. Kincaid phoned a doctor she knew in America and obtained expensive drugs which were not available on the island. His condition began to improve almost at once. One day when she was at the hospital she felt a surge of love for him and there was real contact between the two which had never occurred before. Back with her family in New England though her feelings were rather different:

> I missed my brother, being with him, being in the presence of his suffering and the feeling that somewhere in it was the possibility of redemption of some kind, though what form it could take I did not know and did not care, only that redemption of some kind would be possible and that we would all emerge from it better in some way and would love each other more. Love always feels better than not-love . . . I talked about him, his life, to my husband, I talked about him to people I knew well and to people I did not know very well. But I did not think I loved him; then, when I was no longer in his presence, I did not think I loved him. Whatever made me talk about him, whatever made me think of him, was not love, just something else, but not love; love being the thing I felt for my family, the one I have now, but not for him, or the people I am from, not love, but a powerful feeling all the same, only not love . . . How did I feel? I did not know how I felt. I was a combustion of feelings. (Kincaid 1998, pp. 50–1)

Kincaid pulls us into her train of thought and we feel the 'combustion of feelings' in the repetitions of words and phrases and in the long disturbed sentences which have a poetic rhythm. The whole book is written in this immediate and self-revealing style and in long paragraphs which weave together what is happening with what is going on in her head. Some of the repeated phrases are refrains throughout the book.

For a time Devon's health was better but Kincaid's ambivalence towards him grew even though she tried to focus on the positive in his character, especially his love for plants and gardens – a love which she shared. She was forced to see that he had never lived independently nor had a proper job and was upset that he went back to sleeping casually with women in spite of the dangers his illness posed. She traces her feelings during the last months of his life and describes her shock when she discovered during a chance encounter with a woman from Antigua that Devon was a homosexual but had kept it secret.

The book reflects Kincaid's need to keep returning to her relationship with her mother as well as to recount her brother's life and his harrowing death. In this compelling memoir there is also frequent reference to her closeness to her husband and children. It is a strong affirmation of the relationships Kincaid made in her adult life.

Close friendship is a very important aspect of love. In 'Old Friends' Susan Jordan speaks directly to a friend she has known most of her life. She describes the history of their relationship and its strengths, faces its limitations and celebrates what it means to them.

Old Friends

People don't say so often now
'Oh, but you must be sisters'.
Ageing marks our differences: bodies droop
or stiffen in their own shapes, faces sag
more into themselves, minds run deeper
in their tracks, lives set like drying clay.
Jokes are our meeting-ground, gardens
shelter us from our discrepancies;
we cherish these pieces of our shared life.
We ask where our likeness lies:
you partly German, I mostly Jew,
except where unknown Poles
have bequeathed me hair fairer than yours.
Your wholesome Christian childhood,
where everyone was polite
and nobody got too close to one another;
my raw-edged family, over-fed
on Karl Marx, *kneidlech* and smother-love,
jostling for space inside each other's hurt.
You the musician, who didn't need to be clever,
whose Oxford was a place and not an aspiration.
I, aching to write, who learnt to cut myself
on the sharp edges of my own mind.
You so clean-fingered, smearing nothing,

I still the child, marking the world with messes
you hate to clean. These thirty years
have earned us both the right to irritation.
We have worn each other in those years
as comfortably as clothes, talked one another
through deaths of parents, lost loves,
work, illness, builders, dentists.
Outgrowing each other, we expose
extremities our friendship does not cover.
We tug it to fit, knowing still
that without it we would both be naked.
Impossible that when I lift the phone
My 'hello sweetie' would not be answered by yours.

Dilys Wood investigates her relationship with two friends and discusses the poems she has written about them. In the process she also writes very perceptively about the concept of friendship.

Friendship: Dilys Wood

For me writing about the deaths from cancer of two close women friends, Veronica and Maxine, meant not just writing about loss but about friendship – and how large the subject proved! Poems written over ten years included a sequence of fourteen poems about Veronica, a corona of sonnets (fifteen linked sonnets) and another long poem in a looser form about Maxine. I found that the subject of friendship widened out, became something of a philosophical study, but rooted in my friends' personalities, their life-histories, and my very different relationship with each. The friendship poems are, inter alia, portraits and include elements of narrative.

Before beginning writing, I realised that my friends' long illnesses had offered rare opportunities for closeness. I had observed our reactions minutely and now used (exploited?) the experience in my writing. As a human being, but also as a poet, I needed to know more about how close affection and understanding can transform ordinary events, such as the day-trips taken with Veronica, a distraction from her illness. Here is part of my poem, 'Veronica'.

The places you want to go! –
  the Thames by bus

sun throwing linked shapes
  as we lean on fluid time

and melt, as cloud
  turns the river to dark glass

and, later, sun projects each leaf
    again, softens rough skin . . .

Our arms linked – see, twinned!
    and on numb current floating.

(from In The Company of Poets)

I see the word 'link' appears here twice, the second time with 'twinned' – a flaw in the poem, perhaps, but an instance of many references to sitting close, standing close as we cooked a meal, physically in touch: 'Your son/drowsed over your held hand.//I took the other'.

Three aspects stand out in all my writing about friendship: 'sharing' and the qualitative difference when even the simplest action is shared; the attractiveness of very open, confessional relationships; the danger of betraying friendship – instanced, of course, by deciding to write about essentially private, confided moments. In this respect poems about lovers and poems about friends share a dilemma.

Writing the poems took my ideas further. I learnt, I think, that full and free communication with friends contributes to spiritual awareness. The possible depth of the experience of friendship when one is about to lose a close friend is expressed in the first sonnet of 'Letters to a Dying Friend' (a poem addressed to Maxine):

I turn from the post-box. Words fly overhead,
transmit the energy of migrant birds.
'Cancer is a world apart', someone said.
Between us, there's a wild journey. My words
imagine new compass-bearings, hang in there.
Words, like a friend who knows she's dying, must
lose old meanings, get new ones in the air,
use up summer stores to the last and trust
there will be more. As I write, bones seem hollow –
love equals (I think) the longing to be light
as death is also weightless. Straight as arrows,
words learn the use of flying. When? In flight?
I see you look up sharp, hear a letter
fall, or, signalling, migrant birds fly over.

In the last long poem I wrote on this theme, 'Lament Based on a Corona of Sonnets' there are also a noticeable number of images related to sky, travel, migration, floating, free-fall –

. . . knowing how ungrounded we were, we asked
    how you were? like us, were you drawn
        to floating landscapes of clouds . . .

Some of these images relate primarily to disorientation and loss, but the focus is equally on the intimacy of friendship and on escaping into the weightless world of two people in tune with each other.

> . . . . . On the phone
> we became bodiless, in one head together,
>   serious thoughts swinging loose,
>
> *swing, swing*, not meaning to be idle
>   but not purposeful either. Children would not think
>   to pass such tiny
>
> folded notelets as we did in the last phone call,
>   on cloud-nine, light-headed, laughing weakly . . ..

Like all forms of love, friendship is about risk and all close friends probably 'use' each other. Feelings of friendship are, I think, quite distinct from feelings towards blood-relations and lovers. But there is overlap. All the questions we may have about love relations arise in this context also – are our feelings selfish, unselfish, truthful, reliable, what does the friend really think of you, where do you stand in his/her hierarchy of commitments, and how do you feel towards eg the friend's partner, children – jealous?

I often puzzled how to define feelings of physical closeness not – at least apparently not – sexual. In the end I hardly touched at all in the poems on these particular ambiguities in friendship. I was more concerned to celebrate the freedom from such 'complications' and to express the joy of communication without reserve.

Jenna Bailey's book *Can Any Mother Help Me?* further attests to the significance of friendship. It grew out of research she did at the Mass Observation Archive at the University of Sussex and it presents, with background information, the writings of the Cooperative Correspondence Club. This club was set up in 1935 in response to a letter from a lonely mother which had been published in *Nursery World*. The members were a group of women who lived in different parts of Britain, most of them isolated, well educated, bored and with young children. They circulated a magazine with a stitched cover in which each of them regularly wrote a long letter under a pseudonym. A member who used the name of Ad Astra was the editor. The women wrote openly, much more openly than was usual before the 1960s. They discussed coping with children, their day-to-day lives, sex, marital relationships, extra-marital relationships, the Second World War, their professional work which was mainly taken up in their forties and fifties, interests, and facing old age. Here is a short extract from a letter written by Roberta in 1953 after her husband left her:

I can truthfully say that such peace within me I have not known for years. I have been torn, all twisted inside me, mentally at sea, never at rest, seeking what I did not know, but I was terribly restless mentally, and I know at one point I would have cracked up and was terrified. I did not sleep properly and woke thinking of Walter and the future and writing imaginary letters to him, one day all loving and one day all hatred and bitter; one day begging him to come back to me and the children . . . another time hating him and thinking all the most fearful things I could, full of self-pity and martyrdom stuff, but now I have floated free, free, free . . .

Thank you all of you, for all you have done to help me, for your loving and encouraging words. (Bailey 2007, pp. 189–90)

Through the magazine close friendships were formed and over a period of time most of the women met. Once the war was over there were annual get-togethers. The Correspondence Club is a remarkable example both of writing your self and how writing can sustain friendship. It only came to an end in 1990 after many of the members had died. Bailey notes that after the 1930s other women started private correspondence clubs, some of which are still in existence. The correspondences which develop from message boards and the like on the internet might be considered a modern equivalent.

Finally we look at friendship forged in a time of extremity. Such a friendship is likely to be a very powerful one. For Brian Keenan and John McCarthy, who spent nearly four years imprisoned together as hostages in Lebanon, this relationship was hugely important in helping them survive their ordeal.

Keenan's book, *An Evil Cradling*, which is an account of his four and a half years in prison, begins by re-creating the first appalling months when he was shut up alone. He writes about his fear and despair and the ways he found to re-possess himself: dancing round his cell, for example, and secretly keeping a diary on pieces of paper from his briefcase which, surprisingly, had not been taken away from him.

His total isolation came to an end one day when, without warning, he was blindfolded and driven far away from the noise of Beirut. He was left, still blindfolded, in a new cell but he had a sense that someone else was in it too and as soon as he judged it safe he lifted a corner of the wrapping over his eyes. He saw feet, a smart blazer and then the head of a man who was doing the same thing. Journalist, John McCarthy, introduced himself and they quickly exchanged details. Keenan notes: 'Perhaps the suppressed joy of being able to speak to someone, to have a meaningful conversation, perhaps also the fact that the room was quite large and we could walk about in it, made us both very relaxed' (Keenan 1993, p. 92).

In spite of this immediate connection there was also a wariness. Keenan felt a desperate need to be honest and saw they could only get to know each other properly by being open about the isolation they had both been through and what they had come to understand from it. However, he was 'afraid of exposing myself, afraid of seeing the hurt, the pain that so preoccupied me in isolation. I imagined that my new friend would be feeling the same things' (ibid., p. 95).

One morning, in order to intimidate them because they had asked for cigarettes, a guard pointed a gun at them and shouted that they should pray to God. This reminder of their possible fate removed a barrier:

> The floodgate began to open. We eased ourselves out of our quiet and unspoken apprehension of one another. We began slowly, carefully but honestly to tell one another of the things we felt, the things we thought about, and our experiences during that time alone . . . We gave honestly of ourselves and of our experience and each received from the other . . . On occasion there would be discussions on vaguely religious themes . . . We had each gone through an experience that gave us the foundations of an insight into what a humanized God might be. (Ibid., pp. 98–9)

In the weeks and months ahead Keenan and McCarthy shared their life stories including difficult memories. They devised chess boards with scraps of paper and made up other competitive games. They interlaced much of their conversation with grotesque humour and swearing. Doing this was both a release and a support. They also made up exercise games although these came to an abrupt end after a time because they were put in chains. When McCarthy went through a period of deep despair Keenan supported him by making him do visualizations. One night he insisted until McCarthy pictured a room and what was in it, then imagined going into the room and finding out who had been there until he became involved in making up a story about it. When Keenan woke the following morning and saw John was deep in sleep he felt: 'the huge relief that a parent might feel when their child had passed through some crisis of fever' (ibid., p. 130).

Every time the pair were moved there was tension until they found they were still together. Whenever one of them was beaten up by the guards the other suffered the pain which was inflicted. In the later part of their imprisonment Keenan had a severe stomach virus with diarrhoea. McCarthy cleaned him up and nursed him. Keenan saw his friend in a new light:

> The buffoon, the fool, the comic was a man of vast tenderness, a man of compassion . . . I believed John thought I was sleeping, then I felt his hand lie gently on my stomach, and it remained there. He was praying. I was overcome . . . I wanted to thank him for this huge and tender gesture. (Ibid., p. 251)

When, after four and a half years of imprisonment, Keenan found he was going to be released without McCarthy he felt he would be leaving part of himself behind and he seriously considered resisting.

Inevitably there are descriptions of violence and suffering in an *Evil Cradling* but the writing in this deeply humane book is full of humour, poetry, close observation and probing thought. It traces a spiritual journey and it is a testament to the closeness which friendship can offer, a closeness which is rare in any relationship.

4 Abuse

In this chapter we are looking at ways in which people have written about sexual abuse. However, we are very aware that abuse takes many forms and we have focused on the subject in several other places in this book. Sadly, physical and emotional cruelty to children is widespread. In Chapter 2 our account of *A Lie About My Father* refers to ways in which John Burnside was seriously mistreated by his father. In the same chapter we describe abusive behaviour by Mark Doty's mother. In Chapter 7 we note how neglect and bullying affected Les Murray. Long-term cruelty by a parent has been recorded in a number of popular memoirs such as *Ugly* by Constance Briscoe which records a girl's remarkable ability to survive and make a life for herself. Certain abusive practices are rooted in cultural tradition and in Chapter 2 there is reference to female circumcision in our account of *Desert Flower* by Waris Dirie.

Abuse of adults is not at all uncommon and in this chapter June English writes frankly about a very destructive marriage. In Chapter 5 John writes about the need he felt when working in prisons to counteract the abuse he saw within the prison system. In the same chapter our account of *Life and Death in Shanghai* by Nien Chen describes the abuse inflicted by an extreme political state. In Chapter 3 we describe how friendship helped Brian Keenan and John McCarthy withstand brutal treatment during their years as hostages.

Sexual abuse usually entails other forms of abuse: emotional blackmail, the threat or actuality of violence and betrayal of trust. When sexual abuse occurs in childhood there is often collusion which is also a betrayal. This was so in the case of Jacqueline Spring. She was the youngest of seven children in a large, well-off Glasgow family which had no open discussion and was dominated by her father. *Cry Hard and Swim* describes the journey she made in adult life to come to terms with the way her father sexually abused her and also the anger she felt with her mother for not preventing it. The book traces with extraordinary honesty and insight the different stages she went through with the help of a sensitive therapist. Gradually she was able to talk about what had happened and understand how this was affecting her adult feelings and behaviour. With further help she began to change the way she related to her husband and children. Writing her story was a final stage in the healing process and she hoped that sharing her experience might be helpful to others.

Spring's therapist suggested at quite an early point that she might like to write to her mother and keep what she had written. Writing these letters and re-reading them were important elements in her recovery. The first two parts of this insightful book are a series of 'secret letters' to her mother, the first about her memories of childhood, the second about her experience of life as an adult. Here is a short excerpt from the first set of letters:

> Do you know, Mama? I am never sure. It is unthinkable. I am just His little girl. He is my Daddy. We love each other. We are never challenged. No one, not even you, especially you, would dare. I myself don't dare to take the centre of the story, the meaning, and tear it out for myself, like twisting the stone free from a sweet plum. He alone knows for sure . . .
>
> It is early morning, and He is calling. I am asleep. I will be asleep, no matter what. The others are not going to go. But He is calling . . . He demands that I kiss his lips, and I give Him the vile kiss, pretending that it is a child's. But He will not let me pretend. With Him there is no pretence at all.
>
> Where are you, Mama? You are downstairs doing motherly things, clearing dishes, washing up, drying cups. Instead of upstairs doing the wifely things I am doing for you. (Spring 1987, p. 8–9)

The second part ends with a long letter to her father which gives a picture of the damage he did to the whole family as well as herself. Spring finishes the letter with the thought that she may be able to forgive him one day and then says: 'And now I want to stop looking back. I want to look forward instead' (ibid., p. 46). The rest of the book is an in-depth account of her journey. It includes in the text, as do the earlier parts, a number of poems. Some of these are direct, some use oblique images to express feelings and experience. *Cry Hard and Swim* shows in graphic detail how sensitive therapy can help change a life and what a powerful therapeutic tool writing can be.

Poet Pascale Petit turned to poetry to write about her relationship with her father.

The Zoo Father: Pascale Petit

When my father, who I hadn't seen since I was eight, who I believed I would never meet again, suddenly summoned me, I rushed to Paris to visit him but returned angry and disturbed, though I wasn't sure why. He was dying of emphysema, so over the next two years I went back and forth to his tiny flat in the Latin Quarter. It was next to the Jardin des Plantes and its Ménagerie where I started writing *The Zoo Father*.

In this collection I wanted to transform my personal experience of an abusive father into art, to turn him into a book. I wasn't interested in a realist narrative – the therapy was in trying to make magic out of pain. I worked on the music and lineation of each poem until it felt like a chant, hopefully with some primitive quality from childhood.

He was too ill for visitors in the mornings, so I gravitated towards the zoo where I found many of my favourite Amazonian species which I had already encountered on my recent travels in Venezuela. I portrayed my father and myself in a series of animal-masks because I love animals. Someone said to me that the animals were a kind of tribunal, and I like that idea, that I was putting him, and myself, on trial. Here is the opening poem where his face becomes a shimmering mask of hummingbird feathers:

The Strait-Jackets

I lay the suitcase on Father's bed
and unzip it slowly, gently.
Inside, packed in cloth strait-jackets
lie forty live hummingbirds
tied down in rows, each tiny head
cushioned on a swaddled body.
I feed them from a flask of sugar water,
inserting every bill into the pipette,
then unwind their bindings
so Father can see their changing colours
as they dart around his room.
They hover inches from his face
as if he's a flower, their humming
just audible above the oxygen recycler.
For the first time since I've arrived
he's breathing easily, the cannula
attached to his nostrils almost slips out.
I don't know how long we sit there
but when I next glance at his face
he's asleep, lights from their feathers
still playing on his eyelids and cheeks.
It takes me hours to catch them all
and wrap them in their strait-jackets.
I work quietly, he's in such
a deep sleep he doesn't wake once.

When I wrote this poem I had no idea what these images meant. I came across a photo of forty hummingbirds sleeping in a suitcase, and an account of how the Brazilian hummingbird fancier Augusto Ruschi stored them live in suitcases for air travel and kept them in the hold. Hummingbirds go into torpor at low temperatures to conserve their energy, and Ruschi used to wrap each one in its strait-jacket to protect its wings. The photo and its caption spoke to me, and I knew I had to take this suitcase (metaphorically) to show my father. Perhaps the forty hummingbirds symbolised forty years: I didn't take him a suitcase of hummingbirds, but I did bring him photo albums of my life.

Hummingbirds are tiny dynamos and when I write my aim is to capture life force, make poems intense and alive. They are beautiful (to make my father beautiful), jewel-like, and aggressive, attack owls fearlessly. They are penetrators, penetrating flowers with their bills to drink nectar. They breathe supernaturally fast and my father breathed painfully with the aid of an oxygen recycler, which reminded me of the Amazon rainforest, the threatened lungs of the planet.

I wrote a sequence of these animal masks to depict our troubled relationship, then my mother died, leaving me a trunk of letters containing shocking revelations, including that he had raped her and that I was the result of that pregnancy. I couldn't make myself visit him afterwards, as there was the possibility he had also abused me. So I began reading about initiation rites that turn boys into warriors. The purpose of these rites is to acquire strength and that's what I needed. The tribes I studied were the Pemón (of Venezuela's 'Lost World'), the Yanomami, the Sateré Mawé (who use the excruciating ant glove ritual), and the head-shrinking Jivaro or 'People of the Sacred Waterfalls' now known as the Shuar.

My poems got fiercer. At the core of the book there's a set of rite-of-passage poems: 'The Ant Glove', 'A Wasps' Nest', 'Trophy', and 'My Father's Body'. These poems were violent but crucial for me to write. I felt overwhelmed by my parents, and what these poems did for me was to reduce my father's power, sometimes by literally shrinking him. Here is how one poem starts:

My Father's Body

As I sit here holding your hand
knowing that you were once a rapist,
I think how it isn't enough
just to shrink your head.
I could shrink your whole body
with the skills I learnt as a sculptor.
I'd use volcanic heat,

> water from Fire River,
> hot sand from its bed
> and I'd sing to my materials.
> They'd sing back, glowing.
> Even Jivaro headhunters
> would be shocked at how easily
> I'd slit the sides of each limb,
> peel the skin from your neck
> and torso down to your feet.

The young Jivaro warrior has to undergo a seclusion ordeal before he can shrink an enemy's head, enduring the fasts and sleep deprivation a shaman goes through to enter a trance. He then has to sit facing a sacred high waterfall. There, he receives a terrifying vision: a ball of lightning, or two fighting black jaguars, or two coiled giant anacondas attack him, and he has to touch his vision, which dispels it. This is how he gains *arutam* – soul force and killing power.

The years preceding my father's reappearance I'd had an obsession with waterfalls and sought out the highest in the world – Angel Falls in Venezuela. I flew over the kilometre high plume plunging from Devil's Mountain and canoed to the base. I was ill and feverish while there so looking at the falls was disorienting. Then, just before my father made contact, I dreamt about being back at the base where, out of the blue, his head appeared in the falls like a premonition.

There are gentler poems in the book, and some where the ferocity and tenderness are intertwined. I believe that human beings are born good, and felt that my researches into the South American jungle and its tribes were a journey to explore my father's behaviour and the reasons behind it. After shrinking him to a manageable size I could go and visit him again before he died. Here is the last part of 'My Father's Body':

> I wouldn't stop until
> you'd shrunk enough to be my doll.
> I'd hang you from a hook
> and stare at my naked Papa –
> your miniature penis
> that couldn't hurt a mouse.
> I'd take you to a part of the forest
> where only children are allowed.
> Walking there, I'd listen
> to what your soul had to say.
> When I arrived at the clearing

I'd lay you out. And stay
as the children gathered around
whispering, touching your tiny fingers.

We now look at June English's account of her relationship with her first husband. She describes the different ways in which she tackled writing about this damaging marriage and how the process of producing poems helped her.

The scattered self: June English

Marital rape is, apart from physical and sexual violation, a betrayal of trust, of promises made and of the children of the marriage. It makes the victim question the fundamental values of life. A Catholic, brought up to believe marriage was forever, I could see no end to the situation – writing about it did not come easily. Before I met A, my first husband, I was a habitual scribbler. Yet during the ten traumatic years we were together, I wrote nothing. It was almost as if by committing anything to paper the nightmare would become real.

People react to stress differently. Their backgrounds, beliefs, the precise situation, and the support of family and friends are of paramount importance. A and I, both Catholics, were married with the full ceremony of a Catholic mass on 7th May 1959. Four years and two children later he left me to live with my best friend. Divorce was rare in those days. I fought for him and won. Desperate to make a fresh start, I agreed that we should emigrate to Vancouver Island: 'and so we flew to Canada, six thousand miles from family and friends. What God had joined together – our private purgatory?' I wrote in my notebook much later in 2000.

The following extract from my 1999 notebook is from a fifteen-line litany which poured out of me in a few minutes. These words were among the first, written or spoken, for over thirty-five years:

I remember the strain of those long, lonely years
when I followed you blindly, when I did as you asked,
when I'd no one to turn to, no one to tell . . .

The line, 'when I followed you blindly, when I did as you asked', provoked several poems. Often they'd tumble out whole – but not, I suspect, without a lot of inner fathoming. An example of this is 'Bunny Girl' which began: 'I keep finding bits of myself / scattered like chewed up papers'. When I wrote this I had no idea where it might lead. In hindsight I realize that, subconsciously, I'd begun to look at what had happened. We, myself and two sons, had returned to England believing that A would follow us. The Dear John letter I received told me he'd shaken us off 'like old rags' as I later wrote in a poem. Caught up in the traumas of a new life, a sister's death, a mother's illness, money to earn, children to care for, I buried what had happened for over thirty years. In 'Bunny Girl' I saw:

> . . . a girl frozen in time,
> naked, except for a white fur coat,
> her woman's eyes startled as a skinned rabbit's,
> starting out, waiting for the pot to boil.

(from *The Sorcerer's Arc*)

Locating the girl and putting her back together was a different matter. The innocent Catholic was dead; the girl 'who followed you blindly' learned a new language, found an angry voice:

Whore Games

Talk about sex, scandal and locked doors,
fishnet-tights and bare buttocks,
rumpy-pumpy on the ironing board
with you in your Argyle socks.

Talk about me playing the fish-wife,
screeching for a taste of your cod;
talk about settling for whelks,
when I find that the cod's served cold.

Talk about playing at whore games
with you as an ironmonger,
and me on a bed of nails,
pretending I'm good at yoga.

Talk about power struggle,
talk about wolves baring fangs,
talk about vixens as playthings,
talk about hammer and tongues.

Talk about sex, scandal and locked doors
with you as a power-monger,
talk about bullies and bond-slaves
and the death of anger.

Talk about me as your whore,
mocked, degraded and beaten.
Talk about talk, you couldn't,
and my blouses cover the blows.

(from *Sunflower Equations*)

I wrote this poem, using the patterning device, during a workshop run by poet, John Whitworth. The repeated phrase: 'Talk to me' opened the door of silence, allowed me to give vent to repressed anger and self-loathing. The key line, 'Talk about talk, you couldn't,' came later and with it the first hope that what had happened wasn't all down to me. The rhythmic insistence in the defiance was a cogent and therapeutic release. Seeing the poem published, receiving letters of admiration and support from other poets, played an important part in the rehabilitation of my self.

The poems discussed so far were all written on impulse. Strangely, the next step came when my home was burgled. There was no sign of entry, just the gradual recognition that valued items had gone. This violation – rape of my home, opened closed doors. Memories of those 'long, lonely years' unnerved me and filled me with self-doubt. But this time I told my story, told it in dribs and drabs to family and friends – allowed it the credence of words in my notebook. This entry was made in 2005:

I'm alone at Whiffen Spit, that graveyard of the dead, head and arms bruised, black as the pebbles embedded in the sand; a dumb, and senseless thing . . . I can see the back of your red-checked shirt as you turned from us that day – the day that ripped belief and murdered youth. You're standing on the seaward side, smoking your Players Weight, gazing across the Straits of Juan de Fuca to where the Cascade Mountains rise like demented ghosts of our wedding cake. Look at you standing there, ignoring us. Turning away when our son gets stung, ignoring his screams as he wets himself. I can see you now, standing there cool and unmoved as a bit part actor in a boring play. Your presence will haunt me forever, as will the sound of waves thrashing against the dark rocks, the smell of seaweed, the screech of hawks and turkey vultures – the sea-anemone you found in a rock-pool, the cruel way you poked it with a stick.

Whiffen Spit, the way it reached out, dividing the Pacific Ocean and the straits of Juan de Fuca, embedded itself on my psyche that day. I recall sifting the bleached bones of fish, looking into empty shells, equating the 'lifelessness' of our living lives with them. That I had linked trauma and place became clear in this first piece of flow writing. I had worked with images before but nothing I'd written had been so imbued with a sense of place. Research helped me – the more I read of the habitat, its natural wild life and seasonal changes, the more the events attached themselves to the images. The first two poems which had gone through countless drafts, sat waiting for the un-writable third. Finally, during a gathering of *Second Light Network* poets at Launde Abbey in 2005 I found myself talking to Myra, telling her of Whiffen Spit, the sea-anemone and the rape. Talking of it, finding myself respected, not degraded, I began this poem:

Thanksgiving, October 1970

You at Whiffen Spit, on the seaward side,
where the Cascade Mountains rise
in sheeted skies, like the demented
ghosts of wedding cakes, where hawks
and turkey vultures flay the air.

Too quiet, our children's play
in this graveyard of the sea. Pensive,
they sift the bleached bones of cuttlefish
and conch, find a calcified starfish,
ask me why it doesn't swim.

You move to the harbour side, examine
sheltered rock pools where small fish
dart and hide in seaweed gardens,
find a sea anemone, a pulsating cell, red
as a woman's vulva and poke it with a stick.

Later, in the shell called home,
you strip me; tie me, camera poised,
kneel between my quivering knees,
thrust screwdrivers into my womb,
skewer the woman from the girl.

Writing this was a slow process. Two things were holding me back. The first was the amount of material – so many other instances of mistreatment and cruelty, all threatening to push the rape aside. Even at this late stage it would have been easy to do that. Talking about it, writing it in note form is not final; finishing it, seeing it in print, with the possibility of publication, offered a double-edged sword. Would it lay the ghost or confirm my shame? Sharing draft copies of the poem with loved and respected friends and fellow poets tipped the balance. Bit by bit I pared the material to its core, asking advice, sifting it, discussing it, always conscious and insistent that the final poem must speak my truth, no less and no more. In writing this I had hoped to lay the ghost, allow the past to rest. Publication of all three poems in the journal

Agenda and of *Thanksgiving, October 1970* in *Images of Women*, together with the feedback, helped towards that.

'But she is always there, that younger self . . . / mindful of past bruises . . . fearful for herself and for her children . . . ' ('The Big C', *The Sorcerer's Arc*). And – 'She' has questions to ask, questions which will fuel new poems. Why did he take the photographs? Where are they now? Does he have any regrets? Questions that can't be answered. 'She' finds that disturbing.

We have focused most of this chapter on writings by women but, of course, boys and men are also subject to sexual abuse and Pauline Kirk was very aware of this when she spoke to survivors of childhood sexual abuse during the time she worked for social services. She edited *A Survivor Myself* using extracts from their writings as well as her notes from the stories they told her and she represented both sexes equally in this book. One piece by a man relates his struggle to come to terms with abuse from both his grandfather and his father. Another, by a professional writer identified as Joe, begins:

> With the carrot and stick combination of Mr Biggs caressing my genitals and Dad's impatient tutoring, I was a fairly advanced reader by the age of seven. Mr Biggs wasn't my teacher, but he took a shine to me and literally held me up in front of his class of nine year olds, where I would precociously demolish the book they were stammering through . . . I was aware that what Mr Biggs was doing out of their sight, with his hand ventriloquist-style up the back of my shorts, was probably wrong. (Ed. Kirk 1994, p. 7)

In fact the boy liked this friendship until the day when Mr. Biggs asked him to touch his genitals. Then he panicked and the teacher threatened him with terrible trouble if he ever told anybody and signalled the threat every time he saw him. As a result Joe was emotionally confused and disturbed for many years. In his thirties he began to understand himself and the experience he had been through. He concludes: 'Writing about what happened to me has been therapeutic and if the ghost of Biggs isn't entirely banished, he doesn't cast the same shadow as he once did' (ibid., p. 13).

Displacement and disability

Life, for many people, is affected by some kind of displacement – a circumstance which has a profound effect on their lives, limiting it or forcing it into a particular direction. Very often this creates a problem but many individuals find ways of turning the negatives of their situation or condition into positives. In this chapter we shall look at different kinds of displacement: exile from the country of birth, separation from birth parents including adoption, and imprisonment which can be considered as an exile from freedom. We are also including disability in this chapter because the loss of a faculty or physiological impairment has a displacing effect.

Over and above the circumstances listed above many of us experience a sense of displacement at some point in our lives as a feeling of not fitting in or of not belonging – a need which is particularly strong in children. We begin by looking at Myra's experience of this.

Belonging: Myra

Just before World War II my father, a government scientist, was transferred from the Admiralty in London to be the chief scientist at the torpedo factory in Greenock on the Firth of Clyde. I was three, unaware that I was leaving Hampstead Garden Suburb in London where my parents had a network of Jewish friends and nearby relatives. When I was of school age I was sent to the Greenock Academy which seemed a long journey from our house. It was an all-age school and I was daunted by its large nineteenth-century buildings surrounded by high walls, also by the hundreds of pupils, many of whom seemed huge. Just being at the school filled me with a sense of fear. There was more to take on:

> When I was six I learnt
> according to the gospel of school
> that Jesus Christ meek and mild

was the child of God,
so I was put out,
not to say ashamed,
when my parents gave me the news
that he was not my saviour.

(from *Insisting on Yellow*)

Finding out that I was Jewish was bad news because every now and again I was taken to a synagogue in Glasgow and afterwards I had to play with strange children. All this was 'uncomfortable/like wearing clothes which didn't fit'. Sometimes at school children jeered at me for being English and this added to my general sense that I was different. By the time I was fifteen we were back in England and living in Chichester. I used to sing with the school choir in the cathedral but my sense of not belonging, of being a freak almost, was still very strong. I felt very guilty because although I wanted to I couldn't quite believe in Christianity or any other religion. Eventually I found a sense of meaning in Wordsworth's pantheism but I was well into adulthood before it dawned on me that many people felt 'different' and my sense of being a misfit disappeared. It was then that I wrote the poem, *Belonging*, from which I've quoted above. Here is the end of it:

Now I've gone far enough
not to feel my oddness
obtruding like an awkward corner
though I remain at odds
with all orthodoxies. For I belong
with those who don't belong:
the eccentric, the oppressed,
the over-sensitive, the voiceless
struggling to communicate by finger;
those beset by failure.
Sufficient to me to find
I slot into the human race.

For Eva Hoffman displacement was sudden and enormous when, in 1959 at the age of thirteen, she emigrated from Cracow with her parents and sister to Vancouver because life had become too insecure in Poland for Jewish people. It took her until well into adulthood to come to terms with living in Canada. She examines how she coped with leaving the country of her birth in her memoir, *Lost in Translation*. In the first part of the book she writes about her childhood which she remembers as a paradise although she grew up in an apartment 'squeezed into three rudimentary rooms with four other people, surrounded by squabbles, dark political rumblings, memories of wartime suffering, and daily struggle for existence' (Hoffman 1991, p. 5). What mattered though was her loving family, a wide network of friends including a childhood sweetheart, music and her beloved music teacher.

Exile, the book's second part, details the early effects of moving to another culture and a life in which her family were short of money. In describing the dislocation she experienced Hoffman must speak for many others exiled from the land of their birth. One of the first shocks she had was in the classes she attended to learn English where the teacher changed her name, Ewa, to Eva and her sister's name, Alina, to Elaine. When she learnt English words and expressions they did not feel like real equivalents. The word 'river', for example, sounded 'cold' and had none of the associations of the Polish word. She writes:

> The worst losses come at night. As I lie down in a strange bed in a strange house – my mother is a sort of housekeeper here, to the aging Jewish man who has taken us in in return for her services – I wait for the spontaneous flow of inner language which used to be my nighttime talk with myself . . . Nothing comes. Polish, in a short time, has atrophied, shrivelled from sheer uselessness. Its words don't apply to my new experiences; they're not coeval with any of the objects, or faces, or the very air I breathe in daytime. In English, words have not penetrated to those layers of my psyche from which a private conversation could proceed. This interval before sleep used to be the time when my mind became both receptive and alert, when images and words rose up to consciousness, reiterating what had happened during the day, adding the day's experiences to those already stored there, spinning out the thread of my personal story. (Ibid., p. 107)

The sense of alienation did not wear off. The young girl tried to push memories of the past away but she kept dreaming of Cracow. When she tried to fit in she was constantly aware of using words incorrectly, saying the wrong thing, of being an oddity or of trying to create an impression. In her efforts to assimilate, Hoffman tried to stop herself gesticulating and to cultivate detachment. Often she felt silenced.

The last part of the book traces her slow assimilation. A girl of considerable intellect she went to college first in Texas and then to Harvard where she continued to question who she was. Later she met her childhood sweetheart again and there is a poignant account of how much each of them had changed.

Later still she went on a visit to Poland but the pull of both cultures remained. Eventually she consulted a psychotherapist and by re-living her childhood in English, she managed to knit herself together, though she recognized: 'The gap cannot be fully closed' (ibid., p. 274). However, she saw it was also 'a window through which I can observe the diversity of the world' (ibid., p. 274). She remarks too: 'Dislocation is the norm rather than the aberration in our time' (ibid., p. 274).

Lost in Translation is not a narrative autobiography. It gives an impression of the stages of Hoffman's life but the main focus of this perceptive book is the investigation of her feelings, behaviour, questionings and the gradual shifts which took place in her inner life.

Leaving the land of his birth was a happier experience for artist and poet, John Lyons. However, his memories of life in Trinidad and Tobago are indelible and over a long period of time they have been the main source of his creative work.

Exile: John Lyons

My exile, if it could be regarded as such, was self-imposed. In 1959 I came to England in pursuit of an art education at Goldsmiths College in London and was confronted by the awe-inspiring reality of an English art college society, to say nothing of the world outside that social microcosm. The poems I had brought with me from Trinidad were imbued with the legacy of a colonial literary education: Shelley, Byron, Tennyson and others. The students of my year considered them archaic and a source of much amusement. That traumatic experience resulted in my destroying all the poems I had written up to that time but the desire to write poetry remained compelling. I attended creative writing workshops and grew to understand that poetry springing from a psychological and emotional base can often act as a cathartic means of coping with the vicissitudes of life. The strangeness of the new cultural environment, coupled with the physical and psychological distance from my native Trinidad, telescoped into sharp focus what I had left behind. Here is an excerpt from the 'Lure of the Cascadura', the title poem of my first collection:

> Exiled under silver birch and conifers
> see the poui and immortelles blooming;
>
> the mistle thrush sings,
> but I hear the kiskadee . . .

I began exploring the folklore and legends, the vibrancy and drama of carnival, the street theatre of everyday life. A deluge of childhood memories and images came flooding back:

> Amidst bush and bramble
> I grew wild as rocksage, learned
> how to avoid stepping on snakes.
>
> I taunted squirrels:
> ate mangoes on their stems,
> braved pikant patch for gri-gri,
> got bunged up with guava seeds;

('Tobago Days' from Lure of the Cascadura)

I remembered as a child sitting with friends on the backdoor steps of our house in the moonlight gleefully scaring each other with jumbie stories, the exploits of the blood-sucking Soucouyant, Loupgaroo, Papa Bois and a host of other folklore characters. In 'The Game-Keeper' I present Papa Bois, sometimes called Maitre Bois, as the protector of animals in the forest:

> You stalk hunters
> in the green dusk
> beneath balata trees,
> mahogany and cedar.
> The macaw's screech
> is your fanfare:
> you materialize
> clothed with the forest
> and the odour of animals.
>
> We don't know
> who you really are;
> but you are real enough
> to the killer hunter,
> his last words muffled,
> his weight on a strangling vine.

(from Voices from a Silk-Cotton Tree)

Carnival is a festival of hedonistic abandonment and in the poem, 'Carnival', I tried to convey this very feeling with the use of the Trinidadian vernacular and onomatopoeic rhythm:

Oh Gaard! Oh Gaard!
Pan sweet, sweet yuh hear:
LISTEN, LISTEN
to dat beat:
Biddin-ki-diggidin, biddin-ki-diggidin
biddin-ki-diggidin, biddin-ki-diggidin . . .

(from Lure of the Cascadura)

But not all my memories of life in Trinidad were happy ones. At the age of nine my mother died after a very short illness. My world of warmth and emotional comfort was completely shattered. Much later in England, remembering her death, I wrote 'The Parting', in which I described the view I had of her as funeral attendants performed the accustomed ritual of passing me three times over her coffin displayed in the drawing room, apparently to establish in my child's mind the finality of her death:

After all these years
your blood-drained face is still
cradled in coffin mauve.

You look so far away
lying there.

(from Lure of the Cascadura)

My father, who was determined that we should stay together as a family of brothers and sisters, sent us to Tobago to be looked after by our paternal grandmother. It was in this period of my life that I developed a habit of going off on my own into the forest where I found some comfort in the closeness of trees and shrubs. My other escape was into the world of novels, Sir Walter Scott's in particular. As a boy of ten reading fed my imagination and it was from that time that I felt the urge to write.

Love of language, I do believe, comes naturally to peoples of the Caribbean. Official, Standard English is a legacy of the British to its colonies. I use both languages. Some memories of my life in Trinidad naturally invoke the colour and rhythm of language used in everyday communication, the full force and theatricality of which, with its accompanying facial expressions, gestures, inflexions and intonations of the voice, is difficult to convey in written form without the support of performance. I delight, nevertheless, in its use as in the poem, 'Livin In Bonne Langue':

Look how he limin,
rhymin life wid language:

Coonoomoonoo
soften vexation wid music.

For seduction,
punkaloonks and doodoo
slip off de smoodness
of he tongue.

(from *Voices from a Silk-Cotton Tree*)

I have been living in England for forty-eight years and have returned to Trinidad several times. The colour, smells, the brilliance of its sun, the sudden downpour of its rain even when the sun remains shining, the vibrancy and hedonism of its celebrations remain indelibly etched in my psyche.

Tariq Latif is a poet who feels strung between two cultures. He was born in Lahore but has lived most of his life in Manchester. His poems look affectionately at the life he left behind. They also cast a sceptical and often perplexed eye over his adopted country. In a sequence, 'The Outsiders', which is in his first book, *Skimming The Soul*, he considers the dilemmas of Pakistani people in the United Kingdom. Some keep themselves to themselves and create a little Pakistan in their houses, work and worshipping places. Some, like the poet, venture forth and encounter prejudice and abuse. He cannot find his place anywhere, and in the final poem gives full expression to his anguish over the situation in which he finds himself:

If I take the chance
And sever my roots
    will they grow
In the warmth of your white arms?
Does the fear in my face show?

What do I do now that I
Am hung upside down over grey
Muddled space? My feet are roped
Into family blood. My arms have
Grown wings and I just hang, limp,
Swaying between two worlds.

Exile had a profound effect on Elke Dutton. She was sent on the Kinder-transport from Czechoslovakia to England at the age of fourteen months, just before World War II began. For the next few years she lived in orphanages and it was not until she was seven that she was re-united with her mother. This double displacement left her with no memory of her early childhood. She felt a strong need though to retrieve it and writing has helped her to do so. Flow-writing exercises began the process. Here are two short extracts:

> In the silence, in the silence, why do I chatter so if silence is good. I dare not face myself . . . Don't run away – watch, tell, observe. The bird that flutters on the branch is shot and splintered mindlessly on still afternoons, in silence. The child playing in the quiet dust is maimed and disfigured by a malevolent mortar shell . . . A nebulous something that has a negative feel – links in the silence . . .
>
> I leave it for another day. Yet what is it we fear the most, the tiny child who could not sustain her very being without her mother – left to cope in a strange land, all alone. Strangers, strangers, who are these starchy strangers in white starched uniforms . . . ?

These potent pieces together with what she had learnt about her early years enabled her to create memories in poems. She commented: 'Creating finished pieces of work out of my personal world is important, as if by giving the writing shape I also create an inner sense of completion and order'. Here is one of the poems:

Among Strangers

Who are these strangers
in white starched aprons

armed with flannels
in scrubbed hands

bright smiles
stitched onto their faces

their noses tight
against her leaking smell?

Elke Dutton's childhood was strongly affected by being parted from her mother for several years. A baby or child separated from his or her birth parents and adopted also undergoes a displacement. This may cause very little dislocation but there can be problems. Kate Foley writes about her process of adjustment.

Myths and secrets: Kate Foley

'Good God, Elsie! You don't want that! Take it back', said my Aunt Margaret to my mother, who was timidly clutching the squawking bundle she had taken delivery of from the Adoption Society that very day. But despite the massed ranks of disapproval from her relatives – the blood-is-thicker-than-water hisses from thirteen siblings and assorted grandparents – my mother did want a baby of her own so much that she braved family, class and wartime difficulties to get one. Unfortunately, although she had great courage she didn't get any help to understand just what she had taken on, with the result that for a long time we were both haunted by the suspicion that I was the wrong baby and she the wrong mother.

In the 1930s and 40s the norm was not to tell a child it was adopted, so that for me the feeling of being an awkward fit in the family was compounded by an atmosphere of secrecy so dense that I was perpetually afraid of accidentally crashing through its skin and finding out something I'd much rather not know. However, when following up a broad hint from a school teacher, I rifled through my mothers lisle stockings and knickers and found my adoption certificate, after the initial crashing shock, my feeling was one of immense relief. Now I could be free to fashion my own identity – the first of many such seductive myths.

When I told my mother I was going to be a writer, she sniffed. 'How're you going to pay the rent?' 'I shall starve in a garret', I announced, only half whimsically. It took me a long time to write myself out of the myths of abandoned child, child of *real* parents (i.e. middle class and better off than my working class set), misunderstood artist . . . At the core of this, my purple period, there was, of course, a very real pain, one which I believe all adopted children suffer, however open and loving their new parents are, which has to do with forging an identity and coming to terms with an absence so deep it seeps into everything, like the milk disappearing in my father's mahogany tea.

Little by little I discovered through writing, voracious reading and much later therapy, that writing is *not* therapy. It is the hard task of seeing. It may well include passing your own experience through the sharply focused lense of reality but it is never simply bleeding onto the paper. I began to want my writing to be styptic and astringent. I needed it to tell me the truth about myself and the world. I began to appreciate the richness of my own background and to see that like it or lump it I had been mothered by the woman who identified herself as my mother. The poem I've chosen to include here, which is in my book *A Year Without Apricots*, starts by describing my own lacks but I'm glad I couldn't end it without a tender eye on my mother's. What do you do when, after a long journey, the absence you are used to becomes a simple space? Well, you could write about it . . .

Milk

She never smelt of milk.
Sweat and sometimes fear
crackled like burnt paper
behind her overall.

When the doodle-bug's clock-work
stopped, quiet as a feather
and she crammed my face
into butchers' sawdust,
pine and greasy blood,

when I coughed
or wouldn't coax
cold gobs of cod
into my mouth
squared off to cry,

when in my new stilettos
and sugar starched slip,
creaking like ice,
I limped home
after midnight,

when my father, twisting
in the smoke of pain,
refused to die
until she said the word,
crossly, at last,

when lavender soap,
clean sheets, stale air
and disinfectant replacing sweat,
she stared down death
like jack in its box,

but worst, when her breasts ached,
I roared, the landlady tutted,
my borrowed father sighed,
she never smelt of milk.

Imprisonment, being denied the freedom to move about as you please, to
decide where and how one spends one's time, is another area of displacement.
We consider first of all the imprisonment of people who have committed a
crime against society.

Write inside: John

Prisons are about locking people up as a means of punishment. Writing is about the freeing of the spirit from the limitations of the social environment and the unfettered exploration of the imagination. It is a paradox that one activity should take place inside the other.

For a period of fifteen years I was Prison Education Officer in three different penal establishments, followed by Writer in Residence in a fourth. Working in such places is like time-travelling. It is like being transported back into a nineteenth-century ethos (and often physical conditions too). It is all locks and bars and keys; it is shouts and commands and abuse; it is negative and primitive and punitive. In theory it might seem that the atmosphere of an open prison would be very different from that of a closed one, but in reality that does not appear to be so. As one female inmate wrote: 'An open prison is a prison ruled by unseen bars; these are within people's minds, behind their eyes'.

Although my role in the first three prisons I worked in was not that of a writer I ran regular workshops for prisoners to encourage self-expression. In all four prisons I wrote myself. The challenges to make sense of my surroundings, to explore the predicaments of those in my care, and to counter the threats to my own sense of identity, never lessened throughout this period.

My first concern was always for the inmates, who could not withdraw to a comfortable environment at the day's end. The second place I worked in was a young offenders' institution. This made a particular impact on me because the minds of those in my charge, many on full-time education, were still at a formative stage. This was the period when our political masters were experimenting with a militaristic regime for trainees. My own feelings about this are encapsulated in the poem I called 'SHORT, SHARP, SHOCKING'. I am looking out of my office window onto the parade ground:

> The trainees, sad inner city saplings
> stunted by lack of cash compost at the root,
> are here staked out sternly in rows
> according to alien rules of nurture.
>
> Only a few weeks of pruning, dragooning,
> of testing the strain, and force-feeding them,
> and, despite the inadequacy of the stock,
> see – the hardy perennial offender!

Female prisons are emotional, highly volatile places. Women in prison often experience multiple problems: many have been abused, and have been trying to sustain one-parent families; now their children may have been taken into care. I tried to reflect their predicament in this poem:

Women Inside

These have left behind at the gates
their lovers, husbands and friends,
their children, broken promises,
misunderstandings and mistakes.
Now there is nothing they can do
that will make the least difference.
Here they are confined within
a casualty ward of the mind
endlessly resolving traumas in sutures
that inexorably melt away
when exposed to the normal airs
leaving a gaping hole for pain
and confusion to rush back in.

The poems so far quoted have been generalized, attempts to sum up situations in common. I also wrote many poems and pieces of prose about individuals. In such places one comes into contact with a cross-section of people one might not otherwise encounter, and there is a rapid broadening and deepening of one's responses. There also has to be a coming-to-terms with the control side of prison: made up of the staff, including governors, prison and probation officers. Relations can easily become fraught, and 'fighting one's corner' in the face of indifference and sometimes hostility to one's ideal of rehabilitation is an essential part of one's role. The reflection, and sometimes safety-valve opportunity, afforded by writing was for me an essential tool for survival on a daily basis.

I have said that there is always the underlying tension which comes from the nature of incarceration and one's personal response to it. There are many occasions when the realization comes to you with a sense of shock that you are serving a sentence too, and have absorbed some of the attitudes of the long-term inmate. The poem I wrote after re-entering prison, this time as a writer, a couple of months after leaving as an educator, reflects this most poignantly:

Inside Again

I'm giving in my name at the gate
I'm handing in my tally
I'm receiving my keys
I'm breathing in my nostrils
that familiar stale smell.

Inside me there must be
a kind of longing for
the bars that exclude challenge
the rules that inhibit choice
the dress that proclaims deference.

I'm seeing the danger signs
and now I'm up on the Wing
the most alarming thing
is how my mouth keeps opening
and speaking the lines.

I showed many of the prisoners I worked with that writing has the capacity to relieve tensions and help one attain some kind of perspective. The notebook in the cell and the sharing in the group became a kind of lifeline. One man summed up what it meant to him in the following words: 'Poetry is the heart of expression, the true confessions of mind-beat'.

To be able to express the basic fear of being locked in with the clarity which Bernie achieved in his first piece of prose constituted for him a profound internal sense of unlocking:

Locked In

BANG! Small and weak, helpless. Lost, forgotten. The walls slope over me bringing the ceiling lower and lower till I can feel its weight. The dull glow from the light throbs in my head. I close my eyes but I can still see it; and the room, and the cold hardness, stark and bare. I feel that if I screamed no-one would hear me. Sunlight, if only I could see sunlight. A fear envelops me. I feel that I will never see day again. Air: I feel that which I breathe to be warm and suffocating.

Connie was one of those people who discovered a writing talent while 'inside' and who continued to exercise it after release. She wrote a number of moving pieces about the process of going back into her community and reconnecting with the life of her relations. 'Coming Home' is one:

I'm coming home now and I'm trying not to poison this beloved air with my feelings of bitterness, but a weekend alone with my family has never been easy.

On Sunday when I had been there twenty-four hours I could feel the resentment growing cancerous within me, and with every thoughtless remark they made tears of frustration and humiliation pricked at the back of my eyes.

At 7pm I could no longer stand the strain and I sought sanctuary in the dark, brittle January night on the pretence of needing some cigarettes, and alone in the carpark at the back of the building I gazed up at the TV flickering window, the illuminated pane that protects the world from my family.

On turning I spied a wispy rice-paper moon, then something primeval surged within me and, still gazing at the moon, I fell to my knees and howled with pain. From the frost-ridden town I heard the howling, yelping replies, a chorus from the bowels of humanity. Far above me a window was flung open and a voice bellowed 'Shut those fucking dogs up.'

Writing is the art form of most practical use to prisoners. The tools are of the simplest. The other requirement is time, of which (alas) they have a seemingly endless supply!

Sadly, in many parts of the world people are imprisoned for political reasons. In these cases the prisoner is likely to have no idea when or, even if, he or she will be released and may well be subject to brutal treatment. Those inflicting cruelty may themselves be victims of a political system.

This was very much the case during the Cultural Revolution in China. Nien Cheng, a wealthy Chinese woman who had lived abroad and who worked for Shell after her husband died, was denounced in 1966 as a capitalist spy. Most of her belongings, which included many books and works of art such as fine pieces of porcelain, were confiscated or destroyed. For a while she lived under house arrest but when she went on insisting she was innocent she was taken to No 1 Detention House. For the next six and a half years she remained there in solitary confinement.

Life and Death in Shangai bears witness to her mistreatment and her grief about the death of her daughter, Meiping, who was killed while she was in prison. At the same time it is an in-depth account of living through the Cultural Revolution. It reveals Cheng's extraordinary courage, also the ways in which she used her intelligence and sense of humour to resist her tormentors and hit back at them.

When she was taken to prison she saw it as an opportunity to study a detention house at close range. She was given a number instead of name and locked up in a filthy cell yet she notes: 'For me, crossing the prison threshold was the beginning of a new phase of my life which, through my struggle for survival and justice, was to make me a spiritually stronger and politically more mature person' (Cheng 1995, pp. 119–20)

Because of poor food, the winter cold, harsh questioning and threats, Cheng's health broke down after a time but she continued to deduce the situation from the propaganda newspapers which were given out and to calculate how best to look after herself and outwit her tormentors. At one point she wrote:

> My persistent efforts to maintain sanity had a measure of success. But there were still moments when I was so burdened with hunger and misery that I was tempted to let go my tenuous grip on the lifeline of survival. At those times, I had to depend on conflict with the guards to stimulate my fighting spirit.
>
> 'Report!' I would walk to the door of the cell and call out with all my strength . . .
>
> 'How long do I have to wait for the government to investigate my case? It's illegal to lock up an innocent person in prison. It's against Chairman Mao's teachings.' In fact no mention was ever made in his four volumes of such practice, but I was pretty sure that the semi-literate guards had not read Mao's books thoroughly . . .
>
> 'Lower your voice! You mustn't shout! The interrogator is busy.' I knew very well that there was no interrogator working at that time. She knew I knew it, but we kept up the pretence.
>
> . . . I knew the other prisoners were listening, as they had nothing else to do. I also knew that they probably enjoyed hearing another prisoner being defiant, just as I felt encouraged whenever I heard another prisoner brave enough to answer the guards back. (Ibid., pp. 186–7)

Because she continued to resist she was beaten up and left for eleven days in handcuffs which cut deeply into her hands. Nevertheless she wouldn't confess and when the handcuffs were removed she devoted herself to tending her badly wounded hands and building up her strength.

At last when the political situation had eased a little a fudged document, which Cheng disputed, led to her release and she was given living quarters but kept under watch. She was officially told that her daughter, Meiping, had committed suicide but she did not believe it and surreptitiously she began to uncover facts about Meiping's murder. Eventually after Mao Tse-tung's death she managed to obtain a passport to go to America but she was sad to leave her country because it still mattered to her so much. In the epilogue to her memorable book she says:

> Writing about the death of my daughter and my own painful experience during the Cultural Revolution was traumatic. Often I had to put the manuscript away . . . But I persisted in my effort. I felt a compulsion to speak out and let those who have the good fortune to live in freedom know what my life was like in Communist China. (Ibid., p. 488)

We move on now to consider disability. If one is without full use of physical or mental faculties then integration in ordinary life presents problems which others do not have to face. For Wendy Lawson there was a further difficulty. She was well into adulthood before her disability was recognized and properly diagnosed.

Life Behind Glass: Wendy Lawson

I wrote *Life Behind Glass* because I wanted to help others understand autism better and I didn't feel there was much out there that was easy to relate to. As an autistic individual it was my attempt to put into words my everyday experiences using both prose and poetry. Sharing my story and my journey towards a diagnosis of autism spectrum disorder (ASD) cost me heaps of anxiety and discomfort. Most of the discomfort was due to revisiting both childhood and adult memories which were very painful but the effort helped me clarify many of those experiences. I find it very helpful to write things down and I actually think in rhyme at times. My love for words and poetry are a useful medium for connecting emotively and so I had a real sense of achievement when the book was published.

I was forty-two years old when I was appropriately diagnosed with ASD. I had been battling confusion and seeming mental illness for more than twenty-five years. The reality that I wasn't 'mental', that there really was a reason for my confusion and difficulties, was a huge relief. However, my new diagnosis brought fresh challenges and I began to explore what being autistic actually meant and how it could be applied to my life. At the beginning of my book I describe what it is like to live with the difficulty of not being good at defining one's emotions and of not recognizing emotions in others:

> One of the best ways of understanding what autism is like is to imagine yourself as a perpetual onlooker. Much of the time life is like a video, a moving film I can observe but cannot reach. The world passes in front of me shielded by glass.
>
> On a good day, I can smell the flowers and taste the inviting aromas. What I cannot do is fully participate in the complexities of apprehension, interpretation, communication and comprehension.
>
> According to the impressions of those around me, my experience of living with autism is like being a written sentence that is incomplete . . . But who can say what is 'complete' and what is lacking? It may be some of us just view life differently and therefore, actually help to make up for the 'lacks' that others experience . . . (Lawson 2000, p. 1)

People often thought me to be rude, egocentric and odd. Actually I don't believe I was any of these things. I was just not in touch with what was happening for me or for others. I used the video description because it was as if life was going on in front of me, sometimes at a very fast pace. I could watch it all happening but I couldn't connect with what it all meant. Quite often other people just expected that I would understand and would know how to respond. For me, the only way of knowing was to do what I always did; if my routine or expectation was changed it caused me to panic. How could I work out what to do or say if the order or expectation was changed? I couldn't.

When things stay the same it is easier to feel safe. Other individuals appear to have the resources to forward-think and this lets them plan ahead, organize themselves, explore alternatives and so on. These are things I find almost impossible to do. My way of coping today is to ask questions or tell someone that I don't understand and I need help. This is vastly different and a great improvement on the lack of skills I had ten years ago, when I might flap and panic at changes I didn't understand. I now understand that I might not be good at 'reading' the emotive states of others, but, once informed, usually verbally, of what is happening for others I can adapt my behaviour accordingly.

One of my first ever experiences where I felt a real connection with another person was as a teenager. I described this later in the book:

> The sun was warm on our bodies and the dappled shade of nearby trees flickered across our faces as we laughed together. It was good to laugh and to feel accepted in the company of another. (Ibid., p. 64)

Today I know acceptance and love by both friends and family. They accept me for who I am and they accept my autism too. Being accepted and having my particular learning style valued and accommodated has been very important. Sharing my experiences with others and aiming to shed light on much of my autistic world is my passion. I love teaching and helping others to 'see' something that, perhaps, had held them in the dark for some time. Writing other books and using words as a tool to build connections to autistic experiences and understanding our 'normality' is very important to me. I see this as a way to building a more inclusive society and a better future for the autistic children of our day.

The problems of becoming disabled after living a normal life are different from those of growing up with a disability. American artist Andrew Potok who had an inherited eye disease, retinitis pigmentosa, found that his eyesight deteriorated rapidly when he was in his forties. He tried to adjust to the fact that he was not going to be able to paint, read, get about unaided and do the many other things which sighted people take for granted but he often felt very depressed and as if his essential personality was being destroyed. When he heard about Helga Barnes, a woman in London who apparently had extraordinary results in curing blindness with the use of bees, he determined to visit her.

His book, *Ordinary Daylight*, is structured round his few months in England, 'the cure' with bee stings and his eventual recognition that the treatment was fraudulent. Potok relates his encounters with the bee woman and his attempts to investigate her authenticity as if he were writing a strange and often comic novel. However, the book, based on his diary, is far more than a colourful story. It is written with extraordinary honesty and in the end Potok's explorations and growing self-knowledge help him to cope with his condition. Here is an excerpt from a visit to Helga at a time when he was still trying to believe in her:

> . . . as Helga was putting fourteen bees in my hair and down my neck, she said: 'Yes, cherub, that is how the bees work sometimes. Especially on you poor depressed people – and who wouldn't be depressed going blind? It will go up and down, up and down, then the ups will be longer and the downs shorter, and one day soon, it will be *whoosh!*' and she stepped in front of me and made an arc from floor to ceiling with her arms, like a conductor driving an orchestra to the final tonic chord, 'All up, angel, all up!'
>
> For a brief moment she seemed to recognize my despair, though always in her own special, cranky way. 'You know I could see it all in the water . . . I could see the depression fighting the improvement all the while.' (Potok 2003, p. 117)

We end this chapter by looking at an extraordinary account of multiple disability:

> Have you ever been at sea in a dense fog, when it seemed as if a tangible white darkness shut you in, and the great ship, tense and anxious, groped her way toward the shore with plummet and sounding-line, and you waited with beating heart for something to happen? I was like that ship before my education began, only I was without compass or sounding-line, and had no way of knowing how near the harbour was. 'Light! Give me light!' was the wordless cry of my soul, and the light of love shone on me in that very hour. (Keller 1996, p. 11)

That is the way Helen Keller celebrates the arrival of her tutor Anne Sullivan in her first volume of autobiography, *The Story of My Life*, originally published in 1903. She was to go on to write twelve further instalments, but none is more vivid than this account of her first twenty-two years. Suffering a severe illness at the age of nineteen months which rendered her blind and deaf, Keller tells a story of courage, faith and optimism which is one of the most inspiring in all literature.

The process of learning with Miss Sullivan is one of great empathy and persistence on the teacher's part. Helen Keller was not always an attentive pupil and sometimes threw tantrums which challenged all in the household. But gradually progress was made. One day she was set the task of stringing beads of various sizes in patterns; this she carried out with minimal concentration and commensurate lack of success, when:

> Miss Sullivan touched my forehead and spelled with decided emphasis, 'Think'. In a flash I knew that the word was the name of the process that was going on in my head. This was my first conscious perception of an abstract idea. (Ibid., p. 15)

Eventually Helen Keller learned to read, write and even speak, and found constructing her narrative and making it come alive through the full use of her other senses a life-enhancing project. Here is part of a lengthy description of her first encounter with a major snow-storm, notable for the immediacy of its telling:

> Narrow paths were shoveled through the drifts. I put on my cloak and hood and went out. The air stung my cheeks like fire. Half walking in the paths, half working our way through the lesser drifts, we succeeded in reaching a pine grove just outside a broad pasture. The trees stood motionless and white like figures in a marble frieze. There was no odour of pine-needles. The rays of the sun fell upon the trees, so that the twigs sparkled like diamonds and dropped in showers when we touched them. So dazzling was the light, it penetrated even the darkness that veils my eyes. (Ibid., p. 29)

Illness 6

In this chapter we are considering ways in which people have written about serious illness: how it helped them express shock and cope day to day, how it supported them in coming to terms with their illness. Physical weakness forces one to live in a narrower frame. This affects terms of reference and if prolonged can change one's sense identity. In a time of illness, though, it is possible to find a range of coping mechanisms, to draw on unexpected strengths and discover new perspectives.

We begin by focusing on diagnosis. As one gets older, of course, one has to face the fact that illness is more likely, but whatever one's age it is a shock to find oneself faced with a major illness which totally disrupts one's life. Here is a poem by Gill McEvoy which encapsulates the sense of disorientation she experienced when she was told she had a life-threatening illness. The short sentences add to the sense of dislocation:

Diagnosis

Outside the window, huge clouds toil by.
I stare, my eyes blind as oceans.

Inside, the air waits for someone to say something.
No-one speaks. My tongue is nailed down.
Words have swum away.

The room turns under me, tick, like a clock.
How strange that is, when here
all clocks have stopped.

The air goes on waiting, stupidly.
No-one can rescue it.

(from *Uncertain Days*)

Myra turned to writing while she was being treated for cancer and found it extraordinarily supportive.

Writing My Way Through Cancer: Myra

When I was told I had breast cancer I was afraid I'd been given a death sentence even though the consultant said the prognosis was good. I learnt later that my reaction was not unusual. Two days after the diagnosis I decided it would help me to turn my writing notebook, in which I sporadically jotted ideas for poems, into a journal. I had no idea then that this would form the basis for a book, *Writing My Way Through Cancer*. That same day I wrote an entry which included a piece about some snow-drops I'd seen in a garden. I knew, even as I started, that it was important – the beginnings of a poem:

> Drops of life on this distressed afternoon. Everything grey – the concrete frontage with miserable sticks like bunches of deadness. The small white bell heads could be gathered together – could be layers pressed to my breast – could fill the space that will be left by my missing breast. These drops are not drops. The weak heads are not weak, not drooping, not dropping. They are hanging bells with thin rims of green on their delicate undersides. They have pushed through the lumpy earth and stand unmoved by the thrusting wind, the bites of cold air. They are stronger than cones of buddleia, than the can-can poppy – a brazen girl kicking. Very small, they bend but do not give way, they refuse winter, silently they remind me it can end. (Schneider 2003, pp. 22–3)

As the words rushed into my head I felt a glimmer of hope that I would write the poem, that my life would continue.

The night before mastectomy I was so frightened I couldn't focus on anything. I took out my journal and told myself to write down everything I was afraid of whether it was rational or irrational. Without thinking about it I began writing sentences in a pattern by repeating the first three words. In fact this was a technique I'd often used in writing workshops because the repeats create a rhythm and a sense of direction. Here are a few of the lines:

> I am afraid of the anaesthetic.
> I am afraid of the period after coming round.
> I am afraid that I'll have difficulty with breathing.
> I am afraid of being very weak and muzzy.
> I am afraid of not being in control.
> I am afraid of being seen as a feeble coward. (Ibid., p. 27)

After a while I found myself writing: 'The operation is a gateway through which I must pass and my life will be longer if I do pass through it.' Then I wrote four sentences in a new pattern:

I want to pass through it and I want it to be tomorrow.
I want to fight my fear.
I want to make the best use I can of the rest of my life whatever it is.
I want to write about cancer in different ways including writing poems about it.
(ibid., p. 27)

When I shut my notebook I had an enormous sense of lightening, a sense that I could cope with my fear and that if I wrote about my progress through illness I wouldn't be dominated by it. I had always believed that writing had a therapeutic element but here was proof that the most mundane words could have an immediate and potent effect. I was elated by the discovery.

During the next twelve months writing was my mainstay. I used my journal for dumping my feelings, writing poem notes, describing incidents in my life and noting my reactions to books and films. I also wrote fourteen poems which were connected with cancer and I finished the last third of a long poem that was a fictional narrative I had started several months before I was diagnosed.

The first poem I wrote also had a useful practical effect. The breast cancer nurse came to see me three days after the operation and encouraged me to look at the wound, saying I must come to terms with it. I immediately felt slightly faint. She didn't insist but said it would be better if I did so before I left the hospital. The next morning I woke up earlyish and in the dark I gingerly touched my chest. Feeling my shape made me begin to cry but it was a relief to be alone with my feelings in the silence. Images started to form in my head and it was soothing to sort them. Five hours later I'd drafted a poem in my notebook. Here is the poem which I finished soon after I went home:

Today There Is Time

to touch the silken stillness
of myself, map its landscape,
the missing left breast, to lay
my nervous palm softly
as a bird's wing across
the new plain, allow
tears to fall yet rejoice
that the surgeon scraped
away the killer cells.

Today there is time
to contemplate the way life
opens, clams, parts, savour
its remembered rosemaries,
spreading purples, tight

> white edges of hope, to travel
> the meanings of repair, tug
> words that open parachutes. (Ibid., p. 39)

The next time the breast cancer nurse came I had no problem in looking at the wound.

For a while I wrote mainly about the preciousness of life, the sense of renewal I felt and the fact that the experience of cancer had added a new dimension to my life. Then anger began to surface. One morning I let rip in my journal:

> Cancer and jam, cancer and anger.
> The anger keeps oozing out like pus, breaking out like a rash.
> I'm angry if I drop something.
> I'm angry because I keep losing my glasses.
> I'm angry because the skin of my fingers is sore from chemotherapy.
> I'm angry because my life's been interrupted. (Ibid., p. 85)

After several more lines I started writing notes for a poem: 'What does it feel like, this anger? What does it smell of? What does it sound like? It is bubbling in my body like a mob of prisoners', and I ended: 'It feels as if – well I am – taking energetic action with my anger and it's incredibly releasing, exciting, fun!' (ibid., p. 86). When I wrote the poem I called it 'Release'. Here is the first verse:

> I'm going to slap my anger onto a wet slab,
>   put it through a mangle,
> hang out its long line of eccentric washing.
>   I'm going to fly its flags
> from my windows, smack it into surprised faces,
>   push it up noses,
> smash green bottles of it to smithereens
>   on pavements, daub its shout
> over walls, hurl it down a football field,
>   kick it into goal,
> empty it into a dustcart's masticating jaws. (Ibid., p. 91)

During my illness, while I was writing – whatever I was writing – I felt I was my whole self connected with the world outside me and not my weak ill self. When I stopped keeping my journal I started fleshing it out into a book: *Writing My Way Through Cancer*. I was so struck by the way writing had carried me that I wanted to share its potency with other people and to offer ideas for writing to those who maybe hadn't written before. Later I realized writing the book was also a way to assimilate more fully the trauma I had been through.

Illness and death are the predominant themes of the poems of Frances Bellerby, as they were of her life. They are full of powerful feelings and sometimes are highly dramatic. 'Convalescence', in her *Selected Poems*, is one of her calmest and most measured works. It mirrors the stages of recovery with its slow tread and many repetitions. It contains another voice, but the speaker is not identified, though their role is clear. There are many words about time in this poem, and distance is measured by specific objects which the poet uses as markers for her painfully executed walks. The poem holds out the hope for a return to normality, and the regaining of a healthy perspective on death. Its movement is therefore towards the embrace of positive emotions:

Convalescence

Yesterday, as far as the broken foxglove;
Today, on to the glittering in the hedge;
Tomorrow, right to the first tree
Of the wood in the valley –
Yesterday, as far as the broken foxglove;
Today, to this glittering tin in the hedge;
Tomorrow, right to the first tree
Of the wood in the valley –

And after that? After that the day will come
When I shall go on and on and on, my lost home
Found in my heart; I, a king bearing his kingdom
Within; never again to turn, never to re-trace,
Never to pass any more through the same shadow twice;
Free and light as the dying, in Time; as the dead, in Space.

But I must turn here today,
Turn and go back, as yesterday,
And tomorrow, treading the same way
With everything changed, the freshness gone,
The dripping arch cold, its green
Bright slime dangerous, all vain
The blazing glory of the path at the foot
Of the golden embankment, where my steps obliterate
Outgoing footprints and outgoing thought.

'Did you go too far? Lie down
A while.' 'Has walking brought on the pain?'
'I'll put your tea by the bed and turn
Your bath on early, so rest until then.'
A patient; cared for, protected; love
So passionless and scatheless learning to receive.

Today right up to that glittering tin in the hedge
Though yesterday only with effort as far as the broken foxglove
Tomorrow tomorrow to the shadow cast by the first tree
Of the wood in the valley
And soon after that soon soon the day will come
When I shall go on and on and on my found home
Held in my heart.
        A child again? Too sure, too tireless;
And friends with death.

Stubborn patience and grit is needed not only to fight a major illness but also to cope with well-meaning people with an agenda of their own who offer inappropriate encouragement or advice. Here is another poem by Gill McEvoy which makes its points in a short, sharp monologue:

Message To the Well-meaning

It's not 'being positive'
that gets you through. No,

it's something grittier – sharp, capable of hurt:
it would have you grabbing the very last crumb
from under your best friend's nose,
it's savage, stubborn, it's made of steel –
if you were in business the whole world
would hate your guts. So,

the next person to come along and say
'Think positive' and all that sort of crap
will get it right between the eyes.
For I'm a hard woman now:
I am diamond, carborundum,
and I wipe out fools.

(from *Uncertain Days*)

It is one thing to use writing as Myra did to support yourself through a difficult illness if you have good reason to believe you will recover, quite another to turn to it if you are totally incapacitated and the future is very uncertain. At the age of forty-three Jean-Dominique Bauby, editor-in-chief of *Elle*, suffered a severe stroke which left him sound in mind but without speech and only able to move his head slightly and blink his left eyelid. However, his speech therapist devised a communication system for him using an alphabet set out from left to right in the order of the most frequently used letters in the French language. By means of blinking when the correct letter was pointed to Bauby was able, if slowly, to converse. But he did much more than this. Six months after the stroke he began dictating a monthly letter to his friends and then over a period of two months he dictated *The Diving-Bell and the Butterfly* to Claude Mendibil.

This is an amazing book. The writing is highly polished. Bauby worked out each short chapter in advance and memorized it. He describes the hospital building, staff and patients with acute observation and humour, his massive stroke with irony. In the past he says, '. . . you simply died. But improved resuscitation techniques have now prolonged and refined the agony. You survive, but you survive with what is so aptly known as "locked-in syndrome"' (Bauby 1998, p. 12).

He kept his sense of wholeness by allowing his mind to take flight like a butterfly. Using the technique of visualization brilliantly he re-visited distant countries and books he had read and pictured himself as a character in *The Count of Monte Cristo*. Fed intravenously, he used his imagination to enjoy food and translated this to his book: 'You can sit down to table at any hour, with no fuss or ceremony. If it's a restaurant, no need to book. If I do the cooking, it is always a success. The bourguignon is tender, the boeuf en gelée transparent . . . ' (ibid., p. 44).

Bauby started ALCIS Association du Locked-In-Syndrome and in his writing he underlines his determination to remain fully alive:

> I need to feel strongly, to love and to admire, just as desperately as I need to breathe . . . But to keep my mind sharp, to avoid slumping into resigned indifference, I maintain a level of resentment and anger, neither too much nor too little, just as a pressure-cooker has a safety-valve to keep it from exploding. (Ibid., pp. 62–3)

He writes about the letters he receives. Some 'simply relate the small events that punctuate the passage of time: roses picked at dusk, the laziness of a rainy Sunday, a child crying himself to sleep. Capturing the moment, these small slices of life, these small gusts of happiness, move me more deeply than all the rest' (ibid., p. 91).

The Diving-Bell and the Butterfly is a literary masterpiece. It is also a testament to the strength of the human spirit and its capacity for joy.

We end with an account of a very different experience. The neurologist, Oliver Sacks, is well-known for his books which examine what can be learnt from the case histories of his patients about the workings of the human brain. *A Leg to Stand On* is unique because the patient is himself and at one level the book is a personal history of several weeks following an accident. It is also an account of a doctor observing and analysing his own condition.

The story begins with a hilarious description of Sacks on a mountain in Norway running away from a bull. In his haste he fell, injured his leg seriously and discovered the bull was not actually chasing him. Less hilarious was the fact that he was miles from anywhere, that it was cold enough for him to suffer from exposure and that attempting to move was excruciatingly painful. However, he relates, still with humour, how he managed to limp some way down the mountain where he came across a man who got help to take him to hospital.

Back in England he underwent an operation but he was shocked to find that he could not move his leg. It was worse than that:

> The flesh beneath my fingers no longer seemed like flesh. It no longer seemed like material or matter. It no longer resembled anything . . . Unalive, unreal, it was no part of me – no part of my body, or anything else. (Sacks 1991, pp. 48–9)

Confined to bed in hospital in a small room with no window, Sacks discovered that the surgeon who had operated on him would not talk to him doctor to doctor and insisted that nothing was wrong. He felt very depressed. However, he continued to observe and analyse his condition. He also experienced fully what it felt like to be a patient. This underlined for him what he had always believed: the importance of listening to patients. Emotionally though he continued in a state of fear and despair that his leg would never function again. In this dark time he found comfort from reading the Bible, especially the Psalms. A turning point came when he listened to a cassette of Mendelssohn's Violin Concerto:

> I felt with the first bars of the music, a hope and an intimation that life would return to my leg – that it would be stirred, and stir, with original movement, and recollect or recreate its forgotten motor melody. I felt – how inadequate words are for feelings of this sort! – I felt, in those first heavenly bars of music, as if the animating and creative principle of the whole world was revealed, that life itself

was music, or consubstantial with music; that our living moving flesh, itself was 'solid' music . . . (Ibid., p. 87)

Two days later, when the cast had been taken off his leg, Sacks felt an impulse to flex it and did so – a movement which until then had seemed 'impossible and unthinkable'. At this point it began to dawn on him that the recovering limb could not simply be willed to move. A couple of days later the physiotherapists got him to his feet and insisted that with their support he placed one leg in front of the other. At first this was like walking with 'a clumsy prosthesis' and he was terrified he would be unable to walk normally for the rest of his life. But then:

into the silence, the silent twittering of motionless frozen images – came music, glorious music, Mendelssohn, *fortissimo!* Life, intoxicating movement! And as suddenly without intending whatever, I found myself walking, easily, *with* the music . . . and in the very moment that my 'motor' music, my kinetic melody, my walking, came back – in this self-same moment *the leg came back* . . . I *believed* in my leg, I *knew* how to walk. (Ibid., p. 108)

For Sacks the return of his leg was a spiritual experience. However, this in no way lessened his interest in his condition and during his convalescence and beyond he continued to investigate the subject of limb alienation following injuries. He discovered, partly through correspondence with an eminent neuropsychologist in Moscow, that this alienation was a common syndrome which had rarely been written about. *A Leg to Stand On* is a remarkable fusion of memoir, personal investigation and scientific record.

7 Mental illness

We begin this chapter with a reminder that what follows must be put into the context of mental *health*. All the writers quoted here were attempting to achieve or regain an equilibrium of sanity and composure – escape from illness was their goal. That said, we are about to embark on a journey into a land of half tones at best, and at worst downright darkness. We have picked some experienced and eloquent guides to this territory. The first of these is Les Murray, but Myra has visited the landscape he describes.

Depression is the most common mental illness. It affects many people in all walks of life at some point in their lives. In spite of much greater understanding the idea is still about that it is not a real illness and that one should pull oneself together. This is an extra burden on the sufferer who usually feels a sense of guilt about his or her condition. Fear and anger are also elements of depression. About eighteen years after experiencing post-natal depression, Myra tried to capture the hopelessness she had felt in the first verse of a poem called 'Flooring':

> The appointment was stapled to my mind
> so I didn't attempt cancellation at the door
> though the man was stiff
> and bald as his flooring samples.
> When the concrete kitchen floor
> threatened to dissolve
> I propped myself against the wall
> while he measured up in ignorance.
> Picking a pattern meant
> believing I would be here
> to wear down flooring
> next month, next year.
> Yet even tomorrow was impossible
> for each second hung

from my neck into eternity.
Sick with fear I pretended
to plump for the bleakest grey.

(from *Fistful of Yellow Hope*)

The world famous Australian poet, Les Murray, has written a searching essay about his long-term depression which was published together with *The Black Dog Poems* in a book called *Killing the Black Dog*. The Black Dog, as he explains, was Winston Churchill's name for his depression. The condition, which overtook Murray in 1988, was severe for several years:

> . . . I would lie curled in a foetal position on the sofa with tears leaking from my eyes, my brain boiling with a confusion of stuff not worth calling thought or imagery: it was more like shredded mental kelp marinaded in pure pain. During and after such attacks, I would be prostrate with inertia, as if all my energy had gone into a black hole. (Murray 1997, p. 6)

He had had a breakdown at the beginning of the 1960s which he depicts in an early poem, 'An Absolutely Ordinary Rainbow'. This is very different from the poems he was to write two decades later. It describes a crowd's reactions to a mysterious man who is weeping and who seems to have a special significance. Weeping is presented as a gift and this beautiful poem celebrates the sacredness of feelings, of accepting the self.

In *Killing the Black Dog* Murray lists what helped him cope with his later breakdown: work, family, routine, talking with other sufferers and the drug, Xanax. At first he could not write in poetry about his illness. He turned away from self 'and tried to enter imaginatively into the life of non-human creatures' (ibid., p. 11). The sequence of poems he produced, 'Presence', formed the heart of his collection, *Translations from the Natural World*. During his recovery Murray began to analyse his own inner history and its effect on him:

> I had to remember what had felt like a growing dislike of me on the part of my poor mother, as her miscarriages ate her happiness away, and to recall a night-mare sense on my part, which I may not have arrived at wholly on my own, that the disasters I was never told about were in fact my fault, for being born and for the circumstances of the delivery. (Ibid., p. 15)

He also discovered:

> I had been furious at my father for sinking into broken-hearted grief when my mother died, a grief he'd nourished and refused to give up till the day of his own

death forty-four years later. I hated how I'd had to become my own parents and get through adolescence with little help, continuing to play childhood games with my cousin Ray well beyond the natural end of those, so as to shut out the helpless half-adulthood that had fallen on me along with the guilt of matricide and the strong family message that sex had now been *confirmed* as sinful by directly causing death. Never do it, my unconscious told my body: you'll kill the victim. (Ibid., pp. 16–17)

All this was compounded by the way he was bullied at school. What he suffered during these years is recorded in 'Burning Want' in which he writes graphically about how 'the kids did erocide: destruction of sexual morale'. This poem, with its high charge of anger, is remarkable for its self-revelation.

In the essay Murray notes: 'I'd disapproved of using poetry as personal therapy, but the Black Dog taught me better. Get sick enough, and you'll use any remedy you've got' (ibid., p.19). Poetry and prose illuminate each other in *Killing the Black Dog* which is a courageous and insightful foray into personal writing. (*Killing the Black Dog* is out of print but the poems mentioned above are also included in Murray's *New Collected Poems*.)

Murray found a salve in writing poetry, but fiction, with its distancing effect can provide for some a less forbidding method of getting in touch with dangerous thoughts and feelings and making an attempt to resolve them. This was certainly the case for Miriam Hastings, as she explains in the following account.

Exorcising the past: Miriam Hastings

Writing autobiography has never come easily to me since writing has always been a means of escape from myself – as a lonely, frightened child, it was making up stories about fantasy worlds and characters that helped me survive.

When I began writing my novel, *The Minotaur Hunt*, I used a first person narrator and I only got as far as four pages when I had to give up, completely blocked. I doubt it was only the first person voice that made me 'freeze'. I think I was still too emotionally vulnerable at the time and too close to the traumatic experiences inspiring the novel. Five years later I was in the middle of a part-time degree course at Middlesex Polytechnic. I had already lost several years of study to the maws of psychiatry and emotional anguish so I applied for a discretionary grant to let me finish the course full-time but I was refused. At first this demolished my always fragile confidence, then I fished out the four pages I had written years earlier. Reading them again, suddenly

I realised how to continue – by turning the narrative voice into a third person form, thus giving me the necessary control and distance:

> Her dreams frighten her – not when she is sleeping but when she wakes. She opens her eyes and the room is filled with wings. Great black wings, as dark as night, that press down upon her, smothering her. And there are voices that whisper malevolently within her head, talking about her, talking against her. She pushes the wings away and listens but the house is very quiet – are they in or have they gone out? She is afraid of the silence and of the voices but she is more afraid of them, her father and her mother, coming in smiling talking probing.
>
> 'I'm sure you'd feel better, darling, if you got up, don't you? It's a beautiful day,' drawing the curtains back letting in the harsh, piercing, hurting light.
>
> She gets out of bed and slips to the door, frightened of making any sound. She opens it an inch and listens – the quality of the empty silence tells her there is no one in the house. No one at all for she doesn't count. She doesn't really exist. She goes back to the bed where the wings still lie in a heap, shrunk now to a small, crumpled, leathery mass. Under the bed she finds the bottle and drinks. The wings dissolve into mist as vodka flows through her. She drinks again and then gets into bed pulling the sheet over her head, waiting tense until the boat comes. The voices rattle in her brain, but she gets into the boat and it moves fast down the racing, spinning river, so dark between the tall chasms of rock. The whispering voices recede and are left a long way behind, and at last she arrives safe in Mythonae.
>
> She had been in the boat many times during her childhood, with the voices counting down the chasm for her death, but she had always held back, never allowed herself to arrive. Then she was eleven and she knew she must get there – she needed to escape and there was nowhere else to go. (Hastings 1987, pp. 1–2)

Liberating myself from the limitations of 'I', freed me to explore several viewpoints, allowing me to develop more than one central character; a fictional device I always prefer. It also freed me from my writers' block and I decided that if I had to spend a further two years over my degree, I would use the time to write a novel as well – and I did, completing the first draft in a year.

There is a psychotherapeutic theory which argues that all the people who appear in our dreams represent different aspects of ourselves, and I think it might equally be argued that all the characters in a novel represent certain aspects of the writer, however this doesn't mean they *are* the writer; a novel by its very nature is a fiction. In *The Minotaur Hunt*, I never identified with one of the characters as 'me', but life is the raw material from which the fiction writer fashions her/his art and I certainly drew on my own experiences, particularly on the traumatic time when, a distressed, self-destructive fourteen-year-old, I was admitted to an adult psychiatric hospital and detained there for over three months. This formative and painful period in my life provided a great deal of powerful material for the novel, however none of the characters portray the young girl I was then, or exclusively represent my inner thoughts and feelings at that time.

From the age of fourteen until I was over thirty, I had a recurrent nightmare in which I was imprisoned in some vast institution, running down endless corridors, desperately searching for a way out, or looking for a telephone – any link with the outside world. In some of these dreams I did find a phone but only to realise that it was a payphone and I had no money, or that the phone had no dialling tone. *The Minotaur Hunt* is saturated with the atmosphere of this dream, but after it was published the nightmare gradually ceased to trouble me. Writing the novel exorcised the trauma of my hospital admissions at fourteen and at twenty-three.

I do think it's important to stress that creative writing can be beneficial and healing even when it isn't directly autobiographical. The very act of creation is therapeutic: taking the raw material of real life and shaping it into something different and powerful is a magical, transformative process. In my personal experience I've found it can not only transform our writing, it can also transform our lives and our selves.

Addiction is a form of mental illness, and can lead to behaviour which is uncharacteristic of the person and the experience of feelings which can be very frightening. In 2004 Chris McCully published a book called *Goodbye, Mr Wonderful*, an autobiographical account of a recovering alcoholic. The book began life in The Priory Hospital, Altrincham in 1999. It was the third time he had undertaken detox, but the first that this 'had been accompanied by psychiatric help and counselling together with reconstructive work in group therapy, which last was based on the first four Steps of the AA 12-step programme'.

At The Priory he was discouraged from engaging in work activities. However, writing was another of his addictions, and he was loath to attempt to counter two simultaneously so he hung onto his laptop and recorded some details of his thoughts and emotions during his month-long stay. This diary was to form an important component of his book, which went on to give an account of how he fared after discharge. As he has commented subsequently:

> I was writing, urgently, in order to collate information, to remind myself (and perhaps others) of key rehabilitative points, and to synthesise those feelings I had in

common with other recovering souls so that those feelings – principally, in early recovery, the doubts and fears – could be recognised and named.

Although he was a well-published poet McCully rejected the idea of writing verse. Some of his reasons are as follows:

I'd have become dazed by the structure of the emerging poem (supposing for a moment I could make the inchoate into a poem), or entranced by rhythmical and/ or metrical possibilities, by lexical choices and thematic coherence . . . I would have become a perfectionist. And perfectionism was exactly one of the sub-set of problems resulting from the addiction I was trying to understand and counter.

McCully makes a very interesting point here, which may explain why some professional writers may find the 'letting go' involved in therapeutic writing difficult to achieve. He did not accept this situation with equanimity, however:

Something very profound has happened to the structure of the imagination. Civil, ironic, humorous, I have become, or seem to have become, a bill-paying citizen, someone who rakes leaves, washes the car, and hangs out with the easier bits of self-assembly furniture . . . I'm utterly and miserably aware that something, and it's something called recovery, is keeping me from the most profound sources of creativity and disturbance. The vision, the compelling way in which fragments of seeing and hearing would speak to each other, the need to express, the ambition, the pride, the way a line fell inevitably right, and all the dislocated happiness of that form of making . . . These are, these seem to be, no more . . . (McCully 2004, p. 145)

He has since summed up his aims succinctly as follows:

I needed to learn to live again – to live properly, abundantly, generously and well. Beyond that I needed to *stay* sober and in recovery. To achieve that I had to *do* certain things, just as, say, a diabetic needs to treat his or her condition on a regular basis. For example, I had to maintain contact with other recovering souls; to evince commitment to a recovered life by making amends to others, and by (if possible) renewing family and other ties; to communicate (if possible, and where feasible) some of the principles of this kind of recovery to those still dazzled to death by their own and others' addictions . . . These things were and are compulsory. They're a set of new habits and circumstances in which I and all my Selves are unable to pose.

McCully's take on the whole writing process in which he was engaged is encapsulated in the following comments:

> Did the writing of *Goodbye, Mr Wonderful* help me? Writing up the entries became a beneficent ritual, a chore with a multiple point. Further, the work is a place where retrospection can become almost accurate, where the shape of events can be reconstructed, where the form of the days can be recognised. Reading back now, I can't evade the Selves I was, including that bastard – Mr Wonderful – the Drinking Self. Yet perhaps the work exists like liver scars in the body of an otherwise well person. It too is a reminder.

(Note: much of the above account draws on a text supplied by Chris McCully to the authors.)

In the case of Clare Shaw, another poet, distress demanded an immediate physical outlet. She found that self-harm gave her temporary relief from her bulimia. It was only later, as she began to recover, that writing took over and she realized that it offered more lasting and empowering satisfactions.

Speaking of harm: Clare Shaw

To the casual observer my depression was not obvious. I got out of bed in the morning, I kept the house clean, I functioned well. And if anyone would have asked, I would have said I was okay. But I wasn't. Every moment was filled with working hard enough to justify the space I occupied on the planet, keeping that space small, with controlling so fully every inch of my body that I didn't have the time to recognise how unhappy I was. Bulimia isn't usually life-threatening. But it is indescribably miserable. Of course, the easiest thing by far would have been to have told someone. Starving and purging yourself is dreary and painful. Cutting yourself really hurts. How much easier to approach someone and say, 'I'm struggling. I need some help'. But the problem was, I didn't feel able, I didn't feel entitled.

As things got worse, my attempts to secure some recognition grew more extreme. Eventually, after years of bulimia and self-harm, I took myself to the university psychiatrist. He diagnosed 'third-year nerves'. Shortly after that I took a big overdose. Thus began several years of admissions to Liverpool's psychiatric wards. Then I didn't just lack the sense of entitlement to directly describe my pain and my need for support. For once in my life, I lacked the vocabulary. Words like distress, harm, pain, were simply not enough to convey what I was going through. I had to make those words visible in the form of wounds which, by their shocking severity, spoke more articulately than I ever could.

And somewhere along the way I discovered that self-harm also made me feel better. Not only did it give me a method of communicating my pain, it also gave me a way of controlling and distracting myself from that pain. Yet, however it helped me to survive, self-injury wasn't an effective long-term strategy. I had wanted to communicate my distress. Instead, I attracted psychiatric diagnoses. I wanted to reach out to people. Instead, I alienated most of the people I knew.

Which is where words come in. Self-harm for me was a kind of wordless language, a way of speaking about my distress and my urgent need for support. As the circumstances of my life began gradually to improve, and as I found a new drive not just to survive, but crucially, to enjoy my life, words took on increasing importance. They were no longer simply a way of recording my life, they were a way of living it. Communication became, and remains, my primary reason for writing. Whether it's poetry, academic papers or journalistic prose, I don't write for the sake of it – I write so that someone will read what I have written, so that someone might know who I am.

Writing is a strange kind of reaching out. At the same time it's also a way of being alone. On the one hand, I'm doing my best to communicate, to put my ideas and thoughts and experiences into words. On the other hand, I'm just putting them on the page – or into the air. I don't have to interact directly with anyone. This is why I'm able to publish and perform poems – or to deliver presentations to packed conference halls – about feelings and experiences I would find it intensely difficult to talk about in close conversation. Also because in writing, and particularly in poetry, I am in control. A poem, with its crafting and drafting, feels like the nearest that a writing form can be to sculpture. This is so much of the satisfaction of the process. At the end of it I'm left with something so concrete I can almost hold it in my hands. Certainly I can feel it in my mouth – the texture of the sounds in their exactly chosen constellation. I choose them for their meaning but equally for how they sound, feel and look.

And then the poem is a thing. Something I made. It gives me the satisfaction of having created an object, something solid and lasting. And whatever experience, feeling or thought it encapsulates is – a thing. It becomes separate to me, it has its own shape and life. And to a degree, it leaves me. Like bleeding. And this time, people notice.

Here is an excerpt from 'Poem for Dee Dee' in my book, *Straight Ahead*:

IV

The day room is a late-night
fish tank of sound
and yellow shadow.
The hum, bang, clatter of the ward.

Dormitories simmer with sleep.
I am wide-eyed with two weeks awake.
Her eyes
are methadone-heavy.

We watch TV in the small hours,
eating Frosties dry from the box.
We know all the tunes to Ceefax,
baiting the glaze-eyed agency staff

with high-risk jokes.
"How about a day out?
It's been three months since I crossed a road
and I'm beginning to lose the knack".

Dee Dee and me are having a laugh
dreaming plans for O.T. –
rock climbing schemes
for the deeply depressed.

A barebacked parachute jump.
A Blackpool trip. Imagine
riding the Big One
with your seatbelt undone.

Dee Dee laughs.
Feels the wind in her hair,
the world spinning its pages
beneath her.

God, we laughed
in there
you could die laughing.

Mental illness is one thing; how society treats those diagnosed with a form of it is another. It may be considered a misfortune to have the symptoms of an illness, but to be incarcerated in an institution which enshrines the practices of ignorance, cruelty and short-term palliation is little short of tragic. Such was the experience of Colin Rowbotham. Colin was a poet who honed his craft over a number of years on themes such as childhood, marriage and parenthood. In the last four years of his life he experienced bouts of what was eventually diagnosed as manic depression and was in and out of mental hospital. The twenty-five poem sequence 'Fugue' (published after his death in his selected poems, *Lost Connections*) derives from this and constitutes one of the most powerful expressions of confusion, distress and anger that we know of. It also makes a devastating indictment of the system put in place to deal with those suffering such traumas. It ranges from the rumbustious Gilbertian rhythms of 'Insanity Rag':

> When you try to write about it two years later –
> an explorer who dispensed with taking notes
> as he journeyed up the pole to the equator,
> his safari dogged by bearers in white coats,
> (and think: *Oh lucky me, I missed the realm of ECT*) –
> you may wonder why you undertook the quest
> but though the ramblings of a nutcase aren't an open and a shut case
> are they odder than the rat-race of the rest?

through the bleakly laconic portrayal of 'Blackout':

> I get them getting out of bed
> a buzzing noise inside my head
>
> my body tingles swells I fall
> or ricochet against the wall
>
> unconscious for an instant find
> myself upon the floor with kind
>
> attendants bending over me
> it lasts for an eternity
>
> inside an instant filled with fear
> they'll never let me out of here

and the excoriating portrayal of the doctors in 'Ward Round':

> Oh doctors all, the good, the rotten
> the useless and the simply bad
> the ones who never ever cotton
> on, the kind, the misbegotten
> I hope that *your* consultant's not un-
> sympathetic when you all go mad.

and takes in wandering the corridors of an institution in 'Lost':

> I knocked on frosted glass windows,
> entered an empty office and rang
> home – got the answerphone. A gang
> of security men took me under their wing

nodding and shaking heads
at each other, smiling as if
it couldn't happen to them. Did one say *let's duff*
him up a bit first? Now I can't believe

that – though I heard it then all right.
Oh, but it was hard
to be led back under guard
back to the chaos of that safe environment, the ward.

These poems are like pages torn from a notebook scribbled on in extremis. Yet, because Colin Rowbotham was a highly skilled versifier they convince as artistic creations too. We can only speculate as to how much they may have meant to the writer attempting to cling on to his sense of self-worth in the midst of such desolation.

We have seen with Miriam Hastings how fictionalizing can provide an acceptable technique for getting under emotional barriers and meeting one's traumas head on. Poetry too, need not be straightforward in its emotional expression, and such strategies can bring very special rewards. This does not have to be achieved in isolation either. Karen Chase in *Land of Stone* tells the remarkable story of how she and Ben, a hospital patient, communicated largely through writing rather than speech. Another resident from the same hospital commented on the process: 'The pencil lets you say what the mouth does not' (Chase 2007, front page).

Ben may have been schizophrenic, but it seems likely that his near-muteness was connected with childhood trauma. His parents brought him to Rosedale Hospital just outside New York because he had been silent for six years but he also had a history of sporadic violence. The method Karen employed to get through to him was that of dialoguing through verse. They made jointly composed poems, turn-taking without speaking and creating a hundred and seventy-nine works on a weekly basis over a period of two years. Gradually speech came back to Ben, and at the end of the time he was deemed safe to return to his community. He was speaking more: to Karen, his therapists, and his family.

If this story were not remarkable enough, there is also the fact that the content of the poems was never overtly self-revelatory. The subject-matter was almost entirely of weather and landscape, and both participants in the process were happy for this to remain so. For Karen herself had a past of which she never spoke: she had been hospitalized because of polio at the age of ten, and been rendered immobile by the condition. Ben's language when he did speak was colourless, but when they made poems together colour began to flow back into the lines. Here is 'Out of the Blue Fell Snow' which is one of the early poems they collaborated on:

> Out of the blue fell snow
> a cold wintery snow
> that was blinding
> there were blizzards everywhere
> white breezes, the noise of weather
> it was enormously chilly
> not enough clothes to go around,
> people froze
> it was a cold season . . . (Ibid., p. 81 and p. 155)

White is the predominant colour here, but in other later poems the whole spectrum appears. Here is one of these, 'A Magnificent Orange Glare'

> A magnificent orange glare
> filled the afternoon
> one particular time
>
> There happened to be much shine and brightness
> much gleam in the air
>
> It was just a
> particularly cloudy day
> that happened to come along
>
> All the color
> captures the imagination . . . (ibid., pp. 66 and 171)

Metaphor became the means by which both began to express their emotional condition. As Karen Chase comments: 'One reason our work could go as deep as it did without interpretation or explication is that we were drawn to many of the same metaphors' (ibid., p. 59).

There is yet a further layer of complexity to the tale that unfolds. At the hospital there was a psychiatrist, Dennis, who became Karen's mentor for the poetry work and was also one of those responsible for Ben's well-being. In course of time, although he did not write (except reports!), by a kind of therapy by proxy the expressive nexus enveloped him too, and his story of childhood abuse was revealed to Karen.

The lessons for writing of a personal nature embodied in this book are profound. The method adopted by Karen is shown to be mutually beneficial, and no doubt could prove of value in other circumstances. Here is 'The Duet of Voices', the poem in which Ben and Karen comment on it directly:

> The duet of voices
> Much energy is felt
> back and forth
> There is a calm time
> when there are many
> things at one time, simultaneously
> in the midst of this long song
> differences occur
> all over, distinct notes . . . (Ibid., pp. 127 and 176)

Caring and coping 8

Caring for others, supporting them in times of difficulty or illness and coping with the stress entailed are demanding and sometimes all-engulfing activities. Many of us find ourselves in such situations at one or more points in our lives. We feel, therefore, that it is important to allot a chapter in *Writing Your Self* to this subject. Such situations can put relationships under severe stress. The piece by Duncan Tolmie, which describes how he coped when his mother had dementia, shows graphically the almost intolerable strain placed on himself and his marriage. What also emerges is that people draw on extraordinary reserves of strength and find new aspects of themselves.

Becoming a parent plunges one into a long-term situation of caring which, of course, for most people also brings happiness. We begin with a sonnet by Charlie Druce which was published in a National Poetry Competition Anthology. This is addressed to his baby son as he stands holding him in the middle of the night looking at the world outside with its possible dangers. The father's tenderness is very moving:

Night feed

We stand at the door and watch the pale night,
you, my twelve pounds of grackle bird, seagull boy,
oblivious to the moonlight and what lies beyond –
the foxes silently slipping through fences,
robbers waiting in their cars for a gap in their nerves.
A helicopter rides overhead, restless and searching.
It's all right birdie boy, it's not us they're looking for.
But its beam exposes me – how even now
I am preparing you, handing you down my alibis,
already thickening your soft new-leaf skin.
A siren bleeds and the chopper canters away.
You ruffle down in my arms' nest, eyes closing,
so we leave the garden to its own stealth
and the foxes to their rusty shadows in the wet grass.

Parenthood always involves an element of coping. For some parents there are circumstances which mean long-term coping is involved. We have already written about Debra Ginsberg's relationships with her sisters in Chapter 3. As a single mother, determined her child should have a good upbringing, she had many years which were very stressful. She realized her son, Blaze, was unusual when he was very small. He was over-sensitive to noise, spoke late but was able to replicate a huge variety of sounds, showed a great love of music but was uninterested in drawing. At kindergarten school there were immediate problems. He did not want to follow the teacher's instructions and did not connect with the other children. Ginsberg was shocked at the wish to put him in a special education unit. She had no choice but to accept this placement and attend regular meetings to assess his progress.

How Blaze fared in the classroom depended on whether an individual teacher related to him. *Raising Blaze* is an in-depth account of Ginsberg's struggle to get the best for her son during his elementary school life and in his first year at middle school. It reveals her own growing understanding of his strange mixture of talents and difficulties. On the one hand he lacked patience, fine motor control and at times exhibited high anxiety which led to perseveration. On the other hand he revealed extraordinary modes of thought and insight. He assigned colours to the days of the week and the letters of the alphabet. When he told his mother about this she realized she made similar colour connections.

Later, a psychiatrist assured Ginsberg that he was not autistic or educationally backward and that his problems were probably due to oxygen deprivation during birth when the cord, wound round his neck, deprived him of air. Blaze was interested in this information. To his mother's surprise he produced a drawing which led to a discussion which was remarkable for its intuition and instinctive use of metaphor:

> The drawing consisted of five rows of different brightly coloured circles more or less the same size. He had used every marker in the house so that no one color was repeated. Below the circles was a stick figure lying on its side. I looked at it carefully, searching for clues . . . 'That's what I looked like when I was born,' Blaze said . . . 'that's me and that – ' he pointed to the circles, 'is what it looked like.' (Ginsberg 2003, pp. 159–60)

The conversation shifted to Blaze's dislike of loud noises and he asked why there were so many in the world:

'Why do you let them all bother you?' I question back . . .

'I can't help it,' he says, 'my yellow wire is broken . . . When I was born, they didn't put the yellow wire in right so it got broken and now I'm so sensitive to loud noises.' (Ibid., p. 160)

Blaze then explained there were wires of different colours and what each wire controlled. 'The blue wire is for feelings', he said and 'there's a girl in my class who has problems with her blue wire. That's why she cries all the time' (ibid., p. 160). When questioned about repairing a wire he said: 'You have to find a white wire and patch it together' (ibid., p. 161).

To support Blaze Ginsberg put aside her own career and went into his school first to help in his class, later to work as aide to another class. During this time she was backed up by her family, especially her father. The child's final year at elementary school was very successful, thanks to a dedicated teacher but things fell apart when he moved to the bigger world of middle school where no real understanding was shown. Ginsberg worried about Blaze's limitations and what adult life would hold for him. At the end of her tether she removed him from the school altogether and with the family's help educated him at home for some months. The book ends with the first moves to get Blaze back into school and the re-staging of his birth. This was at Blaze's request and to correct what went 'wrong' the first time.

Ginsberg wrote *Raising Blaze* because she felt 'our story was compelling enough to commit to paper' (ibid., p. 291); also because she had searched for a book that would support her but never found one. She worried about making Blaze's life public even though she had explained to him what she was doing. As she neared the end of the book he insisted on seeing it. He liked it and became totally involved in the writing, sometimes arguing about his mother's interpretation. He also asked for one or two incidents to be removed which they were. This memoir certainly is compelling and it reads as a strong case for not labelling children. It is also a testament to Ginsberg's devotion, determination and to her belief in her son.

Raising Blaze is an in-depth, chronological prose memoir about caring for a child who does not fit into any category. 'Sundays', Mimi Khalvati's poignant sequence of three poems about her adult son, Tom, who has mental health problems, is built round three particular Sundays. At first the poems, written in iambic quatrains, appear low key. The tone is conversational, much of the matter is everyday. They are linked by a focus on the cooking of food and Khalvati's strong desire to nurture her son. This underlines her concern about his illness and its effect on his eating. Music also links the three poems – Tom playing the piano in the first and third poems. In the second, which is about a Sunday when he ate very little, music is related to the rain, and grief surfaces when Khalvati shifts from rain to youth that has gone 'to rack and ruin'. By this point the reader understands the significance of music to Tom. The imagery and detail which evoke his playing in the first and third poems raise hope of renewal and wholeness. These subtle poems, which provide a frame for Khalvati to write about her feelings, echo the movements in a musical work. Here is the first:

Sundays

for Tom

i

Together, we have made sour cherry rice,
rolled minced lamb into meatballs and listened
to the radio while eating, him to stall
hallucinations and me to respect his silence,

the time he takes to eat. We've strolled slowly
in the park together, our favourite park,
lapsing into pauses with the falling light –
tennis in the distance – as we slowly climbed

the hill. I've left my shoes at the door, him
reminding me, to scrub off the dogshit later
and now he's at the piano in the nowhere hour
before TV. These are the things that make him

well – company, old and easy, recipes
old but new to him. His playing brings
the night in. Turns the streetlamps on, makes
the kitchen clock tick. Softly a chord falls

and out of the ground grow snowdrops, fat
and waxy, with green hearts stamped upside down
on aprons, poking their heads through railings.
Between his fingers things grow, little demons,

fountains, crocuses. Spring is announced and enters,
one long green glove unfingering the other,
icicles melt and rivers run, bluetits
hop and trill. Everything talks to everything.

(from *The Meanest Flower*)

We now look at the ways in which a writer has written about her adult daughter's schizo-affective disorder and the behaviour it led to.

The worry of words: Maggie Sawkins

Driving to work, worrying about words for a poem I am maybe working on, I sometimes wonder about the nature of obsession. Is it any crazier for someone to spend hours, days, weeks stalking a single word than for someone to imagine they are being followed? And if it wasn't for poetry, what horrors might be stalking me?

Beside my bed I keep two notebooks. One has a gold hardback cover and contains tissue-thin paper: this is where I keep my dreams. The other is a spiral bound A4 notepad: this is where I keep bits of my life. During the summer of 2000 my daughter began to lose her mind. As her behaviour and world became evermore fragmented, the contents of my notebooks seemed to blur into one subject. Eventually she was hospitalised and diagnosed with a schizo-affective disorder that was, and still is at the time of writing, exacerbated by a dependency on street drugs.

There had been signs. A year or so earlier, in the midst of a word storm, she had begun to write on the walls of her flat. On one occasion she showed me a ten-page poem – rich in myth and imaginings, the language sang. Since her teens she had experienced mood swings. Her recent behaviour however – the grandiose ideas, the terrible moments of despair – reminded me of my father's manic-depressive episodes. During that time I wrote a poem, later published in my booklet: *Charcot's Pet*, in which I personified the illness as a 'rogue gene' passing from generation to generation:

Rogue Gene

For years they had me talking
making stories out of ink spots.
But when they found it,
it wasn't in me at all.
    It was in my daughter.

When they caught her
she hadn't slept for weeks.
They found pieces of dreams
scrawled across her room:
on the flaps of airmail envelopes
origami paper, old tissues, even the walls.

There were tales of arsonists
and snake-tossing jugglers
and chimpanzees flying high
on a giant trapeze.

As they approached with their instruments
she stripped off her clothes
and fled, like a goose,
through the window
into the path of a passing car.

   When they found it,
it didn't look like her at all.
It had my father's pixilated eyes
his darkened stare.

Later, when she found and read the poem, my daughter accused me (perhaps understandably) of wanting to kill her off, of 'writing her life'. This happened during a period when she was suffering from delusions of reference, and paranoia: when I was spending hours listening to her, trying to follow her logic. I thought of the poet Philip Gross, who had written a series of poems about his daughter's eating disorder in *The Wasting Game*, and the reading I attended where we discussed whether it was morally right to make art out of someone's suffering. Despite his justifications I sensed he wasn't sure, and now neither was I.

Eight years on and some of my most powerful poems are still being written in response to incidents that have left me at best shaken, but more increasingly numb. The following poem was written after my daughter, during a psychotic episode, assaulted me in the street outside my house:

The Bruise

   arrived a few days later
a bright yellow pansy
on my right arm,
   then it disappeared.
Eventually
I threw away the clump
   of hair.

   Now there's nothing
left to show –
no cause for alarm –
   except for something,
somewhere there's this:
a small persistence,
   a faint hiss of tears.

(from *The Zig-Zag Woman*)

Often when we are in a state of shock what lingers in our consciousness is an after-image: the expression on someone's face, the clump of hair, the bruise, the silence. Perhaps it's easier for the brain, in times of crisis, to hold onto *things* as the slippery world of thoughts and feelings fails us.

'Crossfire' was written after another incident that occurred during the early stages of my daughter's illness. When calm was restored, I found that three images remained: the debris from the pot that had been used as a missile, the exotic lily lying limp in the hallway, and the trace of blood on my daughter's lip. This last image found its way into the final line of the poem and gains power through its literal and metaphoric truth.

The poem begins by describing a state of stasis. Unsure of how to develop these first three short lines, I read a little about lilies and discovered that they were known by different names. Perhaps this was the connection I had been looking for. Once I began to address the plant by its various names I became aware of a shift: as if the poem had found its voice. Reading the final draft later, I realised that through the process of personification, not only was I addressing the lily, but also my daughter and myself. The three of us had become one. Struggling to write the poem had enabled me to arrive at a nub of truth: that inherent in us all, is a capacity to be both perpetrators and victims. But more importantly, by remembering my daughter as she once was, before the time of speech, before complications set in, before she was troubled by 'this dark ceiling without a star' (Sylvia Plath, 'Child'), I was able to reach a place of compassion and a place of healing:

Crossfire

It hasn't moved for months.
It knows its place – on top of the dresser
facing the door.

Arum Lily
    the Afrikaans have a name for you:

Varkblom
Pig's Ear

no wonder you poke out
your yellow tongue.

Calla Lily
one day you will be caught
    in our crossfire.

Someone will wrench you
from your terracotta pot
and hurl you to the floor.

Names will fly.
Fists flail.

My Little White Hood

I will remember you
mute and beautiful –
   bite my tongue.

(from *Charcot's Pet*)

We move on to look at two examples of adults caring for elderly relatives. There are times, of course, when people find themselves looking after a sick or disabled partner, a sibling or close friend, but it is those at or near the end of their lives who most commonly need caring for. A frank and involving account of such caring is provided by Elaine Marcus Starkman in her book *Learning to Sit in the Silence*. This is described as 'A Journal of Caretaking' and consists of selected entries from the author's journalling over a period of four-and-a-half years, during which time she cared for her mother-in-law in the home she shared with her husband Maury and their children, and in the nursing home where Ma eventually died. These first entries are from the period when Ma had only been recently been welcomed into the household:

Maury spends more time with her than he does with me. Does his devotion stem from the fact that she nurtured him with unconditional love? Hate to admit it, but am disappointed in myself; I feel both jealous and guilty. (Starkman 1993, p. 18)

Over four months since Ma's arrival. The whole family is talking about what a good son Maury is. They should see him put Ma to bed. I'm just the daughter-in-law who begrudgingly allows her to stay. (Ibid., p. 28)

And the following entry is from later in the Journal when Ma has been three years in the nursing home and has only a few weeks more to live:

Went with Maury; my last few months of stubbornness have passed. No matter how hard he tries, talks about the kids, their schooling, their adventures, she won't open her eyes, smile, respond, take his hand. I stroked her cheek and her hair this time. As long as the aides get a bit of water and food into her, she continues to hang on. He simply can't bring himself to tell them to stop.

'There's a difference between denying and not offering if she asks' he says. (Ibid., p. 151)

The book also contains a handful of very vivid dreams in which some of the author's issues are highlighted; here is one of them:

> I'm alone with Ma in my old childhood apartment. She's on a pull-out bed and keeps slipping off. Stick-like legs hang out of her nightgown. She shouts. 'I want to sleep in your parents' bed!' Astounded, I try to help. She pushes me away, rummages through my mother's dresses, throws everything around. Then her body transforms itself into one of my young black students, Hattie Gray. Ma is Hattie. I watch the transformation amazed. We go outside into the black ghetto and Ma/Hattie talks to a small black kid on a go-kart, saying, 'Be careful, darling, I want you to go upstairs and eat.' We start up. By now I'm not sure if Ma is Hattie or not. The living room fills with people who sit on folding chairs, as if this were shiva, and we're mourning the dead. I tell them about the transformation. No-one believes me. There's Ma herself in her nightgown, weak again. I scream, 'She was Hattie just a minute ago. She was walking around!' People think I'm mad. I begin to think so too. (Ibid., p. 74)

Although these quotations relate to caregiving, Elaine Marcus Starkman's journal explores a wider canvas. One of the themes is finding meaningful activities to occupy you in later life. The author identifies her own goal as: 'Gaining inner peace is what counts now. How to get, how to hold on to it. My writing seems more important than ever' (ibid., p. 147).

We end this chapter with an in-depth account of a son caring for a parent. In an unpublished manuscript Duncan Tolmie has chronicled in great detail a deteriorating situation within a family caused by the increasing incapacity of one of its members. 'Driven' would not be too strong a word to use of his attitude towards writing at this time. In the following piece he describes the circumstances, his motivation for writing, and also provides two extracts from the text he completed.

Writing myself sane: Duncan Tolmie

As 2002 drew to a close, whatever passed for normality in the relationship between my elderly parents was coming to an end. I looked on helplessly as my mother's benign forgetfulness and idiosyncratic behaviour of a few months' earlier mutated effortlessly into full-blown Alzheimers. Unceremoniously, she was stripped of her ability to laugh, love and communicate. I became no more than a visiting stranger.

My once-teetotal father, unable to cope with the burden of around-the-clock dementia in his life, quickly drank himself to the verge of alcoholism. His increasingly frequent trips to the local off-licence coincided with my mother's increasingly frequent black eyes. Although any fool would conclude that the two events were connected, Social Services insisted on hard evidence to support my accusations of physical abuse.

The evidence finally presented itself on New Year's Eve when my inebriated father grudgingly admitted to punching my mother full in the face, causing an injury that warranted police involvement. Social Services immediately placed her in a local Nursing Home, never to return to the home that she had shared with my father during the previous fifty years. Shortly afterwards he suffered a succession of strokes and was admitted to hospital where he almost died a few months later. On his recovery, he publicly discredited me as part of his campaign to be reunited with my mother.

For almost a year I struggled to cope with the resulting difficulties, and stress eventually took its toll on my mental state. I became an emotional wreck, constantly tearful and depressed, consumed by negative thoughts. Consequently, my work, my friendships, and my marriage began to suffer. As time dragged on with no improvement in the situation I struggled to get through each day. I began to suffer from extreme headaches, my head so full of troubles that it felt like it would explode. As the situation worsened I came close to a complete mental breakdown and only cowardice prevented me from taking my own life.

More by accident than by design I discovered that I could reduce the pressure inside my head by transferring my thoughts onto paper. I had very little experience of writing so was not following any established process. I simply considered that if I stored all my problems on paper then I had no need to keep them stored in my head. By writing everything down I was effectively activating a release valve, emptying my head of stress, preparing to face the problems of each new day on a non-cumulative basis.

In this first extract I am visiting my mother, who has been admitted to the local hospital for a month's assessment:

> 'How has she been?' I ask. How many times have I posed that question in the past three weeks? 'She's fine now', replies the nurse, 'but she was quite aggressive last night.' 'Aggressive? How? Why?' 'She had a nurse pinned to the wall.' I don't want to hear these words. Words that lend credence to my father's argument. Pinned to the wall. Is it possible that, all this time, I have allowed myself to be misled? That I have undermined my father, have refused to consider that he was telling the truth? The words flash in my head like a crimson neon sign: *PINNED TO THE WALL – PINNED TO THE FLOOR – PINNED TO THE WALL – PINNED TO THE FLOOR*. 'Is it possible that someone was invading her space?' I ask . . . clutching wildly at any excuse that might justify my mother's *aggression*.
>
> Despite affording my father no such tolerance in similar circumstances, I truly believe that my mother's actions *are* excusable, and that her circumstances *are*

extenuating. For is it not the case that protecting one's territory is regarded as normal behaviour? We all do it, every day of our lives, without question. Then why is such behaviour regarded as abnormal just because the victim of trespass happens to suffer from dementia?

I attempt to clarify the nurse's take on events: 'Is it likely that staff were making her do something she didn't want her to do?' I ask. 'We can't have her stripping off' says the nurse in misguided justification. 'We have the other residents to think of.' Then, tired of my leading questions, she walks away, leading us in my mother's direction. 'Were you knocking the nursing staff about last night?' I ask of my mother, making light of a heavy situation. She looks at me, eyebrows lowered, mortified by such an accusation. 'No' she replies, indignantly, and by the look in her eyes I know I have disappointed her by asking.

I have said that the circumstances at that time put a great strain on my marriage. In the second extract the stresses I was under are shown to be taking their toll:

My mother is *my* problem. Not my wife's, not my children's, not my friends'. I brought the problem into our house, poked it and prodded it, kicked it, analysed it and complained about it every waking moment. I wrote about it, spoke about it, from early morning till late at night. Every phone call I make. Every phone call I take. Every single person who enters my life or enters my home becomes a sounding block for *my* problem. *My* problem about *my* mother.

I can stop all that now, it's not too late. But not while my wife and I are in a state of silent limbo. I phone her at her work. Her pleasant greeting turns sour at the sound of my voice. She is no less angry. My request to speak is granted with silence, so I begin:

'This is not an ultimatum', but we both know that it is. 'I understand that you're angry with me, but I can't deal with your anger on top of everything else that is happening.' I begin to get emotional as I speak. It's unintentional, but I know it will come across as phoney. I take a few seconds to steady my voice.

'If you intend to stay angry with me' I eventually continue 'then I'm moving out of the house. Today.' I really do mean what I say. But my wife doesn't appear affected by my words, anger still apparent in her voice. The conversation moves forward, gains momentum, but remains in stalemate. 'I really don't think you know how close I am to snapping' I say, feeling myself lose hold on my emotions. 'I'm not going to be here . . . ' I sob into the mouthpiece. 'I'm not going to be here . . . ' And, no longer able to control myself or finish the sentence, I hang up the phone.

It wasn't only the actual act of writing that kept me sane. Just as useful in preserving my sanity was my discovery that I could 'step outside' myself while events unfolded. On numerous occasions I involuntarily participated in what can only be described as an out-of-mind experience. Without any effort on my part, my capacity for thought would split into two separate entities. While I trekked between social work departments, hospitals and care homes, discussing each of my parents' progress with various members of staff, I simultaneously stood back from my physical self, emotionally detached, clinically recording everything that was happening and being said, memorizing the facts in readiness for writing down afterwards. I had no control over the process, and never once instigated it. It simply happened and I was grateful to be an invisible observer in situations that would otherwise have been impossible to deal with.

During that period I became the owner of a photographic memory. I could remember conversations with nurses, doctors, carers, and social workers, word for word, including medical terms and technical jargon.

Throughout almost a year of dealing with the full-time job that my parents' difficulties had become, I emptied my head of almost 300,000 words by means of the writing process. Curiously, my skill for retaining masses of information tailed off at the same time as the situation became more manageable. I'm convinced that I unwittingly tapped into some unknown latent capability that stayed awhile before slipping back into dormancy. Like a surge of adrenaline it came to my rescue when I needed it most, then vanished as soon as I was able to go it alone.

Having regained complete control of my life, I now prefer to write for pleasure rather than survival. I still have my notes and occasionally dip into them, a reminder of how I made it through the darkest year of my life, the year in which I wrote myself sane.

Loss is intrinsic to the human condition. Its most grievous form, bereavement, is our main focus in this chapter. However, loss affects us in many other ways and is a subject we consider throughout this book. We have already written, for example, in Chapter 5 about Eva Hoffman, who recorded in detail what losing the country and language of her birth meant, and also about artist Andrew Potok who lost his sight in his forties. In Chapter 6 there is an account of Jean-Dominique Bauby who lost mobility and speech as the result of a stroke. In Chapter 4 June English describes how her security and self-belief were destroyed in an abusive marriage.

Before turning to bereavement we want to look at three other areas of loss. The first of these is deprivation of opportunity. Not being able to conceive a child is devastating for many women. Jacqueline Brown's book, *Thinking Egg*, is a sequence of poems which depict impressionistically, and with reference to fairy stories and rhymes, her own experience: medical examinations, longings, a breakdown and eventual adoption of children. There is mention too of other losses. The recurrent image of 'egg', with its different meanings and associations, binds the poems together. These are mostly written in the third person which gives them a universality. The writing is subtle yet frank. In 'Poaching', with its play on the word 'poaching', Brown depicts the deep need a childless woman feels and how it might drive her to steal a baby:

Poaching

You could assemble a whole catalogue of do's and don'ts on the subject of poaching eggs . . . Don't attempt to poach more than two unless you're a really experienced hand. (Delia Smith's Cookery Course Part 1)

She has heard the women whispering
in hospital rooms of suffering,
pain, blood.

She has stood palefaced in the margins
looking and listening, separate
from them.

While they slept, she has walked in her head
through the bluelit quiet ward, skirting
the nurse,

toe-stepped along the white corridor,
keeping to walls, to where milky kids
snuffle;

she's walked further to a flurried place
where infants lie flat under glass, taped
to tubes.

Sleepwalking, she has understood theft,
the urge to prise open, steal and hide,
not care

that another woman is crying somewhere
just so long as her own boat of arms
is full.

There is always a sense of loss when one person leaves a shared home. This occurs in various situations: when a relationship splits up, even if there is mutual agreement, when friends move apart after sharing a flat because of changing circumstances, when an adult or near-adult child leaves the family home. In this last case parents or a parent may be glad their child is going out into the world, relieved even that the house will be quieter, but there is likely to be sense of loss too. Denise Bennett anchors the feeling in the image of her daughter's ankle boots as black shells:

Black Shells

I found them washed up
at the foot of your bed
after you'd gone;
laceless, gaping, ankle-boots,
discarded like two black shells.

Fingering the soft hollow,
the indents of your toes
I know your whole world is weighted here.
The gospel of your life.
I can still feel your first kick,
the quickening.

But you have outworn
these black boots –
are making new impressions now.
Perhaps tomorrow I will wrap them
in paper and place them with
your doll's crib, your tea-set, your books.

The loss of part of one's body has a psychological effect as well as a physical one. In the next piece Myra describes the feelings she had after her mastectomy.

Amazon: Myra

I didn't give much conscious thought at first to the fact that I had lost a breast. I was too preoccupied with recovering from the operation, coping with the follow up treatments and being determined to make the most of life. Beneath the surface though I was acutely aware of being different. Fixed in my mind was an image of a world full of two-breasted women in which I was an oddity. This view surfaced in a poem called 'The Cave' in which a voice accused me of being 'one-breasted' and 'hardly a woman'. I confronted the voice but this didn't dispel my image of myself. However, my friend, poet Grevel Lindop, read the poem and wrote to me to point out that the Amazons were considered by the Greeks to be the most powerful women of all and that this was precisely because they were one-breasted. His sensitive words opened a door. I saw myself in a completely new light and soon afterwards I wrote 'Amazon' which like 'The Cave' is in *Writing My Way Through Cancer* and also my poetry collection, *Multiplying the Moon*:

Amazon

for Grevel

For four months
all those Matisse and Picasso women
draped against
plants, balconies, Mediterranean sea, skies
have taunted me
with the beautiful globes of their breasts as I've filled

my emptiness
with pages of scrawl, with fecund May, its floods
of green, its irrepressible
wedding-lace white, buttercup gold,
but failed to cover
the image of myself as a misshapen clown

until you reminded me
that in Greek myth the most revered women
were the single-breasted
Amazons who mastered javelins and bows, rode
horses into battle,
whose fierce queens were renowned for their femininity.

Then recognising the fields I'd fought my way across
I raised my shield
of glistening words, saw it echoed the sun.

(Schneider 2003, p. 103)

We look now at different ways in which people have written about bereavement and begin with C.S. Lewis and the way he recorded his feelings. He married late in life, and for a few years enjoyed a deeply fulfilling relationship before his wife died of cancer. *A Grief Observed* is his account of the process of coming to terms with his loss. It is a strangely titled volume, because the word 'observed' suggests either a token account or an objective discourse on the mourning period; the book is neither of these things but a brief yet intense series of insights into his mind and emotions in the aftermath of her death. It is drawn from his journals and is very much a rollercoaster of private distress. Lewis struggles to come to terms with an experience which continually confounds all his attempts to attain equilibrium.

One of the most interesting passages occurs towards the end of the book, where he is reflecting on the process he has undergone so far. He says of his journalling:

I will not start buying books for the purpose. In so far as this record was a defence against total collapse, a safety-valve, it has done some good. The other end I had in view turns out to have been based on a misunderstanding. I thought I could describe a state; make a map of sorrow. Sorrow, however, turns out to be not a state but a process. It needs not a map but a history, and if I don't stop writing that history at some quite arbitrary point, there's no reason why I should ever stop. (Lewis 1961, p. 50)

The above constitutes a valuable corrective to the notion that an endless outpouring of feelings onto the page can complete the healing process. For that a number of other factors, time and fresh experiences among them, need to be present.

In contrast to C.S. Lewis, who rigorously omits all mention of time and place from his account, Joan Didion in *The Year of Magical Thinking* gives in great detail chapter and verse for every event in the unfolding story of the twelve months of her life which saw the sudden death of her husband, John, with a heart attack. It also encompassed the prolonged life-threatening episodes of flu, pneumonia and septic shock of their only daughter, Quintana. The 'magical thinking' of the title is the name for the strategies Didion adopted for coping, which included setting herself to learn as objectively as possible all the details of the medical conditions involved, and an avoidance mechanism for places and situations which might carry challenging memories for her; even more it refers to the denial involved in such decisions as not to get rid of John's shoes or erase his voice from the answerphone message in her flat: she is unable to accept that he will not return.

Although this is a book of much greater immediacy than *A Grief Observed* it is not without its moments of profound reflection, which are all the more striking for their contrast with the seeming matter-of-factness of the rest of the text; here is one of them:

> Grief turns out to be a place none of us know until we reach it. We anticipate (we know) that someone close to us could die, but we do not look beyond the few days or weeks that immediately follow such an imagined death. We misconstrue the nature of even those few days or weeks. We might expect if the death is sudden to feel shock. We do not expect this shock to be obliterative, dislocating to both body and mind. We might expect that we will be prostrate, inconsolable, crazy with loss. We do not expect to be literally crazy, cool customers who believe that their husband is about to return and need his shoes. In the version of grief we imagine, the model will be 'healing'. A certain forward movement will prevail. The worst days will be the earliest days. We imagine that the moment to most severely test us will be the funeral, after which this hypothetical healing will take place. When we anticipate the funeral we wonder about failing to 'get through it', rise to the occasion, exhibit the 'strength' that invariably gets mentioned as the correct response to death. We anticipate needing to steel ourselves for the moment: will I be able to greet people, will I be able to leave the scene, will I be able even to get dressed that day? We have no way of knowing that this will not be the issue. We have no way of knowing that the funeral itself will be anodyne, a kind of narcotic regression in which we are wrapped in the care of others and the gravity and meaning of the occasion. Nor can we know ahead of the fact (and here lies the heart of the difference between grief as we imagine it and grief as it is) the unending absence that follows, the void, the very opposite of meaning, the relentless succession of moments during which we will confront the experience of meaninglessness itself. (Didion 2005, pp. 188–9)

After she had finished the book Didion suffered a further tragic blow: Quintana died. The fact that she was able to turn her book, and this second loss, into a new work of art – a play (with the same title) which was performed to acclaim on the New York and London stages, is a tribute to her honesty and courage.

We turn now to Penelope Shuttle's moving and in-depth account about the stages of grief she went through after her husband, the poet Peter Redgrove, died.

Redgrove's widow: Penelope Shuttle

'Poetry is a way of talking to people we've lost when it is too late.' These words of Ted Hughes sum up the desperate desire to continue a conversation that, in my case, had been going on at many levels for thirty-four years, and only ended with the death of my husband Peter Redgrove in 2003. (We had been together since our meeting in the summer of 1969.) After his death I was far too distraught to write any poetry or indeed read poetry or anything, even a newspaper. There is much truth in the old cliché that a bereaved person needs to travel the cycle of one year, season by season, and to be with their loss intensely, unremittingly, before any diminution of emotions such as sorrow, anger, guilt, shame, can be hoped for. The world, for me, during that first year of numb wordless pain, was devoid of colour. The summer of 2003 was a beautiful summer. But the blinds, actually and metaphorically, were down in my house. I wasn't aware of the summer except as something that had to be blocked out. It was a summer without colours, a summer in black and white, like an old-fashioned newsreel film. But, as wise Shakespeare says in *Macbeth*, we need to:

> Give sorrow words: the grief that does not speak
> Whispers the o'erfraught heart and bids it break . . .

In a master drama such as this, everything that happens is condensed, compressed, woven and fast. In the lives we lead, offstage, it takes much longer for us to reach a place where we can give our sorrow words. We have to get through the time when, literally, we suffer in silence. It was only after that first year of silence had so achingly and slowly revolved, bringing around the first anniversary of Peters' death, that I began writing again. Our daughter Zoe had closed the door of Peter's study bed-room soon after his funeral, and no one had set foot in it since then. One day, without planning to, I opened that door and went in. There was no sense of Peter's presence lingering in his room, and I wasn't especially moved or distressed by going in there. It was just a room. But on his desk there was a file containing the poems he'd been assembling for a new collection. I sat down, began reading. Here was his presence, his voice and all the complex energetic scope of his vision and sensibility. Reading these poems didn't make me sad. They reminded me of things I'd forgotten, particularly the transformative and intensifying magic of language. Loss takes away so much. I'd been suffering from emotional amnesia. Now I remembered who Peter was – a poet. I remembered who I was and would be again – a poet. I felt with a sense of wonder that Peter had left these poems here on his desk to help me through the hard place I was in. And so he was talking to me, even though it was too late for us to talk in this world, in the flesh. Our conversation had resumed.

Here's one of Peter's poems from that magical folder; about his own grief for his late father. It has now been published in his book, *A Speaker for the Silver Goddess*.

One Wedding, One Funeral

Beware the meat
                    in this restaurant, choose
                                        the vegetables
Which are the flesh transformed . . .
                    Waking from a nightmare of a forest
                                        every tree of which
Is changed into the coffin
                    that could be made of it:
                                        there is no way out
But through these rough doors . . .
                    If you want very clean bones
                                        use a chalk-lined box,
Chalk is prime skeleton,
                    gives immaculate bones if you have need
                                        of old bones spotless as porcelain

His mourning skin all changed to wood,
                    glued,
                                        buttoned up over the head
With nails; the ultimate sleeveless
                    suit made of imploded trees; look!
                                        the lady mortician enters the wood,
Bearing kindling, and more grief . . .
                    I pause, and rap on the box-from-the-copse,
                                        I listen,
The family skin is mine now,
                    he's in the box, he is all he has got, taking
                                        His wooden turn in the stuffy waiting room.

'There is no way out/ but through these rough doors . . . ' What moved me then and continues to move and inspire me about these last poems of Peter's is his unflinching way of looking at loss, and, as his health failed in his last years, of confronting his own mortality. Those rough doors are the wood of a coffin. So there's courage in these poems, which lifted me from the depths. Now I was able to start writing again, at first feeling my way very tentatively, in a very halting and unformed way. Gradually I found my way back. Poetry can create a living mirror, a steady reflection in which we gaze to discover how loss changes us, and the whole world. The mirror of words, of imagination, is a paramount tool in the healing of our selves and of those with whom we share loss, and then the wider community beyond, for who has not been touched by loss.

The first sustained piece of writing I felt I could share was a sequence of twenty-four poems addressed to Peter, called 'Missing You'. It was begun almost a year after Peter's death and finished in the summer of 2005. Only then did I realise that unconsciously I'd written a poem for each of the twenty-four months after losing him. At first I wasn't ready to go into print with this poem, and so I read portions of the sequence to audiences I knew would be supportive if emotion overwhelmed me. These audiences were colleagues at a Lapidus Conference, friends in Cornwall, and fellow poets at a Second Light Network Launde Abbey gathering, and I am grateful for their kindness. Eventually I felt strong enough to publish 'Missing You' in my 2006 collection *Redgrove's Wife*.

Here is the first poem and the concluding poem from the sequence.

1

This year no-one will ask how you voted,
or if you know the way to town

No-one will call you as an eye-witness
or teach you how to train a bird of prey

No-one will bring you your New Scientist,
try to sell you double-glazing
or tell you their secrets

People will write to you
but you won't answer their letters

The high sheriff of mistletoe
will never catch your eye again

No-one will peel apples for you,
or love you more than you can bear
No-one will forget you

24

A world's daylight was not enough to keep you here,
nor the night's secret of success

Summer will never forget you,
nor friendly autumn

They'd stop at nothing
to keep you where you belong

Every afternoon reads between the lines
for news of you

and on the spur of the moment
evening welcomes you, who are never there

Next week knows his fatherland is too small for you,
and next year knows it too

No city working till late at night could keep you,
nor the happy endings of the sea

The theatre sold-out every night couldn't hold you,
nor the long disobedience of the truth

Today,
who is a shadow of his former self,
lets you go,

and so do I,
all my schools closed for summer,
silent for weeks

So a dialogue begins with the lost and loved person. Poetry lends itself greatly to this way of talking to the people we've lost, because it combines everyday life experiences with the heightened language of the imagination. This can be done by the simple keeping of a notebook that acts as a letter addressed to someone we've lost. It doesn't have to be for publication. Keeping such a notebook works towards personal healing, gaining insights, the forging of a new self from the wreckage of the old.

I worked on the poems for my 2006 collection, *Redgrove's Wife*, from about 1998 to 2005. At the middle of this time span came Peter's death and my year of silence. But the title poem was written in 2001 as a light-hearted wedding anniversary poem for Peter, before his health had begun to deteriorate seriously. It sprang from a little private joke between us, with me pretending to be this person 'Mrs Redgrove', wife with a capital W. Whereas in reality I always used my own name, never my married name. I told Peter it was to be the title of my next book, and he was very shy about that, and said, 'Oh no, don't.' But I was determined. Then his health worsened. Now, several years after his death, this title poem, written back in happy circumstances, has become an unintended elegy. But it can, I hope, still be read with echoes of the happiness I knew with Peter. (The poem is included in Chapter 3.)

The Jungian John Layard said, many years, ago: 'Depression is withheld knowledge'. For me, there was a lot of withheld knowledge within my grief. Grief shares so many elements with depression. Once I was able to write into the grief, I found that I possessed the grief, the grief no longer possessed me. I don't think I've found acceptance of loss, perhaps that never happens, but I'm working strongly towards emotional equilibrium, still writing about the ways in which we experience grief differently as year follows year.

In the initial stages of grief, there are some things you dare not think of. For me one of the places I couldn't go to in my mind was contemplating what happened to Peter between his death in hospital and his cremation. I mean, what happened to his corpse. We were one flesh, and then we weren't. There's a huge amount of pain within that severance. So I've tried to resolve this by imagining Peter as a man in the prime of life, as he was when I first met him. In this closing poem I look at Peter's naked youthful body, but there are also overtones of his body immediately after his death.

The Keening

Yo voy a cerrar los ojos

I close my eyes –
I can see you better like this,
your head and high-domed brow,

your sea-green eye,
your eyelid, patient eyelash.

You are lost to me forever
but I am looking
at your *canst no more* temple,

your ear crammed full of silence,
singer's blank mouth,
lips, the upper, the lower,
their rue and rowan.

I feast my closed eyes
on your jaw, throat and neck,
your shoulder turned forever from the wheel,
your right arm so quietly past its prime.

Ah slowcoach,
how clearly I see
your clean-pared fingernails,
your strong wrist,

and resting heart – the vial of your heart
so long our wellkept secret . . .

I can't bear to look there,
even through closed eyes,
nor contemplate the rapids of your bloodstream
stemmed forever,

so I gaze at all your dear limbs . . .

Mine is the hard scrutiny
of the aubergiste looking down
at the small-change tip in her hand,
(though I keep no inn),
or of the captain searching no-man's land
for snipers, were I a warrior.

I look at your flanks
where my smoothing hand so often lingered,
loving your human body,
and at your sex
to which we gave no nickname,
at your skin's familiar landmarks,
frecks and specks and brindles –

I yearn over the vineyard of you . . .
not forgetting to look
at thigh, poor knee and calf,
your feet Time is not fit to wash.

Your bones, the fallen mast of your spine,
yes, those also I see –

I'm forbidden to touch you,
for we're no longer one flesh;

I may not give you a kiss of life,
nor my westerly bring joy of rain

to your parchlands,
but I am allowed this second sight of grief.

Day and night I look –
your head, your heel, your heart –

for love blindfolded is love still –
This looking is what is called mourning,
and this is how I have learned to mourn.

Sometimes it is impossible to write directly about a strong feeling or trauma. Caroline Price found the way to write about the loss of her father was through a parallel situation. In her poem, 'The Day My Father Died', she describes the dying of a greenfinch which she saw six months after her father's death. The detail is painful yet it brings out the beauty of the bird, her empathy for it, the shock and suddenness of death and her helplessness in the face of it. At the end Price brings the two deaths together in simple statements of fact which carry great emotional weight.

The Day My Father Died

And what I can't get out of my mind
is the greenfinch one moment
chipping at the peanut feeder
and then, in the blind spot of an eye,
tricked away, a thud on glass,
the delayed action
of a few feathers drifting down.

It's lying on its back on the patio,
legs drawn up, a flicker
in a visible eye.
It is a breezy mild March day.
A sudden gust
rocks its tiny weight, blows its wings
half open – and at this reminder of flight

its feathers twitch, it turns its head
from one side to the other,
slowly shifts itself
a quarter-circle in the dust.
And if this struggle
is great, the next is even greater,
its breathing growing faster

until the whole body shakes
like a feathered toy wound up
and not released – and it stretches out
its legs and opens both wings

wide, like fans, and arches its back
in a single effort
to meet or resist the end

which comes then, the shuddering
stopping abruptly, wings
folding, eyes slipping shut.
It lies warm in my hand, almost
weightless, head lolling back
in the crook of my fingers, claws
still extended, stiffening

on something just out of reach.
I stroke the misty greengrey
of its breast, wipe away specks of peanut
still clinging round its bill.
Which was all I could do.
It was a mild day in March.
It was the sixteenth of September.

Finally we look at the grievous experience of losing a child who has reached adulthood. Jocelyn Hurndall's twenty-one-year-old son Tom, an English photojournalist student, was shot in the head in 2003 as he tried to rescue a Palestinian child from the fire of an Israeli sniper in the Gaza strip. He died in a London hospital nine months later without having regained consciousness.

Those are the bare bones of the story told by the mother in her book, *Defy the Stars*. Actually it tells two stories: the political one of the background to the shooting, and of the struggle for justice in the case by taking on the British and Israeli authorities; and the personal one of the emotional effects of their loss on the Hurndall family. Her skill in keeping both narratives going is formidable.

At one point in the story the author is wrestling with the intractable problem she shared with her husband of whether to give the doctors the instruction to let their son die. She is wandering aimlessly down the hospital corridors turning the dilemma over and over in her mind when a significant encounter occurs:

Professor Gurman's door was open, and he was already at his desk. I stood in the doorway, obviously distressed, and when he saw me he rose and came towards me.

'Please,' he said, indicating a chair, and pulling up another in front of me.

It was a minute or two before I was able to speak. 'When you bring a child into the world,' I said finally, 'you never expect to have to make the decision to end that child's life. Is this really what we have to do?'

Professor Gurman simply inclined his head, looking at me quietly. 'I can think of no greater sadness than the loss of a child,' he said at last. 'Does it help at all if I tell you that I too have lost a child? But in my case there was no decision to make. My son died in a motor accident.'

Suddenly we were no longer doctor and client, but simply two parents, sharing our desperate feelings of loss, and I listened with a different kind of sadness. (Hurndall 2007, p. 117)

The book ends twenty-one months after Tom's death. In the intervening period the truth has come out about most of the details surrounding it, and a member of the Israeli Defence Force has been sentenced for manslaughter. The author is still carrying the burden of grief at her profound loss when she sets out to drive through Glencoe in Scotland:

Nearer to the pass the mountains began to close in. As I entered the pass, I began to feel an almost physical pressure, as if a great force was bearing down on me. Again I wanted to stop, but I somehow knew I must go on, through the narrow passage in the mountains. My face was wet with tears, and I heard a voice, which was my own, calling out 'Thomas! Thomas!' It was an anguished, involuntary cry that came from the depths of my being, like a cry of birth. I remembered the travail of Tom's birth, the moment of first holding him, vulnerable and restless, and the overwhelming feeling of wanting to protect and nurture him. Now I knew that I must let him go and return to life, that it was part of loving to be able to let go. *What will survive of us is love*. I thought of Tom's 'Rules for Life', which he'd written in his teens, and I seemed to hear his voice saying to me, *None of us deserves this life, and one single minute on this planet is an undeserved blessing*. And I drove on through the pass until finally the mountains parted and I found myself on a plateau, with fresh green countryside opening out before me. (Ibid., p. 304)

With this magnificent passage, so passionate, and so metaphorical, Jocelyn Hurndall brings the personal strand of her narrative to some kind of resolution.

Facing death **10**

Both the instinct and the overt desire to cling to life are very strong and maybe the stronger because we cannot escape knowing that in the end we must face death. Death, of course, is a central subject for writers and artists of all kind, a central subject for scientists, religious thinkers and philosophers. In the previous chapter we have looked at coping with the death of partners and also of an adult child. In this chapter we are focusing on writing about the idea of death. We are also looking at the ways people have coped, especially in writing, with the knowledge that they have a limited time to live either because they have been diagnosed with a terminal illness or in the case of Diana Athill, because, at eighty-nine, she recognizes she must be near the end of her life.

A child's first recognition of death is often a sharply painful experience. When Myra was about eight a child she sometimes played with fell into an open manhole and died soon afterwards from her injuries. Shocked, Myra was haunted by this death until she had a dream in which she was gliding over the moors behind her house hand in hand with the girl and a figure who she knew was death. Forty years later the death and the calming dream were still with her. The memory made her write a poem.

We begin here with a piece by John in which he writes about some of his responses to the idea of death. Childhood is his starting point.

Exploring death: John

I had gone through a period of personal crisis, and decided to look at death in different forms. Another factor which may have influenced me was all the communication work I was doing with people at the very end of their lives. I began with the deaths of significant others in my life: parents, my brother and a close friend, then moved on to contemplation of my own death. I started with the first death of any significance to me – that of my grandfather:

> My grandfather told me stories. I sat on his knee in the big leather armchair with the brass plaque on the side commemorating his years of service to the state.

I was there to hear the fantastic stories he made up or read from *Wee Macgreegor* by J.J. Bell. I adored them and him: his wonderful lined face, blue eyes that twinkled, a browning moustache that looked as if it had been used as a strainer for various liquids. Although we lived in Lancashire he was a Scotsman from Boness and had worked as an exciseman inspecting distilleries.

Now he was a storyteller and he took this responsibility just as seriously. I remember the thrill of waiting for the next twist in the plot or the next vivid burst of Glaswegian dialect. I remember the smell of Rennies, small peppermint tablets he took for his indigestion; sometimes he gave me one which I pretended to enjoy as a sweet.

Increasingly grandad took little turns in which he temporarily lost conscious-ness. I needed to hear how the story ended so I ran for granny and the sal volatile. I never thought these little episodes might lead to something more serious.

One day I shook him and ran for granny as usual. But neither granny, nor my mother and father, nor the doctor, could wake him. My grandfather finally fell asleep telling me a story, and I believe that is how he would have wished it. But I cried at the knowledge of a closeness now denied me.

I began to look at what death might mean in terms of the physical. This came to be represented most strongly for me by some photographs I had collected which I find deeply uncomfortable in their starkness. They are from Mexico, and one is called *The Day of the Dead*. This is the day people put a skeleton outside their house on a chair. Another is a death-mask. There was clearly here nothing left of the person. These images are frightening and I can't look at them for very long. For over a decade I worked as a writer in residence in nursing homes, and with some of the people I encountered it was possible to see how the flesh was shrinking from the bones. Sometimes when I look in a mirror I know that is where I am headed too.

I moved on to contemplate the possible circumstances of my own death. This was aided by a dream I had one night. I was in a bustling railway station, and as I passed through it I was greeted by a variety of people, all from different stages of my life – there was warmth in their various greetings but I could not stay to reminisce. The poem I wrote about this I called 'Central', not only because it seemed a major termi-nus but because of the special significance this image of my journey held for me. The poem ended as follows:

I approach the barrier –
I don't seem to know this line.
But who do I find standing there
but you – quizzical, amazed,

as if to say 'so it's true
on this part of the journey
you've found a companion.'

We link arms and stride
out. There is no train,
the lettering on the destination
board's illegible, but
there's lots of strangers waiting.
They greet us as if they know us
as ourselves, and that feels good.

And now our perspective
narrows to the empty end
of the platform, beyond
which lies the tunnel mouth.
We turn, embrace, I let go
of your hand, and wave, then
walk on into the dark.

I don't know who the significant other was in the dream, but it seemed important that I was being accompanied as I approached the end. There was no disguising from myself, however, that at the very last I was journeying on alone.

I went on to contemplate what might follow. The bleakest expression of this came in the poem, 'Last Wish':

Unyielding to the rain's caresses,
unflinching at the eye of the sun,
Tombtop, I would be as you,
tilting to earth in some neglected
graveyard corner where the trees
dip obeisance to my otherworldliness,
my past – a scribble that's inscrutable
as the silver of snail-trails
that criss-cross the striations,
no more personal than the lichens
that in time will cover all.

I also looked at the spiritual. As a non-believer I wanted to find out if there was any sense in which the concept of immortality could be meaningful for me. The only aspect I found I could identify which carried conviction for me was encapsulated in the following poem, which is, of course, about love:

End Note

Somehow you are no longer living just for yourself
and that is what makes all the difference.

The other is moving around in the world casting light
and, though absent, you have a part in this.

Sometime when you have gone into the night,
the other will still be here, carrying forward

what you together began. And this is more
than you could ever have deserved or hoped for.

We turn now to coping with the immediate prospect of death. Barbara Feldt, who lived in Michigan, experienced a serious heart attack in 1980 at the age of forty-six. She was to live as a semi-invalid for the next thirteen years before dying three weeks after her sixtieth birthday. Thus she faced on a daily basis the imminent possibility of her life ending. Mentally she was completely alert during this period. This state of affairs concentrated her mind (and those of the minds of her husband and three children) on the significance of life and death in a remarkable way.

In the last four years Barbara and her husband Allan attended a poetry-writing group, and both began composing poems about what they were going through. Their daughter, Linda Diane, also wrote, but her reflections were in prose. The book, *Dying Again*, is narrated by the daughter but gives extracts from the writings of all three. As well as some of Barbara's poems it contains journal entries by her, and extracts from her dream diary. It is a unique document, chronicling as it does a journey from the perspective of three travellers. In order to bring their shared predicament into some perspective all three examine family history as well as immediate concerns. Linda Diane comments as follows on her mother's embracing of the new activity of writing:

> She found that writing about her ongoing depression, her occasional thoughts of suicide, her past difficulties with raising her children, her disability and struggle to cope with a terminal illness – all of these subjects had audiences she found were eager to hear another person's intimate perspective. She hoped that she could help others by writing about what she was experiencing. When she heard from other people that they had been touched by her work she was overjoyed. It meant everything to her. (Feldt 1996, p. 3)

Barbara attempted a self-portrait in the following poem:

Portraits

I am an opal
an iridescent jewel
confetti colored
softly glowing
lighted from within.

I am a pot of stones
polished by much buffeting.
An ample container,
unadorned, enfolds
my independent parts.

I am an Oriental poppy,
a brilliant orange flower
which brightened the lives
of those who experienced
my full blooming.

As my petals dropped
they formed a pleasing
pattern. Now just a pod
subdued in colour, poised
among green leaves

I am pregnant with words. (Ibid., p. 54)

She also found a metaphor for her condition in this extract from 'The Unweaving':

The essence of my being
appeared as a basket
woven of thin willow strips.

My heart stopped
my lungs filled and I gasped
for air. With each breath
I saw a strip spring free.

All were released
the empty base revealed
I recognised the end.

"I'm dying." I said
but my heart disagreed
and resumed its work. (Ibid., p. 61)

The widower Allan addresses his wife, and his own grief, in the poem 'Thirty-Nine':

> Over a month after your death
> I've learned to live without you.
> Cooking, cleaning, shopping, laundry
> all fit into a weekly pattern.
> Your papers are sorted and boxed,
> jewelry distributed to children and friends,
> wheelchair disposed of, oxygen tanks
> and hospital bed advertised for sale.
> Gradually the tokens of our
> thirty-nine years together disappear.
>
> But on the 39th day
> I walk idly along a Florida beach.
> Spotting a beautiful shell,
> I pick it up without thinking,
> in order to bring it home to you. (Ibid., p. 138)

There are few deaths as prefigured as this one, and few accounts as multi-faceted as *Dying Again*.

Like Barbara Feldt writer Julia Darling lived the last years of her life knowing she was terminally ill. A talented writer, still in her forties, she used her time to stand up to her illness and live life to the full. She wrote, taught and involved herself in many arts projects. She also had two collections of poetry published. Her pared poems are brimming with life, realistic about her situation, witty and poignant. We include one from the second collection, *Apology for Absence*. The writing is sharply comic in the way it characterizes the nurses and her defiant self. The poem ends with a sting:

Nurses

> Slope-shouldered, bellies before them,
> the nurses are coming, garrulously,
> they are bossing me in and out of clothes
> into windowless rooms, tucking me in.
> Nurses are patting me, frowning,
> then they guffaw in another room.
> They have flat footed footsteps
> and very short memories.

But I am the woman who won't take off her bra,
the one who demands that you look in her eyes.
Miss Shirty, they call me, I know my own veins;
when they come back for me, I'll be gone.

Anna Adams sees death as a release from destructive illness in her tightly written, rhymed lyric, 'Dead Letter'. However, this poem is no easy accommodation with death. Adams may 'pick no bones' with it but she has still to come to terms with the loss of her 'dearest lifelong friend':

Dead Letter

1

I pick no bones with death;
endless supply of breath
would be a worse design.
Death is benign.

I throw no stones at time.
It is the spacious room
roofed by a stormy sky
in which we learn to fly.

I have not shed one tear,
my eyes are desert-dry;
nor have I yet, my dear,
quite said Goodbye

because, towards the end,
my dearest lifelong friend,
you could no longer hear;
you were not there.

2

Disease is like a worm
that robs us from within
of what makes up a man;
good humour, kindness, dream;

all notions, words, all skill:
only the will to be
stripped of all courtesy
torments us still

till our last energy
escapes with our last breath.

I pick no bones with death.

We end this chapter by looking at Diana Athill's book, *Somewhere Near the End*. At first glance this appears to be a cosy memoir by an eighty-nine-year-old author about growing old. In the first chapter she describes with humour a writer who feared ageing so much she never mentioned it and she is very witty about another writer who insisted that he 'rejected death'. Athill's good sense and wit are, in fact, a frame in which she faces ageing and death very frankly. In the process she examines the sexual relationships in her life, how she cared for her mother during her last illness and also how she looked after the lover she'd lived with for years to whom, in effect, she became a spouse when they were both old. She examines the practicalities of coping with old age and the satisfactions she has managed to find in it. Spirituality is also an important element. The book is far from a cosy read but its combination of pragmatism, humanity and zest for living do offer comfort.

There are points when Athill looks unflinchingly at death. She writes graphically about seeing a dead person for the first time which was in a mortuary when she was in her seventies. Later, when her mother was dying, she remembers this and how she'd told herself: '. . . it is possible not only to acknowledge the ordinariness of that dissolution [of flesh], but also to feel it' (Athill 2008, p. 63). She also describes how as a result of the mortuary visit she had got into the habit of recognizing the vans used for carrying dead people and it reassured her to say to herself: 'There goes death . . . about its daily work' (ibid., p. 64). She articulated all this in a spontaneous poem she wrote during her mother's last illness. At the end of the book Athill considers the legacy of living beings:

> . . . minuscule though every individual, every 'self' is, he/she/it is an object through which life is being expressed, and leaves some sort of contribution to the world. The majority of human beings leave their genes embodied in other human beings, other things they have made, everyone in things they have done: they have taught or tortured, built or bombed, dug a garden or chopped down trees, so that our whole environment, cities, farmland, deserts – the lot! – is built up of contributions, useful or detrimental, from the innumerable swarm of selfs preceding us, to which we ourselves are adding grains of sand. (Ibid., p. 180)

She then focuses specifically on what dies:

> What dies is not a life's value, but the worn-out (or damaged) container of the self, together with the self's awareness of itself: away that goes into nothingness, with everyone else's. That is what is so disconcerting to an onlooker, because unless someone slips away while unconscious, a person who is just about to die is still fully alive . . . I remember thinking as I sat beside my mother 'But she *can't* be dying, because she's still so entirely here' (the wonderful words which turned out to be her last, 'It was absolutely divine,' were not intended as such but just part of something she was telling me). The difference between being and non-being is both so abrupt and so vast that it remains shocking even though it happens to every living thing that is, was, or ever will be. (Ibid., p. 181)

Athill is always direct. Often it is as if she has invited the reader into her flat and is talking, simply following her train of thought. However, the planning and writing are skilful. Honest, often self-critical, this woman – who admits to being 'somewhere towards the end' and 'hopes it won't be too soon' – pulls one up short, makes one laugh and think. This is an exhilarating book.

11 Spirituality

For many people spirituality is that aspect which gives most meaning and purpose to life. For some organized religion provides them with a philosophy and a code of conduct. For others it is the quality of search that is all-important. We have already met with spiritual concerns in the writings of Jocelyn Hurndall in Chapter 9 and Diana Athill in Chapter 10, and in one sense the journey described by Brian Keenan in *An Evil Cradling* (Chapter 3) is one of the soul as well as the body.

John considers his communication work with people who have dementia, a calling he experienced late in life, as a breakthrough to a more profound human engagement. He has expressed this in the second part of his poem, 'Getting Through':

> I'm a prospector of the soul,
> using human tools to hand
> of touching, listening, seeing
> to explore the seam. The goal:
> to strike gold in each being. (Killick 2008, p. 24)

Myra says:

> In my teens I searched desperately for the meaning of life but it wasn't until I read Wordsworth's poetry that I felt I'd found some kind of answer in his pantheism and this has sustained me ever since. I also need writing to explore my relationship with the world, to feel complete. I've come to think of consciousness, of energy to create, as a gift. All this seems to fuse at the end of my poem, 'Bird':
>
> And I will be
>
> here, there, within you, everywhere,
> my flung wingtips longing to come together,
> striving to complete a shape as I pierce and pierce the blue rush.
>
> (from *Circling the Core*)

There are a number of nature writers in prose today who express a deep sense of wonder at the universe without needing to display orthodox religious credentials. One of the most outstanding of these is the American Annie Dillard. Her book *Teaching a Stone to Talk: Expeditions and Encounters* contains a number of examples of this characteristic. In her Author's Note she proclaims the central significance of these brief essays to her work: '. . . this is not a collection of occasional pieces, such as a writer brings out to supplement his real work; instead this is my real work, such as it is' (Dillard 1984, front of book). She often starts from mundane details of life and suddenly takes off into spiritual exploration. 'A Field of Silence' evokes the atmosphere of a farm where the author lived once. She describes the sounds of the farm, in particular a rooster and some of the farm animals, and these constitute noise. Contrasting with this is the almost supernatural calm of a particular field close by:

> There was only silence. It was the silence of matter caught in the act and embarrassed. There were no cells moving, and yet there were cells. I could see the shape of the land, how it lay holding silence. Its poise and its stillness were unendurable, like the ring of the silence you hear in your skull when you're little and notice you're living, the ring which resumes later in life when you're sick. (Ibid., pp. 135–6)

In the following account Mary MacRae describes how for her writing poetry has become the embodiment of the search for enlightenment.

The spiritual self: Mary MacRae

Given my upbringing and temperament it seems inevitable to me now that eventually I would be drawn to poetry. I grew up in a church-going family in suburban London; nobody talked about spiritual matters but my mother and I would go to our High-Anglican parish church at least once, usually twice, every Sunday. So from a young age I was exposed regularly to church music and to the language of *The Book of Common Prayer* and *The Bible*; these lifted me out of the narrow everyday of family and school and gave me something that I craved. Very soon, however, I was aware that I couldn't share my mother's deeply held beliefs; wherever the music and the beautiful language led me it was not to Christian faith. As a child I found this quite worrying.

However, I soon discovered poetry – or poetry discovered me. And while for many writers poetry provides a way into the inner self, it may also allow us to explore and give voice to those moments that might be called 'spiritual', when something outside oneself is given, 'something understood'. In the act of writing lyric poetry we may be able to unlock our deep irrational core and make connections through intuition and imagination as we try to seize a perception in language.

In common with many writers I find the initial impulse for a poem is often a response to the natural world, particularly to birds or the sea. The following poem, *Gannet*, started as a response to the beauty of the bird's flight:

Gannet

This is what I came to look for
     from the rocks at the very tip
        of St David's Head, this bird,

this gannet, so white it reflects the light
     from far out on the open sea,
        one continuous line of body

aimed towards
     the questing head and sharp beak,
        its whole being flowing forward

like Braque's bird, bleached
     and flying over the bay,
        back to Grassholm.

Suppose I could be re-born
     into that frame, what might I find
        in the huge plunge seaward,

the crash of entry, the long
     descent to semi-darkness?
        What fish emerge with?

Although I wasn't aware of it as I drafted this poem, it seems now that the word 'questing' is a key one; I had deliberately gone in search of this bird, and saw in its outstretched neck and sharp beak an image of the questing self. The bird has stamina and seems at one with the open sea. The leap then happened as I asked myself the question: 'Suppose I could be re-born/into that frame', as I imagined the gannet's dive underwater in human terms of terror, darkness, dissolution, and wondered what fish would be brought to the surface. This poem was first published in the third Poetry School Anthology, *I am Twenty People*, and I chose it to end my first collection of poems, *As Birds Do*, in the hope that the gannet would fly into a future second collection with a startling live fish in its beak.

A few years ago my central vision was under threat, first in one eye and then the other. I was very frightened at the possibility of losing sight of colour and all the beauty of the material world. My poem, 'Blue Tits', began as a response to the vibrant colour of some anemones in a vase and a fear not just of partial blindness but also of death itself. As I wrote, however, I was also watching birds in the garden, blue tits, darting in and out of the bay tree that they habitually feed in and use for shelter:

Blue Tits

No need to look for colour,
it searches me out, crimson

and white anemones
fixing my eye as I read

the fine cursive on the underside
of cupped flower-heads

wanting them to last and last
in a greed for eternity

so that even the slightest crumple
on a white petal touches me –

and I cram it all in, wondering
how I could live without colour

feathering the air, afraid
of blue and brightness, of losing

sight of the material world
as I stare into the garden and follow

small birds along invisible tracks
inside the bay tree

until they conjure themselves
out of the leaves,

their eyes excited
by wavelengths of green light.

(from *As Birds Do*)

The use of the word 'feathering' seems to have helped me to move on in the poem from a feeling of incipient loss to something more positive, as imagination takes over and I 'see' the birds hidden inside the tree, feel their eyes 'excited' by a green light we're unable to see.

In my poem 'By Faversham Creek' I try to record what was to me a very strange experience indirectly associated with my lack of religious faith. At the time my sister who lives in Canada was seriously ill; I was walking alone on Faversham Marsh which seemed alive with autumn colour:

> . . . and the thought
> of my sister who's ill and so far away
> is the shadow of this, the under-drawing.

> (from *As Birds Do*)

Unable to overcome my misery, unable to make contact with anything outside myself, I walked through what seemed an increasingly desolate place until

> a wild rose-bush suddenly opens
> and blossoms with birds, goldfinches
> packed close on every twig

> dazzling even among rose-hips
> as they extend yellow wings to preen
> bowing their scarlet heads.

Through the writing I try to understand why that sudden vision gave me some respite; how the birds bowing their scarlet heads could be set against my own inability to pray.

In the following piece Grevel Lindop describes in detail the experience of writing a single poem which has significant spiritual content.

Night – Finding the poem: Grevel Lindop

'Night' was written in a single evening. I felt that I wanted to write a poem, or *could* write one, but had no idea of its subject. In a kind of frustration I found myself watching the sky above the houses opposite the room where I write. I noticed that a star had 'come out', as we say; and then another. The opening words of the poem began to appear in my head in much the same way, imperceptibly, just being there where they hadn't been before. The image of the 'peacock-tail' was suggested, perhaps, by the wonderful peacock blue of the twilight sky.

I decided not to impose any rationality upon the poem but to let its sounds and images come as they would. This was made easier by using rhyme and short lines, which helped the intuitive, associative processes.

The first star I saw may have been Venus, 'the evening star'. Venus and Mars are often visible from that window. Lovers in classical myth, their appearance helped to give an erotic tinge to the poem. But the night itself, as it came on, grew into a symbol of many things: quietness (without talk or papers), and also timelessness. Clocks run at night just as during day, but contemplating the night sky seemed to take me away from all questions of deadlines and appointments. Giving the non-rational its head, I asserted what I felt: 'the night is timeless'. In this kind of poem – rhyming, traditionally-shaped, non-intellectual – I often let old phrases or proverbs creep in. Here some words, almost a spell, floated up, half-remembered, from a fairy tale: 'Time is, time was, time's past'. I used the phrase, with its repetitious, 'tick-tock' rhythm, to give a sense of the mechanical passage of ordinary time.

As the sky grew darker, a mental picture arose of night as a great blue-black bird preening itself. At the same time, perhaps because I'd mentioned Venus and Mars, I found myself envisioning Night as a goddess. I began to feel that the poem would be a love-poem to her. I found the stars turning into her jewels, and tried to give a sense of scale and depth by reference to the sea.

Now that Night was both sky and sea, it seemed natural that she should be hymned by the earth. Perhaps I heard some mental echoes of Mahler's *Song of the Earth*. So the earth sings to Night; but still the visual sense predominates, so the music is 'a music of all the colours/that can happen on earth'; but with the word 'happen', the colours also become events – like the changing colours of the sky, they are not just there, but take place as a process.

Feeling that the poem risked drifting into whimsy, I drove in a kind of tent-peg by suddenly turning to myself, or the reader, and asserting 'one of them is yours'. Each individual, that is, has their own part in the cosmic symphony. The line puts me, or the reader, on the spot; but I felt impelled to go a step further, challenging rationality by asking 'True or not true?' This connected with the opening points about daylight time and speech and paper. I dismissed the question with: 'That belongs to the day,/speaking its daylight language', feeling that what mattered in the poem was the emotional, imaginative truth, no matter how apparently nonsensical.

By now I had a sense of passionate involvement with the poem. I was praising, hymning, with an intense feeling of love and trust, something entirely beyond me but with which I felt completely safe, and which I experienced as feminine. Looking, I suppose, for a rhyme and a transitional shift towards a conclusion, I came up with what I now feel is a weak line: 'Do not turn away'. I haven't revised it because I don't think I could find anything which would do the job so economically; but I felt it was weak then and I still do. How often is it possible to write a poem without a blemish?

Still, it got me to the final stage, where I found myself seeing Night again partly as Venus, taking weapons away from a Mars who is tired of battle. My own weapons, tiresome as at the beginning of the poem, were words. I sensed that the end of the poem was near and we were approaching silence, so it was almost time to let go of words. Other associations, spontaneous and traditional, were now very strong. I found myself thinking, naturally, about sleep, and about death. The image of Mars and Venus also brought to mind sexual love. Searching almost physically within my body for a concluding image, amongst feelings of love, vastness, humility and many other things, I found the paradoxical phrase, 'enfold her, enter her', which seemed to sum it all up. It was spatially contradictory, because when you 'enfold' you are out-side, yet when you 'enter' you are inside. Yet when a man makes love, both are true. There was a feeling of embracing (in the sense of meeting whole-heartedly) life, death, the divine, spiritual enlightenment – any 'ultimate' you care to name; and also of 'entering' all of these things.

And because there was love for these things, there was also confidence: hence the last line, 'She will not refuse you'. The poem had, unexpectedly, been a process of meditation on the beauty of the unknown and all the half-glimpsed feelings conjured up by watching the astonishing cosmic process of twilight. I found myself shaken and almost tearful with a sense of the vastness and mystery of the world and its miracu-lous divine and spiritual depths. I had instinctively envisioned all these things as a woman; indeed, after finishing the poem, I realised that I had also been writing a love poem to my beautiful dark-haired wife.

I still don't really understand 'Night'. For me it expresses feelings above all; readers will find in it whatever meanings are there for them.

Night

Slowly the night fans out
a peacock-tail of stars,
green into blue between
the eyes of Venus and Mars.

Slowly the sky comes clear,
speech with its disturbance
and all the rustling of paper
falling towards silence.

Time is for the day –
time is, time was, time's past.
But the night is timeless:
nothing first, nothing last,

preening the same black feather
out of her raven wing.
And her jewels are like the sea,
seething, endlessly soothing,

with a gold phosphorescence
poised on their rise and fall,
and a plunge deeper than galaxies
under the dark crystal.

Now everything is quiet,
not even a thought stirring,
the empty miles of the earth
begin to sing her a song:

a mythological symphony,
a music of all the colours
that can happen on earth.
And one of them is yours.

True or not true?
That belongs to the day,
speaking its daylight language.
Do not turn away,

but look into her eyes:
what she understands
is silence, darkness, love.
Give her your empty hands,

let your weapons go,
all the words that confuse you.
Enfold her, enter her.
She will not refuse you.

(from *Playing with Fire*)

We end Part I with Sidney Poitier's autobiography in which he examines his whole life – what has influenced it, what ideas he has tried to live by, what meanings he has found. He was born in a semi-primitive society on Cat Island in the Bahamas and although he grew up in poverty he remembers his childhood as idyllic – his parents were caring, the community was closely knit and he was surrounded by the natural world. He was ten when he first came across white people and it was not until he went to live in Miami at the age of fifteen that he had the shock of finding out that there was such a thing as racial discrimination. Semi-literate, he found the next few years in a society which treated him as inferior extremely difficult but he made his way to New York and eventually into the world of theatre and film. While he was struggling to better himself he was supported by the belief that he was as good as anyone else. He also notes:

> As I entered this world, I would leave behind the nurturing of my family and home, but in another sense I would take their protection with me. The lessons I had learned, the feelings of groundedness and belonging that had been woven into my character there, would be my companions on the journey . . .
>
> Always lurking behind the objects and experiences of the everyday world, there were mysteries. Why is there something instead of nothing? Why have I survived, even prospered? (Poitier 2000, p. 30)

Poitier went on questioning everything. This very much included white attitudes and he refused to take part in any film which denigrated black people. He sees himself as a survivor. Often he is self-critical as he examines the different choices he made. He is deeply concerned with inner life and his relationship with the wider world. Referring to his film, *Lilies of the Field*, he notes it 'had a lot to say about the kind of consciousness I aspire to', ibid., p. 201 and he adds: 'When I cling to the self, I feel neurotic, alienated, insecure. It's when I let the self go that I can begin to realize how fully a part of this grand scheme I am' (ibid., p. 202).

At another point he writes:

> I simply believe that there's a very organic, immeasurable consciousness of which we're a part. I believe that this consciousness is a force so powerful that I'm incapable of comprehending its power . . .
>
> Now, given the immensity of this immeasurable power that I'm talking about, and given its pervasiveness through the universe (extending from distant galaxies to the tip of my nose), I choose not to engage in what I consider to be the useless effort of giving it a name, and by naming it, suggesting that I in any way understand it, though I'm enriched by the language and imagery of both traditional Christianity and old island culture. Many of my fellow human beings *do* give it a name, and *do* purport to understand . . . I just give it respect and I think of it as living in me as well as everywhere else.
>
> The grand consciousness I perceive allows me great breadth and scope of choices, none of which are correct or incorrect except on the basis of my own perception. This means that the responsibility for me rests with me. (Ibid., pp. 196–7)

This is a serious and searching memoir. It is aptly called *The Measure of a Man*.

Part 2

Getting started, image explorations and basic techniques

The aim in this chapter and the next two is to offer a range of techniques to help you explore personal subject matter. It is a good idea to write in a notebook but if you prefer to write on pieces of paper we suggest you keep them in a folder so that you can find them easily whenever you want to re-read or develop your material. There is no *right* or *wrong* way to do any of the exercises we suggest. You can write in notes, full sentences, images or a mixture of these. Feel free to include ideas or thoughts which do not seem to belong to the exercise if you have an urge to write them.

It is likely that what you produce will be uneven: some of it obvious, contradictory, over-explained or incoherent but it is also very likely that you will find material that expresses or begins to express ideas, thoughts, feelings or memories that are important to you. If one of the exercises suggests a completely different subject matter then allow yourself to explore it. You can always try out our suggestion later. You may find you want to take some of the material you produce further and we shall be looking at some ways of doing this in Chapters 15 and 16.

Section 1: Getting started

This first section offers some ideas to help you get in touch with your feelings and what is central in your life. Sometimes it is hard to pinpoint exactly which personal experience one wants to write about and to disentangle it from other material. It can also be difficult to know how to tackle a subject even if one has identified it. We suggest, therefore, that you try out some of the following straightforward exercises in a spirit of adventure without spending too long on them – about ten minutes, more if you want to.

Exercise 1: Desert islands

You are marooned on a desert island, have found food, water and a sheltered place to sleep and you are not in any danger. Write briefly about each of the following: (a) What and who do you most miss and why. (b) What and who are you glad to have left behind. (c) The two things you have been allowed to bring with you – why you chose them (nothing which requires electricity to make it work!) (d) How you would cope with solitude. Here are excerpts from pieces Charlie Druce wrote about the possessions he would take with him and how he would cope with solitude:

> My cello. I used to play it quite well, up until I was about 17. . . But then other things in my changing life took over and I stopped playing it. So I'd try and play it again on the island. It'd remind me of my Mum and Dad and all the ways they encouraged me . . . .
>
> Time on my own these days is precious. So it's easy to say a bit of peace of quiet would be OK . . . But actually, with no one there to measure up to, no one to compare emotional notes with and to share with, or cook up plans for the great escape with, I think I would come to dread the island. I can see myself bound in a kind of straight jacket, bursting with designs and plans, but being chased more and more ferociously by my own demons.

Exercise 2: Patterning

This is what its title suggests – writing in a pattern. Patterning of various kinds is used particularly by songwriters and poets because repetition is satisfying and adds to the emotional weight. It can also be fun. The simplest form of it is to write what is in effect a list introduced by the same word or words. This creates a strong rhythmic effect and could even lead to a poem. The way to use the technique is to write as freely as possible and enjoy experimenting with words. It can be very releasing and surprisingly potent. Choose one of these opening phrases, complete a sentence with it and then add several more: 'Today I am', 'I shall never', 'I want', 'I don't want', 'Because I', 'I am going to', 'I won't forget', 'I remember', 'Every day I'.

Here is an extract from a piece by Celia Cartwright who went straight into her mixed-up feelings:

> I want to take a week off work and do nothing but read and sleep.
> I want to get my teeth into an exciting project.
> I want my mother to lose her voice for a month.
> I want to arrive home without enduring the journey and find no one in.
> I want to find he's in first with a takeaway meal and a box of chocolates.
> I want to go on a diet and lose weight.
> I want to shout: 'Sod everything – let's go to Paris for the weekend.'

Now try this again using a feeling or state of mind in the form: 'Hope is', 'Fear is', 'Determination is', 'Rage is', 'Disappointment is', 'Serenity is', 'I am afraid', 'I love', 'I'm angry because', 'I hope', and so on. Here is an extract from a piece by Tim Jenkins:

> Rage is fire that's swallowing up a block of flats.
> Rage is a mouth which never stops yelling.
> Rage is the sea beating against jagged rocks.
> Rage is what I try to hide from under a table.

In Chapter 6 there is an extract from a piece of patterning Myra did in which each sentence began: 'I am afraid'. Patterning can have a powerful emotional effect in both spontaneous and finished work. In Chapter 4 June English describes how a repeated phrase opened 'a door of silence' for her.

Exercise 3: Here and now

This is a simple way of focusing on yourself. Sit down somewhere comfortable and begin by looking at your surroundings and describing whatever strikes you: a book, a painting on the wall, a letter or an overflowing wastepaper basket. Alternatively write about something you saw, read or heard very recently: a traffic jam, an article in the paper, a conversation overheard on a journey, and so on. Begin with some precise details and then move on to write about yourself now: your mood, present preoccupations, what is going on in your life. Here is an excerpt from a piece by Alan Johnson:

> The remains of my M & S supper and an apple core are staring back at me. Next to them is today's newspaper. 'Failed Again!' says a headline. The cat's vitamin pills are hiding whatever it is that has failed . . . I want to get away from failure. If A. was here there would be flowers in that vase she bought – daffodils. Do I want her here?

Exercise 4: A person in your life

All kinds of influences, often from early in life, profoundly affect our attitudes, feelings and behaviour. Examples are: what social class we grew up in, our religious upbringing and issues about gender. The strongest influences of all though are likely to come from the people who play a central role in our lives. In Part 1 of this book there are many pieces which explore influential relationships. One of these is John Burnside's relationship with his father (Chapter 2), another is the friendship between Brian Keenan and John McCarthy (Chapter 3). Choose someone who has had an important influence on you and describe what he or she means to you, maybe by focusing on a particular incident.

Section 2: Image explorations

This technique gives you the opportunity to use your imagination freely, to travel through your inner landscape and express images, feelings and thoughts that occur naturally. It makes no demand that you stick to facts, explain or analyse. Nor does it ask that you face painful subject matter which you may not be ready to deal with head on. When you use this approach you may find yourself uncovering material and feelings you were not aware of. Equally the technique may release you from an immediate preoccupation such as a serious illness, a very difficult relationship or work situation. As a result you may come back to the problem with a new perspective.

Below are some image explorations to try out. You may find that some of them lead you to write a poem or a story. We suggest you try out those which strike a chord with you. For each image journey we offer a series of prompts. Feel free to mix fiction, fantasy and fact and write as much or as little as you want to. Write in the third person if you would like to.

Exercise 1: An encounter

You are sitting in a café, a hotel, on a train or outside on a park bench. There are people about but you are preoccupied with your own thoughts. Write about yourself and your surroundings with a brief reference to a person or the people round you. You become aware of someone you had not noticed before or who comes and sits near you. Something about her/his expression or behaviour makes you want to start a conversation. What happens next? Here is part of a piece written by Sean Miller:

> I'm on the train. And when I say the train, I mean a train in the sense that I don't think it's the right one. Ask me what the right train is, though, and I wouldn't be able to tell you. I hope to recognize the first stop that we come to, but the problem is the train isn't stopping. It's coming into stations and slowing down . . . then it picks up speed again and we are plunged into darkness. I am aware of a person sitting very close to me. I can feel their breath behind my ear. I think they are whispering something to me . . . After ten minutes, we burst out of the tunnel

and into an impossibly green landscape. I am shocked by the sudden light and the person sitting opposite. The whisperer has gone . . . This is not the whisperer. It is a man not wearing a shirt. Painted across his bare chest in huge red letters are the words: I KNOW WHERE I AM GOING! . . .

Exercise 2: The bridge

You have been on a long journey by foot maybe by yourself, maybe with one other person. Some way ahead you can see a river and a bridge over it. Write about your journey, your immediate surroundings, the view ahead, the weather, the person you are with if there is one and how you are feeling. As you approach the bridge you discover that it looks unsafe and the river and terrain below also make crossing look dangerous. Write about this and its effect on you/your companion. You become aware of a person or people calling to you from the opposite bank. What happens? Here is part of Clive Eastwood's image exploration:

> It's hard to look around, the ground a mesh of tree roots, rocks with their skins of slithery, ankle-breaking moss. The green, the damp, the drops streaming from the branches make this woodland seem primeval, rainforest almost – were it not for the cold. Hart's-tongues line the track, the way ahead is mystery, the plunge of approaching water exhilarating. Yet the river isn't being playful. A mass of wet energy forces itself through the bridge . . . And it seems this walk can't have an ending – I can only go back. I hear a shout above the din. There's a man on the far bank under an umbrella, sitting with easel and board, painting. He holds up what he's done to give me a glimpse, the smallest glimpse of this place from the other side.

Exercise 3: The island

You are on an island which seems to be uninhabited. Write about your surroundings, the weather, how you are feeling and maybe how you came to be on the island. You start exploring and come across a hut or some kind of sheltering place. You go inside and find a piece of furniture or an object that belonged to you or someone in your family or it reminds you of something important. Here is part of a piece written by Sheena Clover:

> I would like to lie in this white sand and bury myself as a turtle buries her eggs, nestle in with my eyes open staring at the vast bowl of the sky and the milky way exploding above me, sleep. But the sun is still fierce and would burn my eyes. I should go to the shadows under the tall trees that cluster above the shore and make a shelter. In that canopy are flashes of colour, yelps and bird calls. The trunks

are covered in vines and marching ants the size of my finger. The ground shifts and moves with the bristle of insect life but the sea's susurration calms me.

From the same exercise here is an excerpt from Kay Syrad's piece. This focuses on the shelter:

There is a hut. It has no door. It cannot be penetrated. There is a hut, a colour – a light – the hut is a colour. It sits on the horizon, alone . . . My mother is the hut, with a little colour, she is there in the light. My mother is there in the light, let my mother be there in the light. Let my let my let my mother, my mother . . . I am inside the hut, still it is dark. I feel, my fingers brush the air, the air is black; black air is thick. My hand meets a chair – a tall chair, its back long, struts are long. The seat – I can feel the smooth, cold wood of the seat, I stroke it and move round the chair—my grandfather chair, black oak, hewn smooth . . . The hut is long and dark; the horizon is long and dark. The horizon speaks. The wind brings light, brings light, brings light. My mother speaks – ah, ah, ah. I am listening, tense with listening . . .

Exercise 4: The safe place

You are hurrying down a road. You feel worried or anxious about something or someone or maybe you are afraid of some indefinable fear. You find somewhere – a corner, niche, cubby hole, bus shelter, room, or some place of refuge and go into it. Gradually you relax. The hideaway may remind you of people who made you feel comfortable or situations in which you felt safe or you may find that you are experiencing a sense of security you have not ever found before.

Now try making up your own image exploration. Here are some possible ingredients to draw on: a high wall, searching a corridor, a rocky shore, flying, someone asking you for help, a river, a tunnel, the seashore, a hothouse, the moon, a crowded station, an escalator, an untidy room, a waterfall, driving a car fast, a voice coming from a loudspeaker, a horse careering round a field, a calm lake, a cave, a bull, a thunderstorm. Enjoy giving your imagination full rein and using these images and others which have a resonance for you.

Section 3: Basic techniques

Flow-writing

This is probably the most useful of all the techniques which one can call upon to access material, buried ideas, thoughts and feelings, and can be employed at every stage of the writing process. It is invaluable for bringing the hidden to light at the beginning of a piece of writing, and can even serve a purpose at the final re-writing stage where a detail proves recalcitrant. Why should this be?

What we are conscious of at any one time is only an infinitesimal part of what is available to us. The conscious mind responds to what is presented to it by the outside world and relates this to what is already known. But this means that the selection process only calls upon what is most immediately relevant and rejects the mass of material that is not perceived to have a bearing on the matter in hand. Of course much of this material is probably not of current significance, but there may also be experiences which are being rejected because they have been forgotten or prove too uncomfortable to contemplate. We develop strategies for the conscious mind to keep the unconscious under strict control. This is a matter of convenience for maintaining equilibrium in our everyday lives, but it is a positive disadvantage if we want to do the kind of creative exploration through writing which will lead to discoveries of value about ourselves.

Psychoanalysts call the process of accessing the riches of the unconscious 'free association'. Quite simply, it is letting the unconscious take charge and following where it leads. The idea is simple but what is involved is not easy at all. We have developed intellectual values and processes which are no less than 'control freaks', and we have to get under their guard. If we let them win we might as well give up the attempt to explore the personal and write a textbook instead. How are we to defeat the 'thought-police'? By taking a piece of paper and a pen or pencil and writing anything that comes into your mind. If it seems like nonsense, do not worry. If it surprises you by its apparent irrelevance to what was in your mind beforehand, good – the method is working. Now just carry on without pause. If it does not seem to be going anywhere, just repeat the words until you move on. The artist Paul Klee called his process of drawing 'taking a line for a walk'. You are taking words for a walk. You have no idea where they will end up.

Sometime you are going to have to stop. We suggest setting yourself a time limit – five minutes would be sensible until you feel comfortable with this way of writing and you could even set a timer so that you do not have to worry about knowing when to finish. The next stage is to look through what you have written. If you have uncovered something you do not feel ready to deal with, cross the passage out, or leave it for a later occasion. In the rest of the material underline any words, phrases or sentences which seem to you interesting or significant. These could form the basis for other pieces of flow-writing. By this means you could be building up a bank of material for use in formulating a poem or piece of prose in the future.

In time you will gain confidence in 'going with the flow' and trusting your unconscious processes to deliver feeling-states and concepts of which you were unaware and which may take you forward in your self-exploration. We should add at this point that the following exercises, in common with the others in this book, should not be attempted on a computer. It is tempting to use the piece of technology at hand, but we strongly urge you to resist. There is no substitute for the physical act of using a writing implement on paper. It is a basic process of self-expression, and it is essential to feel at all times that you are in touch with your self. By all means type something up when you are sure that it is finished.

Exercise 1

A blank piece of paper can give you a fright, so you could start with the first part of a sentence which suggests some kind of possibility and then see where it leads. Here are some openings to try: What I want is . . . When I looked through the window I saw . . . I turned round and saw . . . I hid it in the . . . If I open . . . The most frightening thing is . . .The happiest time in my life was . . . There is nothing more sad than . . . The sound was . . . Supposing I could . . . When the music started playing . . . I love . . . What is silence? Here is what John wrote after choosing one of these openings:

> There is nothing more sad than a sunset, glorious rays shedding red over every-thing, wrenching my heart, beautiful but always the end of something . . . Turner, other artists, the paint spreading, informing the canvas . . . if pale symbolizing loss of power, gradual weakening of grip . . .if red foreboding. Sunsets can never be happy, because of darkness coming . . . my own life, much nearer sunset than dawn . . . beautiful but painful, leaving, life always going away from you, every-thing slipping away, but paint it, write it while you can, leave something behind, even a splodge, a splurge, to prove you've been, a footprint, a handprint, primitive marks, cave paintings, centuries old could have been yesterday, nothing changes, essential urges, get back to basics, stop what you're doing, look at that sunset, make every moment count, don't give up, live your life now . . ..

Exercise 2

Write down a word, phrase, idea or problem which has significance for you or is on your mind and use this as a starting point. Here are some possibilities: tower, steps, wall, cupboards, too much to do, not knowing what to say, burying the past, the moon, body, skin, flying, making a choice, leaving, making a start, facing it, giving up, keeping going, quarrelling, underground, forgetting, confronting and the like.

Here is part of some flow-writing John Mackay did from the word 'skin':

> The skin on my eyelids is paper-thin. So thin. What would it be like to be made of paper, to be clothed in a manuscript, what would be written on that manuscript, what would be the story of my life? The writing would begin neat and well-ordered, and then would become a scrawl, as my life went on, a scrawl, it would be messy and ill-ordered and all over the place, the writing. It would be illegible. And people would come to read the manuscript – they would be gathered round, reading the manuscript that was clothing my body, the paper-thin manuscript . . .
>
> Where it all ended was in a hospital, and my face was falling apart, and I met a friend in the waiting room who didn't recognize me . . . And he was in the mental ward, his brain was falling apart, and he looked at me as if to say, 'Thank God I am not in his position.' The position of what? Lying flat on a bed being poked and prodded, having sections of skin swabbed and taken away, and cut off and put back on, and I was taken apart like a car engine, all my bits of skin and body and flesh and hair were taken apart and removed bit by bit, and when it came to the time to put it all back together, the doctors were no good, they couldn't remember how it all fitted together.

Exercise 3

Write down a feeling you sometimes or often experience or perhaps would like to experience, for example: hope, resentment, affection, anger, anxiety, determination, contentment, confusion, irritation, excitement and so on. Then write down a colour, a sound or a shape and an object which the feeling suggests – be spontaneous about this. Now make up the first sentence that comes into your head using two of the words you have written down and then carry on writing. Here is an extract from a piece of flow-writing Myra did using this kind of starting point. The words she wrote down were: 'anger', 'red', 'shouting', 'long and sharp', 'poker'.

> The anger was a red-hot poker, luminous metal like the iron stick my mother would put into the laid fire to bring it to life. The anger was inside and outside. The anger was all over my body. There was nothing else to me but anger. It was terrifying. And because I had no control of it I couldn't use it, couldn't direct it against the source of my anger. Worse, the anger was in danger of eating me up . . . How could I get charge of these flames of anger, how could I save myself from the fire?

Later, Myra took the final phrase of this first piece and started a second piece of flow-writing which took her off in another direction. Here is a brief extract:

> How could I save myself from the fire? It was creeping towards me – creeping? It was eating whole fields, hedges. It was tiger-leaping into trees. It was fiercer than my anger – this had disappeared as fear leapt up. But I saw the fire was my anger. This, I shrieked at Kate, this is why I cannot allow myself to be angry. If I shout it will backfire, swallow me up . . ..

Exercise 4

When you have had some practice in flow-writing triggered by one of the suggestions above try starting with a phrase of your own or without any prompt at all. It is well worth practising letting yourself go in flow-writing. The results are likely to be unexpected and exciting. There are further examples of flow-writing and how they were used to generate poems in Myra's contribution to Chapter 1 and the piece about Elke Dutton in Chapter 5. Below is an extract from some flow-writing by Rosemary McLeish which began with a phrase of her own. One thought flows into another without punctuation.

> . . . enchanted with the world baskets hot-air balloon must be the most wonderful way to travel travelling hopefully arriving always to disappointment and lack of safety in the asylum where people say you will be safe we will look after you but only on their conditions home is not where the heart is home is in birthday balloons released into the sky home is under the rhododendron bush hiding home is anywhere but here . . .

We end this section with a comment about flow-writing by Susanna Howard, a professional writer, who does writing residencies. It is followed by a short extract from one of her pieces:

> Flow-writing helped me through a particularly difficult point in my life. Sometimes I would be compelled to stop what I was doing and hack up the words forming within me. At other times I would sit and just start my pen moving and see where it led, no judgements – if petty concerns were all that came forth so be it, but sometimes I would dive inside to the world of metaphor . . . The spontaneity of the words helped me in two ways. (1) They had to come out to leave room for a person to emerge. (2) By taking part in the physical action of writing and filling up book after book I was literally writing my self back into existence . . .
>
> (Flow-writing extract) We forget – think people see inside our heads so easily. My head is in a vice and swimming. People's opinions box me into corners and

sometimes I can't move for the loudness of their remarks. Twitchy, twitching in the middle of the square box. Ah! Just to have peace, to find that piece. My box flat silence. It's physical this thing – a barrel of aches and pains, crack me open with an axe and let me run free across pebbles and laminate flooring. Put time aside and dive, dive into myself and come up, hand red and dripping. (Blood and guts having spewed.) Lifeless and yet full of it – full of life – still beating, pulsing, echoing my cynicism, my mistakes.

Clustering

This is a less immediate technique than flow-writing; it introduces the element of pausing to let words and phrases form a chain and then pausing again to allow the mind to set off on a new track. The cluster begins with a word or phrase at its centre. You let this act as a catalyst for further interpretations to suggest themselves. The cluster may well lead in very different, even opposing directions so that a cluster, rather than a line of words appears on the page. A cluster is a map of possibilities. In the example below John began with the word 'stone', and this set him off in five different directions, each subsequent word or phrase giving rise to the next. A cluster can be of any size, and some writers find generating material by this process more congenial than flow-writing.

The cluster is followed by a piece of prose which John developed from one of its strands. The poem, *Last Wish*, in Chapter 10, was developed from another strand.

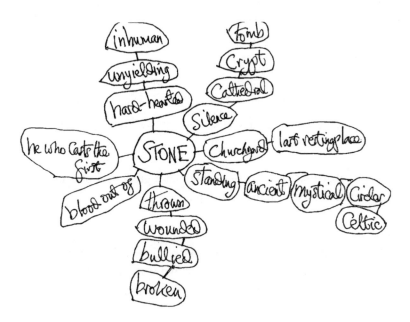

The stones loom up out of the mist, giants rooted in the soil. Four, five, six, seven of them raised to heaven, in supplication to what god? The size of them cows me. The silence around them awes me. The age of them is beyond enumeration. The statement they make is incontrovertible. I withdraw to a distance where I can contemplate them half-hidden by the gloom. What have we come to? My own beliefs are shifting, wind-tossed. My puny lines scribbled on scraps of paper are scattered, rendered irrelevant.

Exercise 1

Attempt a cluster based on one of the following words: home, suspicion, wonder, animal, snapshot, crossing, hands, bars.

The example of John's given above is a very basic one: the cluster is made up of single words apart from twice where phrases are used. Not only is it possible to base a cluster itself on a phrase, but the material derived can be phrases or even whole sentences.

We have met with a piece of flow-writing by John Mackay based on the word 'skin'. He also made a number of clusters with the word at their centre. Here is part of one of them. It is complex, and to make it easier to read each arm has been separated:

Under my skin – People get under my skin – They take advantage of my lack of confidence.

As a child, I looked enviously at people on TV – I envied their perfect skin – I wanted to be reborn with perfect skin.

I attack myself – I attack with fingernails, tear off the surface of my body – My skin is left beaten, then I feel sorry for myself.

Skin is a four-letter word – I see my skin on my face in the morning, and I utter four-letter words – I scratch my skin in agony and I shout four-letter words.

It is my layer to the world – It is my armour, but there is a chink – It lets in the cold – the world can see under my skin.

It is clear that John Mackay has generated a great deal of useful material for developing writing with this technique.

Exercise 2

Use one of the following phrases to make a cluster: shining star, under my guard, cupboard love, a winning streak, out of my mind, on cloud nine, hidden talent, learning to live, opening the door, going round and round.

Clustering can be a self-generating technique: one cluster can lead to another, and this can be a way of accessing rebarbative material. Alice Barton began with the following, based on the word 'Meeting':

Quaker – silence – stillness

formality – minutes – decisions – action

after long absence – tears – embraces – vulnerable

surprise – attraction – future unfolding

intimacy – talk – intensity – discomfort

She decided to take the last arm of this cluster and put 'intensity of meeting' in the middle to see what it might generate:

passion – unfolding – uninhibited

fear – threat – conflict – in your face

analysis – unpacking of motives – taking to pieces – weaknesses –

distraught

It was clear to her that the second and third arms here were leading somewhere, and an image came into her mind which she decided to develop in a piece of prose:

I had been put together like some fine work of art, a fragile vase placed on a high shelf. He took me down and with a little hammer broke me up into small pieces, all the time labelling them for their imperfections. Eventually I was laid out on the carpet at his feet. Then he walked away. I heard the door shutting behind him. I knew he would not return. Despite all my faults having been named, I could not fit myself together again. I was shattered in both a metaphorical and literal sense. How was I ever to go on living?

Exercise 3

Take one of the words or phrases you have not used in the exercises above and make a cluster. Then allow the words of that cluster to suggest a further line of exploration. This process can be repeated (including flow-writing if that would prove helpful) until you have reached the point where you are ready to write something more extended from what you have uncovered. We suggest you also try these exercises with words and phrases of your own choice.

13 Accessing memories, secret letters, monologues and dialogues, visualizations

Section 1: Techniques for tapping into memory

Memories, both recent and distant, tell us who we are and so play a crucial role in our experience of life. Early memories are particularly important because it is in childhood, when we are most impressionable, that our future selves are formed. For many writers the memory of childhood is a key subject. Marcel Proust's *À La Recherche du Temps Perdu* (*In Search of Lost Time*) springs to mind and so do the early sections of Wordsworth's *The Prelude*. In Chapter 5 of this book John Lyons shows how his early life is the source of his poetry and in the same chapter we showed how Elke Dutton created early childhood memories because she had none. Of course memories from later times are also likely to play a key role when you write about yourself.

You may have memories which you want to plunge into or you may have material like a diary or letters which summon them up. There are other ways though of triggering memories. We offer a series of suggestions.

Exercise 1: Objects as starting points

Collect a few objects you own which connect with your past. Possibilities are: your teddy bear, a ring which was left to you, a painting you did as a child, photographs – these are particularly potent, a present from someone important to you and so on.

Begin by describing one of the objects. Then write about any of these: where it was kept and its surroundings, any events, situations or people it reminds you of, the period of life you associate it with, your feelings about it in the past, your feelings about it now. Here is a short piece by Edward Brown:

> This early edition of Keats' poems is weighty, its pages discoloured but the texture,
> the smell and the words she wrote for me inside the cover bring back her attic room,

reading the poems together, the rackety gas ring in the fireplace, the overwhelm of that first night we spent together and the terrible pain of the relationship.

Vary this exercise by listing significant objects you remember from your past but no longer have: your first bicycle, a kitchen table, the settee in your first flat and so on. In Chapter 1 John wrote about a memory which centres on the gate in his childhood garden.

Exercise 2: Sense sensations as triggers

Sense sensations can be very potent reminders of the past. Make a list of sounds, smells, tastes or textures – or, if you prefer, a combination of sense impressions which transport you to the past. Here are some suggestions of smells: dettol, cow dung, bonfires, milk, sweat, petrol, soot, chips. When you think about sound do not forget the voices of people and music which relate to your past. Choose one of your sense impressions and describe it, then write and/or flow-write about what it conjures up. One memory is likely to trigger others. Here is how Anna Avebury used this technique:

> List of smells: Chicken soup – steamy, warm; acrid smell of bonfire night; sulphurous smell of steam trains; Dad's aftershave.
>
> The smell of chicken soup filled the whole house for hours at week-ends. I remember the chicken, bald, on a chipped enamel plate, legs in the air, a gaping hole in between, folds of skin, cold to the touch. Orange yolks sometimes glistened on a small plate next to it. The smell of herbs: parsley, dill, bay leaves filled our nostrils, making us hungry but we had to wait. Chicken soup took time to cook my mother insisted. I have never forgotten that longing, although it lies unheard, unfelt, unacknowledged most of the time, lies in wait to ambush me when I least expect it, bringing it all back: the terraced house, the back-yard, the swing between the front gate-posts, the Sunday walks in the woods in spring to see bluebells, a sea of blue, lapping round the roots of the trees. My mother sitting amid the ferns, showing me how to make a garland, weaving stalks of bluebells through ferns, milky sap trickling between her fingers.

Exercise 3: Place as a starting point

Place can also trigger memories. Choose a room in a house or flat where you lived in your past or somewhere which had significance for you: a garden, a classroom, a work place, a beach, a railway station and the like. Begin by describing it, then write or flow-write about the memories it sets off. Here is a prose poem by Helen Pizzey written in the third person. Sometimes it is easier to use this mode when writing about personal experiences.

Sweet Painted Ladies

A child sits at her mother's fancy dressing table. She dabs thinly-scented cream behind her ears and at the pulse of her wrists, then paints her mouth with fat, greasy lipstick: red, the colour her mother wears when she screws up her face and yells 'No!' Pressing her lips to tissue, the little girl is pleased with the mothy mark that they make – or is it, perhaps, like a pair of blood-streaked caterpillars? Downstairs, a familiar scratched record is slapped onto the stereogram: 'Take these chains from my heart and let me go.' The child gets down and runs outside to the buddleia bush. There she stands with her ruby pout, pulling the wings from butterflies.

Here is Daphne Gloag's very different memory triggered by place:

I can see us now, sitting at a little garden table beneath the silver birch, beside our new pond when it was full of frogs. The tree was really too dense for a birch, but we didn't mind because it was so wonderful in providing food and shelter for birds as well as shade for us; and with its estimated quarter of a million leaves it must have put out a lot of oxygen and mopped up a lot of carbon dioxide. These things combined to add to our feeling of peace as we talked and read a little and ate food we enjoyed. In fact it was more than that because as we watched the frogs getting on with their lives and other small events among the wildlife we had a sense of completion.

In Chapter 1 there is a piece which John wrote about the time he spent in his school sanatorium – the only period he felt any happiness during his time at boarding school.

Exercise 4: Memories of people

Another way of tapping into memory is to write about people who have been significant to you. Make a list of people who have played a key part in your life: parents, relatives, teachers, friends, colleagues and so on. Choose one. It may be clear at once what you want to write about: a teacher who influenced your career, for example. If your relationship with the person had a definite shape: an affair, a friendship which turned sour or one which was supportive during a crisis, there may be a narrative you want to follow. However, you may have a great deal you want to say – several incidents to refer to, ambivalent feelings and the like and not know how to begin. Try writing down the first sentence about the person which comes into your head and then flow-write. Afterwards underline key sentences and use one of these as a starting point.

Alternatively use the clustering method to help you sort out the different aspects of a person you want to explore.

Here are two more prose poems by Helen Pizzey. Each encapsulates a relationship in a few lines.

First Love

In the barn, my brother scattered chickens from the open-top Daimler and cranked her up. The seats were covered in pigeon droppings from the roost above, but the cracked leather was still well sprung behind the walnut fascia and ocean-liner steering wheel. My cheeks flushed when he winked at me as we set off. With outstretched arms he drove like a rally-driver, tossing me laughing first left, then right. I was giddy and reeling, like Dad when he'd been drinking in the cow stalls before lunch. We raced for a while through solitary lanes before having to get back to call cows home for milking. This must be what love is, I thought, when I realised I had forgotten about the guilty boot marks on the kitchen floor. It no longer mattered that Mum would be mad about them when she arrived home from market.

Granny's Party

Granny died aged 102. When I was six, she grew smaller and greyer with every visit. A kindred spirit, deaf to adult conversation, she smiled at me with bleached dentures that slid on shrunken gums. Moving slowly on misshapen feet, she led me into her bedroom to show me the clothes she kept for her 'party': a high-necked cotton nightdress and matching lace bonnet that had ear flaps and ties – like the knitted one on my dolly. I hoped it wasn't a party I would have to go to, or one that I would be forced to have myself.

Exercise 5: Key feelings and experiences

Focusing on key feelings you had in the past such as disappointment, love, hate, humiliation, excitement, panic, curiosity and the like can also be a route to writing your past. Choose a feeling you connect with your past and then write or flow-write about the memories set off. Another starting point is to begin with a key experience or situation and write or flow-write round this. Possibilities might be your first day at school, an accident, a quarrel, being bullied, telling a lie, puberty, a first love affair, leaving home, a failure or a success. Here is a piece by Thomas Roberts:

Mum was definitely peering down at me and I could hear her voice but the words blurred. I turned round and noticed the bottom halves of two men wearing patterned shorts, their legs splaying out in pulses to form triangles. They were at the shallow end of the pool and the tiled floor beneath the palms of my feet sloped upwards.

I don't remember being dragged out but I do remember Mum's face above me crying and shouting blue murder, 'Don't ever do that again, do you understand?' This is my first memory – I was three and a half. We were at a hotel complex and I wanted to experience the water which other people were enjoying so I just ran and jumped in. I have always followed my own path!.

Section 2: Secret letters

We have all written letters to parents, siblings, friends, enemies, employers, the authorities – and torn them up. Sometimes we have written them over and over in our heads. Our reasons for not sending them can be various – cowardice, or the realization that they might do more harm than good, being probably the most common. Composing them, on the page or in our minds, can have a therapeutic effect, whether the missive gets sent or not.

'Secret Letters' is a way of letting our thoughts and feelings pour out onto the page in a very direct and uncensored way. It can be an empowering process, and has the added advantage of giving you the opportunity of looking at the contents of your mind and emotions with a new degree of objectivity afterwards. Sometimes the letter you may want to write expresses anger and disappointment. Here is one John would have liked to have sent to a former employer:

Dear Sandra,

I am writing to tell you how you have let me down. I approached you at first with an open mind, giving you the benefit of all possible doubts, and seeking assurances that you would support me in the direction that my work is taking. You offered those assurances.

I was encouraged to approach you with new proposals, all of which were initially favourably received. Then came that ghastly day when, in a public forum, you laid down a policy which completely ruled out all my plans.

Finally, I came forward with an application for which I had already secured half the finance. You prevaricated over a period of time, changing the goalposts almost on a weekly basis, until you reached the stage of telling me that you were not prepared to undertake the raising of the rest of the finance in the short term, and forbidding me to attempt to do so either. I had had enough, and withdrew.

Instead of offering me opportunities, as a manager should, you have wasted my time and energy on fruitless discussions. Further, because of the way you have treated me, you have raised serious doubts in my mind over your trustworthiness. You have undone in a few months all the good and goodwill painstakingly established by your predecessor. You do not deserve your high office. I never want to have anything to do with you again.

John

Exercise 1

Write a letter to someone you are angry with. This could be a person with whom you have had a bad relationship for a long time, or someone you were close to in the first place. Give full vent to your feelings. Here is an example of a letter provided by Lance Lee:

Dear Martin,

We maintain polite relations with you for our daughter Debbie's sake, and her little boy Joshua's too, and will do so until he is 16 and none of us have to be in contact with you, legally, for his sake, any longer. This is despite your proving a desperately misguided husband who destroyed his family. You did that single-handedly despite Debbie's efforts to prevent your destructiveness. Why? You are a man who is too frightened to look into himself, and so your inner conflicts drive you blindly. You 'cope' with these by picking fights and arguing relentlessly until you win. Winning, for you, means to be in control, and to hurt someone else. But you can't get rid of your own hurts that way, although you never learn: so you are driven to repeat this behaviour ad nauseam. The anger, grief and sorrow you cause you dishonestly blame on anyone or anything else than yourself. Inevitably you drove Debbie to desperation, and then to divorce. You fooled all of us at the start. What a mistake it was to welcome you with open arms into the family! What an irony that it was with Debbie's pregnancy and Joshua's birth that you fell apart, driving Debbie in desperation to take action. One day through another failed marriage, or when Joshua is old enough as a teenager to speak his mind, there will be an accounting. When it comes, you will deserve it.

Leonard

Exercise 2

Write a letter which fulfils one of the following: (a) attempts to reach out to someone you once took for granted but have now lost touch with; (b) addresses someone who is out of reach because no longer alive; (c) reflects the ambivalent feelings you have towards them; (d) offers support to someone who needs it but might well reject your advances.

Here is a letter by Daphne Gloag which is written in the full awareness of the complexity of situations and is also the expression of a deep tenderness:

> Mio Carissimo (that's how I always started a letter, so why stop now?) Of course there's no-one but you I could possibly want to write a secret letter to. But which you? The you I had nearly lost already during those harrowing last days in the hospital; the you who lay on your back, face pointing upwards, eyes closed, no books or papers there to read (you couldn't read them); the you who had been laid on your side by nurses to protect pressure sores, the nurses who you'd said were violent – you screamed in agony when they turned you over; the you who lay hunched up with your shoulders bare above the hospital gown ('Property of the Borough of Ealing') and with your eyes, if they opened a little, perhaps seeing nothing? Or am I writing to the you who still looks from photographs – like the one where you're sitting at a little table writing with the blue water of Lake Garda behind you – and the you who speaks to me still from all the love-letters and the postcards that turn up from all over the house, some with stories on them or references to our adventures? You said that you would always be with me, and I have just looked again at that wonderful book on Chinese art you gave me last birthday, with your inscription: 'All my love for ever'. So you see there's no doubt which you I'm writing to.

Exercise 3

Write the letter which someone who knows your strengths and weaknesses might wish to send you but probably would not attempt because of fear of how it might be received.

Exercise 4

One secret letter may not be enough for all that you want to say. The memoir, *Cry Hard and Swim*, which is described in Chapter 4, begins with a series of secret letters, one of which we have quoted. You may wish to write a sequence of letters to a significant person in your life. Alternatively, you could reply to the letter you have written, which in turn would spark off a riposte. This is a good way of exploring a situation in depth, and it can often be illuminating to find yourself inside the head of someone with whom you have issues, or with whom you are hoping to develop a relationship.

Section 3: Monologues and dialogues

A first person speech which you only deliver in your head and onto the page is an alternative to writing a secret letter. It can be a very good way of getting something off your chest. But it can also constitute a personal outpouring which has something in common with flow-writing. Someone with dementia with whom John was working on communication characterized her speech as 'blethering but from beneath the surface' and that seems a very good description of tapping into the unconscious mind for material. Most of Samuel Beckett's shorter plays partake of this quality.

Exercise 1

Write in the voice of yourself at a much younger age or choose someone from your past and write about them in the way you might have regarded them at the time, using the kind of language you might have used. Alternatively take an aspect of yourself, some distinctive quality, and write a speech about that characteristic. Here is Mike Loveday exploring a childhood relationship which may have been real or imaginary in a freewheeling manner which has a child-like naivety and also imitates the breathlessness of a child's speech when the words keep tumbling out:

> Big Mike plays soldiers with me Big Mike lives in a big house with a swimming pool and the biggest ice-cream machine you've ever seen Big Mike can play piano much better than me Big Mike can ride his mountainbike really really fast downhill with no hands Big Mike drew pictures on my exercise book in class Big Mike is strong and would beat even Pete Hopkins at arm-wrestles Big Mike has been to the moon Big Mike has a girlfriend called Laura Big Mike says it's ok to be six and not have a girlfriend Big Mike has lots of friends but says I'm his best friend . . .

Exercise 2

Many speeches or sermons make use of the rhetorical device of repetition. Here is John using one of these pattern-making devices and seeing where it leads:

> Not that you'd catch me in one of those transparent car-contraptions
>   – I've been sealed in my own all my life.
>
> Not that you'd see me in one of those sleek water-parters
>   – I've been paddling my own all my life.
>
> Not that you'd tempt me into one of those soaring sky-cruisers
>   – I can ride my own thermals any time.

Choose a phrase or opening part of a sentence that has a resonating quality and let it dictate the form and content of your monologue.

Exercise 3

Dialogues have a different quality and a greater potential for variety of use, but they share that important characteristic of dramatization. One of the most obviously effective ways of making use of this device is to imagine a conversation between two people (one of whom can be yourself). This is a good way of teasing out situations, and requires you to put yourself in someone else's shoes. Try writing one between yourself and someone you have a complex or difficult relationship with.

Annabel Close wrote a dialogue between a mother and a daughter; here is part of it, with the mother's words in italics:

> *My scars are hidden.*
> Mine are revealed. I reveal them, for all.
>
> *I wish you would keep your scars hidden.*
> I shall reveal them all.
>
> *The world will know that I failed you.*
> You did not fail me
> These are *my* scars.
>
> *I could not help you.*
> You could not help me.
>
> *I needed to be able to help you.*
> *I am the mother.*
> I am not you.
>
> *I needed to stop you suffering.*
> It is *my* suffering.
>
> *I am angry with you.*
> *I gave you perfect life.*
> I remain perfect.
> I remain your gift.

Exercise 4

Take two different aspects of yourself and let them talk to each other. Alternatively, imagine yourself as a character from literature, and dialogue with another character or characters to explore a personal characteristic or quality.

John decided to write a dialogue between two aspects of himself – the young man and the older; here is an extract:

YOUNG: I'm just setting out. Everything is new. I want to experience and I want to understand. I see you and all I see is lethargy, mottled hands, lined cheeks, a terrible sadness and defeat.

OLD: Your innocence and ignorance are pathetic. You have so much to learn that I don't believe you'll ever know what I know. Your pure complexion and easy rhythms are all you possess. I have a weight that is not just of the body; it comes from suffering. I *know*.

YOUNG: You're just a bag of wind. All puffed up with importance. I know that I know nothing. But I'm open and you're closed. I'm living and you're dying.

OLD: I may not have seen everything but I've seen enough to convince me that everyone's life is a story, with a beginning, a middle and an end. You're boring: just unwritten pages. I have my life-lines. Read me like a book.

Here is a dialogue by Caroline Carver which exploits the second of these techniques:

(On days when nothing makes sense, when I've lost control, I play the Gulliver game, imagining I'm spreadeagled on the shore, with Little People tying me down – 'GU' is Gulliver, 'LP', Little Person).

GU: Little people, if you want to know who I am, start with my feet. Untie me and I'll tell you how they walked and danced through childhood. Back then, I could do anything I wanted. (In my mind I'm already writing about freedom, how I climbed trees, how my mother let me do anything.)

LP: Why did you let yourself grow so big; sail to our island, turn our lives upside down?

GU: I often do things for the wrong reasons. Untie my arms and I'll show you how I stood at the bow of the ship, waiting for your welcome which never came.

LP: You still haven't said why you're so big.

GU: I'm trying to explain. Where did I go wrong? Untie my head. I need to get on top of my life. The computer's crashed, the gasman won't come, slugs have eaten all my lettuces. Try as I might, I can't change anything. Untie me!

LP: We're still waiting for a good reason.

Exercise 5

Create a dramatic scene based on personal experience involving three or four characters. Scenarios you might explore are: a falling-out between school friends; a family row involving parents and siblings; a confrontation between two couples over rivalry in love; an argument between work colleagues.

Section 4: Visualizations

Writing about oneself, exploring complexes of experiences and feelings can, as we have seen at every stage in this book, be releasing and supportive. However, when one is coping with trauma, crisis, prolonged illness or acute stress it can be very helpful to move away from in-depth exploration and use the technique of visualization. This offers the opportunity to put aside for a while a serious difficulty that cannot easily be alleviated and to draw on imagination and memory to conjure up pleasing and supportive images. A visualization can be created first by writing it and then by experiencing it, or it can be summoned up and then extended in writing. Visualizations can offer some protection from acute distress or pain and make it feel more manageable. The technique can be invaluable during a time of illness and it can be beneficial in other situations: separation from a partner, bereavement, a difficult work situation, an overwhelming worry and the like. We offer a series of suggestions to try out.

Exercise 1

Think of an object you find beautiful or appealing in some way: a scarf, a fruit, a small ornament, a plant and so on. You might want to touch your object or hold it if it is small. Focus on what you particularly like about its shape, colour, texture, weight and so forth. What images does it summon up? What do you associate with it?

When she was undergoing chemotherapy Myra wrote in her journal twice about a lavender sleep mask which a friend gave her. Here is part of the first note which appears in her book, *Writing My Way Through Cancer* (see Chapter 6):

> . . . a sachet inside a bag which is deep purple velvet on one side and white cotton patterned with lavender flowers on the other side. The mask can be placed over the forehead and eyes for ten minutes or so while you are lying down. I've already tried it and it's wonderful, soft and soothing and makes me visualize lavender bushes in flower. (Schneider 2003, pp. 104–5)

Later she extended the visualization in a poem called *Lavender* (Ibid., p. 112).

Exercise 2

Now try re-experiencing as fully as possible an activity you enjoy: singing, cooking, swimming, walking, gardening, playing a musical instrument and the like. We wrote about *The Diving-Bell and the Butterfly* in Chapter 6, and the astonishing way in which Jean-Dominique Bauby supported himself with visualizations following a stroke which left him almost totally paralysed. In many of these he played an active role – imagined himself making a film or as a character in a book. We have already quoted the opening sentences of a visualization about food and cooking which was his way of compensating for the fact that he was being fed by tube. Here is a further extract:

> Depending on my mood I treat myself to a dozen snails, a plate of Alsatian sausage with sauerkraut, and a bottle of late-vintage golden Gerwurztraminer, or else I savour a simple soft-boiled egg with fingers of toast and lightly salted butter. What a banquet! The yolk flows warmly over my palate and down my throat. And indigestion is never a problem. Naturally, I use the finest ingredients: the freshest vegetables, fish straight from the water, the most delicately marbled meat. (Bauby 1998, p. 44)

Exercise 3

The next visualization and the two following it invite you to give full play to your imaginative powers. Picture a box which intrigues or attracts you in some way. As you look at it you become convinced that it contains something significant. Describe the box and what you think it may contain. Now imagine opening it and finding inside it something magical and moving. It could be a paperweight, a jewel, a fossil, a letter or, because this is a fantasy, it might contain an object which was lost years ago or that is much too large to fit in a box, or one which changes in a remarkable way as you look at it, or even something abstract. Here is an excerpt from the box visualization by Peter Mitchell:

> I lift the mottled lid – and there inside is a bird's nest and four small eggs, delicately speckled with pale blue. The nest itself is woven with dried grasses, tiny ribbons of plastic, moss fronds, old leaves. I cup it in my hands. I think the eggs will hatch soon. That life so fragile is so purposeful makes me tremble with hope for myself.

Exercise 4

This visualization can be very supportive if a specific anxiety or other destructive feeling is going round and round in your head and you cannot shift it.

Imagine some shape or form for the feeling. It could be a web of tangled threads, a piece of jagged wood with nails jutting from it, muffling layers of cloth, a set of hammers and the like. Now picture in detail shutting away the physical form of the feeling in a box, case or other container. You may have to push it hard to get it in. You may want to lock or even padlock the container. The next step is to picture yourself getting rid of the box or case. You may shut it away in a basement, throw it in a river, bury it in sand on a seashore and so on. Finally replace the destructive feeling with one you would like to experience. As she recorded in *Writing My Way Through Cancer* Myra found this visualization extraordinarily helpful when she was in the early stages of recovery from her cancer treatment. The first time she tried it out she pictured:

> a heavy trunk like the one I used to take to college, stuffing miles of fear into it, banging the lid down, sitting on it to make sure it stayed shut, then fitting the metal clasps and turning its lock. After that I saw myself tipping the trunk into the brook which runs through the park behind our house, waiting while it sank into the stream's muddy bed . . . (Schneider 2003, p. 134)

Exercise 5

A final suggestion for a visualization is to choose a painting or piece of music which suggests a state of mind you would like to experience. An Impressionist painting of trees in blossom, a portrait of a sympathetic face, the first movement of Beethoven's Moonlight sonata, might be possibilities although obviously you may wish to choose something very different. Allow yourself to enter and experience 'the world' of the music or painting and use writing to help you.

Fictionalizing, transforming personal material, dreams, drawing as a starting point

14

Section 1: Fictionalizing

If the material you want to tackle in writing is difficult to face head on fictionalizing can offer a distancing, a way of gaining control over it. Miriam Hastings describes how this worked for her in Chapter 7. The technique can also be helpful if the subject matter is complex, involving many incidents, different people and changing situations so that contemplating it you are immediately bogged down by details. Unravelling these may stand in the way of getting to the heart of what you really want to write about. Fictionalizing is a good idea too if you wish to describe people who you think would be angry or hurt were they to see what you have written. This mode, therefore, can free you to explore aspects of your personal subject matter without having to worry about sticking exactly to the outer facts.

There are different methods of fictionalizing. One is to use a story frame, that is, to take a well-known story – a fairy tale, fable or legend in which you can see a similarity or connection with your own story or part of it. This mode allows you to express the main relationship and/or situation using details from the tale or legend. Furthermore the known story, if aptly used, adds emotional force to your own.

Exercise 1

Think of a fairy story, fable or legend which connects in some way to an aspect of your life. Possibilities might be: *Cinderella, The Ugly Duckling, The Babes in the Wood, Hansel and Gretel*, the myth of *Persephone, Pandora's Box* and the like. Now make use of the story to tell your own. Here is a poem by Barbara Noel Scott in which she depicts her childhood:

Hansel and Gretel

They were not the abandoned ones,
the babes in the wood,
expiring blackberry-stained
under blankets of leaves.

No, they were the cherished ones,
the devoured ones,
fattened for the witch's table,
'parental love' a sugar house to trap them,
the hospitable oven meant for them.

He, with the sweetest flesh
being male, was gorged on witch-bait, caged
for the first kill.
She starved on oyster shells.

There was no come-back this time.

She died a skeleton, he grossly fat.

The Mother, left alone, a tragic figure
wears black now
licks bones.

(from *Parents*)

Exercise 2

A variation of this technique is to make up a fairytale or fable in which to set your experience. We have already seen how John Mackay used flow-writing and clustering in exploring the subject of skin. He also wrote about it using his own story frame – it contains elements we recognize from fairy story and legend:

> I have a terrible skin condition, which blights my life. But then I hear of a magic potion that exists that will cure the condition. So I go on a long journey and begin searching for it. I hear there is a recipe which gives eternal perfect skin. On the epic journey, I meet a strange new person at each stage along the way, who gives me an individual ingredient for the recipe. The catch is – for each ingredient I am given, I have to offer in exchange a section of my skin. This is the risk: at the end of the journey when I have all the ingredients and I mix them all together, will the potion be successful?

There are other ways to fictionalize. One, which is commonly used in an autobiographical novel, is to follow closely what has been experienced in terms of people, situations and events but to disguise all names of individuals, change locations and place names and usually a few other outer details which would make for easy identification. This allows the writer freedom to focus as she/he wishes and to leave out some strands of the story or facts which are a distraction. It also protects living people and rules out the possibility of libel. An example of such a novel is Janet Frame's *Faces in the Water* which is about her experiences in a mental hospital when she was wrongly diagnosed with schizophrenia. One reason for fictionalizing such material would have been to avoid identifying other patients who were in the hospital.

Exercise 3

Think of an episode in your life which you would like to write about but which would in some way expose you or others if you record it directly. Disguise the location where it took place, the names and possibly ages, sex, nationality or other features of some of the people involved. Now try writing about it.

Here is an extract from a piece by a man writing under the pseudonym of James MacIntyre. He noted afterwards that he had changed three details and that putting the incident on paper was a great release:

> I was about five. I followed Tony, my big brother, around all the time, longing to be allowed to play with him and his friends but he rarely let me. Then one day, when we were left alone in the cottage we lived in, he locked me in a cupboard and said he was leaving me there for ever because I was a bloody nuisance. I was petrified, especially as spiders, which I hated, lived in the cupboard. When at last he let me out he said he'd kill me if I ever told so of course I didn't. After that I was frightened of him and I panicked whenever I was in the dark. I'm still afraid of dark places like tunnels.

Another way of fictionalizing is to write an episode in detail exactly as it was but to place it in a completely fictional setting. In Chapter 1 Myra explained the only way she could write about the overwhelming effect of looking at a charity poster was by making the same incident happen to a character in a narrative poem. The fictional character's life had no connection with her own but her personality and what had been hinted at about her upbringing meant her reaction to the poster was appropriate.

Fictionalizing can go further than this. Instead of disguising personal material one can draw on incidents, relationships and long-running situations to create a new fiction. In Chapter 7 Miriam Hastings describes how her novel,

The Minotaur Hunt, only took off when she liberated herself from writing in the first person and created a story which was entirely fictional although she drew on her own experience and knowledge. Novelists like Jean Rhys and many others use material in this way. In Chapter 1 Myra mentions that in her long narrative poem, 'Becoming', it was by creating a fictional parallel for her relationship with her father that she was able to explore the effect he had had on her.

Exercise 4

Make a list of events or key experiences in your life which you would like to write about but have not yet found a way of tackling. Choose one and make notes about how you might create a different story to express the core of it. Ideas for this kind of approach may not come quickly but if the process appeals to you it would be worth developing your notes over days, weeks or a longer period of time.

Section 2: Transforming personal material

We are now going to look at the possibilities of using parallels, images and making deliberate changes in writing about personal subject matter. These techniques offer outlets for feelings which it might be difficult to express in other modes and also the opportunity to view experience from new perspectives.

Sometimes instead of writing a fictional equivalent for a traumatic experience it works better to write about a real incident which connects with it and offers a parallel. In Chapter 9 we included a poignant poem by Caroline Price, 'The Day My Father Died'. This expressed her sense of loss through the description of another death – that of a bird she saw dying several months later. Attention is drawn to the connection by the poem's title and then at the end when the times of the two different deaths are set side by side.

In Chapter 1 John described looking at mussel beds in Normandy and suddenly recognizing a parallel between this method of farming and his own childhood. The result was a poem 'In Noirmortier' which presents parallels between each stage of the farming and his own early life.

Exercise 1

List some graphic experiences in your life and see if you can connect one of these with a striking activity or scene you have witnessed. Alternatively draw a parallel between yourself and another person or creature. These suggestions might feel a little artificial if something does not immediately suggest itself but if you experiment you may be surprised by how well this technique works and you will certainly be alerted to its possibilities. Here is a piece written by Richard Bates:

> It was when Sandra and Harry got a dog that had been abandoned from the Dog Rescue place that things changed. Before that although they were very nice I was always afraid I'd do something wrong and that they'd send me back to Social Services and say I wasn't good enough. The dog was called Hero. He peed on their carpet and ruined their flower beds but they didn't lose their tempers. Sandra stroked him and quietened him down. When I saw they weren't furious if he made a mess it dawned on me they wouldn't send me away if I did the wrong thing. I could see he was in the same boat as me – in fact Hero was another me.

Another way of transforming personal material is to represent yourself, your state of mind or an aspect of yourself as an image. Such an image can be very powerful when writing about a stressful feeling or situation and it may take on a symbolic character. In her poem, 'Portraits', (Chapter 10) Barbara Feldt portrays herself in a series of telling metaphors. In Chapter 1 Myra described how the 'panic bird' image seemed to stand for bullying and fear. When she developed the poem the image took on a mythic quality.

In 'The Nursing Chair' Vivienne Fogel describes buying the chair – a parallel to the way her adoptive mother brought her home when she was a baby. The chair becomes an image for her adoption. In the second half of the poem it becomes an image of the work she does and in a sense herself.

The Nursing Chair

lay hidden under baize in the muddle of the auction rooms,
its cover faded, an arm of rosewood peeping out,
and I knew then that it needed a home.

At first you did not see me, hidden in the corner
under utility beige, you walked right past the muddle of cots –
till my tiny fingers waved, as if to stop you –
and you knew then that you would bring me home,
because I needed you, because of my small and beckoning fist.

Solemn eyes under dark brows, your wiry hair pinned back,
a smell I did not belong to: how could you hold or comfort
when you yourself were exiled and broken?

The chair sits low on the ground, its back straight, a nursing chair
that has midwifed mothers, some eager, some numbed,
others dreaming themselves into another place, another life.

Decades on, the chair listens, solid and soothing,
its seat stained with ink, pawed and clawed by the cats.
It creaks, warmed with laughter, stitches gape, loosen
the fluff and stuffing like a grey frizzed perm,
and bits bulge where they should not.

I pat tenderly, promising to take care of it – soon.

Exercise 2

Think of an animal, bird or plant which might stand for yourself or represent a feeling or state of mind you often experience or connect with in some other way. Write or flow-write about this. Here is a piece by Deirdre Shaw:

> At school they called me bigfoot and my mother was always at me for being clumsy and I came to think of myself as an elephant. Then I met Jim at a friend's party. When he asked me to dance I blurted out: 'I can't – I'd be like a clumsy elephant,' but he said: 'Well I'm a giraffe,' he said, 'so we'll make an interesting pair.' We'd been shuffling round for a while when he said: 'You're not clumsy at all but then elephants aren't.' Thanks to Jim I gradually stopped hating my body, myself.

Exercise 3

Think of yourself as a piece of furniture or a machine in a house which might stand as a symbol for yourself. This could be: a piano, an untidy cupboard, a washing machine, a refrigerator, a spin drier, a television set, and the like. Now write about yourself as your chosen piece of furniture. It can be very effective to do this in the voice of the object. Here is a piece by Bill Woodside:

> I'm a tall rectangular refrigerator with shiny white hard-edged casing. That's what I became the day she snapped: 'You're useless, I'm leaving you!' and slammed out. That was two years ago and I'm frosted up within all that casing. I go through the motions of carrying on with life but somewhere behind my plastic shelves is my heart frozen and unwanted. I don't know if anybody or anything will ever thaw me out.

The exercise can be done with many other images – buildings or parts of buildings, landscape features, items of clothing and so on.

Another way of exploring personal material is to take a painful experience and change its outcome or to visualize the outcome you would like for an intransigent situation. To put into words what you long for but recognize is very different from the reality or unlikely to happen can be a relief even if it is upsetting. It can also be illuminating. It is worth noting that writers, especially novelists, use this technique without conscious planning. Jane Austen's novels ended happily with the heroine marrying the man she loved – that was the convention – but these endings were also a compensation for her own thwarted love life. In Chapter 8 Maggie Sawkins described ways in which she wrote about her daughter who was diagnosed with schizophrenia. She has also written a poem in which she imagines a future when she brings her daughter home from an institution. Here is most of it:

Date Unknown

I will walk up a path
policed by poplars
the sky will be cloudless and blue.

In my hand an empty suitcase
scented with lavender,
swinging.

A patient will skitter past
in raincoat and scarlet slippers
and I'll tip my head . . .

She'll be leaning against
a glass doorway
with lightness in her hair

like a girl from a Hopper painting,
except she is smiling.

I will walk towards her,
take her bundle of clothes,
unbuckle her hands.

A doctor will appear
as if from nowhere to wish
her well.

As we turn to go faces will stare
from darkened windows,
flowers will curtsey

trees uproot themselves
sprout wings
and fly.

(from *The Zig Zag Woman*)

Exercise 4

Make a list of difficult experiences and situations. Choose one and write about it giving it the resolution or outcome you wish it could have. A variation of this approach is to choose a difficult relationship and write about the kind of relationship you would like to have. A further variation is to write about an incident or situation and make the details the opposite of what they actually were. Here is a poem in this mode by Vicky Wilson which makes a powerful impact. The negatives have an emphatic effect and underline the welter of emotions.

Denial

I did not put my mother in a home
never took to the charity shop
boxes piled with Catherine Cooksons and Wedgwood
or walked down the long corridor
to the small yellow room, with the ensuite
where she didn't smear the walls
and floors with excrement
which the nurses never failed to clear up.

I did not watch her lose the power
to walk, talk, feed herself, to distinguish
glass from fork, to remember her age and name.
I did not refuse to pick up the phone at 2am.
I never wished her dead.
I never cried at her funeral – or since.

(from *My Mother Threw Knives*)

Section 3: Dreams

Waking and sleeping are our two main states of consciousness, and we spend almost as much time doing the latter as the former. As writers, and explorers of the self, we cannot afford to overlook the information and inspiration divulged by our dream-states. They are our most direct route to the unconscious. They often speak a symbolic language, as does literature, and a number of writers, Edwin Muir for example, have tapped into it to remarkable effect.

We suggest keeping a dream diary by means of a notebook and pen or pencil by your bedside as a way of building up your own storehouse of material. You can then examine what you have written and use the techniques of flow-writing and clustering to follow the various leads thrown up by it.

Exercise 1: Writing from a dream

Here is one of John's dreams and how he has used it to explore further. A brief account of the dream is followed by part of some flow-writing based on an idea embedded in it, finishing with the poem that resulted:

I was in a kind of travelling therapy circus, going from town to town giving demonstrations and sessions to people, only I wasn't sure what kind of therapist I was. All the other therapists treated me with contempt. There was a large woman, the equivalent of the Fat Lady in the conventional circus, who was particularly abusive, and when the train moved on taking us to the next town, she seemed to seek out the carriage in which I was sitting and claim my seat as her own. Then, at the climax of the dream, she came and sat on top of me. When I protested she said: 'You don't really exist.'

The therapy circus is back in town, roll up, roll up, get with it, see the stalls, the books, the tents, have your money at the ready to buy a little piece, a little peace of mind, that's what you really need, a drug-free heaven, for a little while, will put a smile on your face, drop out of the rat-race, try our oils, crystals, balls, bowls, all things good for the soul, come and meditate at the going rate, we can solve your problems, salve your hearts, set your soul going healthily, let the wounds of childhood heal once for all . . .

Therapy Circus

Roll up! Roll up! The greatest soul
show on earth is here today!
Enjoy a drug-free high.
See set out before you
crystals, bowls, balls, all our oils
essential, all our texts
self-help. So help yourself
to a happier face – lose that frown –
The Therapy Circus is come to town!

> But behind the sideshows,
> tents, swirling banners,
> beneath a trestle table
> loaded with merchandise,
> an old man sits and weeps.
> He's remembering a childhood
> detached in the huge house,
> his companions a china dog,
> teddy bear, trainset, toy telephone.

Dreams often present us with powerful images which stand out from the dreams in which they appear. Choose an image from a recent dream, and flow-write or cluster from it. See if you can find phrases or sentences which you can develop into a longer piece of writing.

Exercise 2: Writing from a painting

Many artists use dream images or produce paintings which have a dream-like quality. Some examples are Chagall, Dali, Magritte and Redon. Find a reproduction which appeals to you and flow-write about it. There may be a phrase or sentence there that you wish to take further.

Geraldine Paine chose a painting by Whistler with the title *Nocturne: Blue and Silver – Chelsea 1871*. This is the flow-write which came from it:

> Blue, at first it's just blue, not Giotto's holy blue but a sort of Air Force blue, then a cover of purple, like a cloak. You take me by the hand and say, walk, it's not deep. I pull at your hand and my watch strap breaks but I leave it and walk into the water with you. My legs are unsteady on the uneven surface. I have my clothes on but I don't feel wet at all, as though I'm walking in shadows, untouchable, the purple is soft now, a stain. I sense the sky darkening; see lights from a small red car in the distance. I know we're walking towards them but they keep moving away. A wind lifts my hair, strands cover my face, but I still have hold of your hand. I want so much to smell the sea, I remember to tell you.

Exercise 3: Writing a story from a dream

Most dreams have a narrative element. Choose one with an already strong story line and either re-tell it or develop it further: what happens next?

Here is part of a dream by Anne Stewart which has extraordinary potential. The story is of three people, two of whom know that they are dead, and the third is unaware of the situation:

Two limos. The two of us who 'do know' are taken to one and the other woman to the other. I did a lot of thinking in this dream. About her going to Heaven and us not. Why my companion died so young. How I had died. I knew compulsively (1) that it wasn't the parachute jump; (2) that hers was a crash, motorbike and car; and (3) that no-one ever knows how they died. I thought a lot about that.

A third car, a lot of animated talk between the men (and yes, all were men) and the cars speed off. Ours arrives at a rickety house with flights and flights of stairs, then a small office, where an evidently 'good', quite handsome man, clearly deeply relieved and delighted, rises to greet us. He's Satan. Seeing him makes me remember a whole rush of things.

This is a welcome-home interview: tea and biscuits, news of Home. Satan treats us differently according to how 'mature' we are. At the end, I know what I've always known: Satan is a loving father to us all. Hell is Home, magnificently beautiful, devoid of riches and greed for power. Heaven is an after-death asylum for those who've become confused. God is a pretty useless psychiatrist whom Satan wishes could do better for his people. 'Living' is a boarding school, each life a different stage of our development.

Exercise 4: Writing a significant dream

Many people have a handful of dreams which seem to carry a special charge. The emotional message in these may be powerful, overwhelming even or the dream may be recurring and this endows it with a special significance. In Chapter 8 we have included an example of a significant dream which Elaine Marcus Starkman recorded in her journal. This surely stems from her turbulent and ambivalent emotional state at the time. Confronting such a dream can have a very powerful effect and it is possible that exploring round it may release ideas and feelings which are difficult to cope with. We suggest you should only embark on this when you feel very ready to and maybe at a time when you have a friend or counsellor you could turn to if necessary.

Exercise 5: Inventing a dream

Using a dreamlike setting can provide a frame within which to write about material which is too difficult to approach directly. Try to envision a situation which you found upsetting, are ashamed of, confused or ambivalent about, and see if you can make up a dream which incorporates it or relates to it.

When he was stranded on a station in the middle of a train journey Paul Sutherland was reminded of another late night journey when he invaded an ex-lover's bedroom. The surreal landscape of the second station and the hallucinatory merging of the two journeys offered him a way to face and write about material he found shameful. Although aware that the poem was 'an exposure of myself' he felt safe enough to take the risk. The surreal nature of the poem, which might be read as a dream and not necessarily as based on personal experience, made him feel safe enough to take the risk. Here is part of the poem, 'The Waiting Room':

> . . . In the dark flat pit
> the double rails
> turn to rust.
>
> A slender-bodied
> signal light
> stands fixated on green
> burns into the distance
> mocking my late journeys
>
> when youth's loneliness
> seemed exhilarating: whole
> metropolises flickered by
> without one waving hand's
> encouragement or welcome.
>
> Where was I going:
> to a fragrant lover's bedroom
> that night?
> who afterwards
> fastened her door hard
> against imagining travellers.
>
> Did I jemmy open the front lock? . . .
>
> (from *Pendulum, The Poetry of Dreams*)

Section 4: Drawing as a starting point

Non-verbal mediums can also offer a route to personal material one wants to access. The visual, in particular, can be an effective trigger. What we picture in our heads connects closely with what we think and language makes constant use of it. We talk about 'looking at something' when we mean 'considering it', express states of mind as: 'seeing the light', 'walking on air', 'being shut in' and so on. It is not unusual for someone in a serious dilemma to do a diagram to try and clarify the predicament.

In this section we invite you to use drawing with coloured pens or pencils as a starting point for writing. This technique often produces exciting and illuminating results. In trying it out you need to be clear that you are not aiming to produce an artistic picture. This is a chance to enjoy using colour, line, shape, size and patterning to represent events and feelings in your life without pinning them to words. Tunnels, turbulent clouds, a great sun immediately overhead, a bridge thin as a piece of string over a wide river, for example, are potent indicators. For the exercises which follow you can use a sheet of A4 typing paper but a piece of cartridge paper larger than this is even better. We suggest too that you equip yourself with a good selection of coloured pens or pencils.

Exercise 1: A significant place

Choose a place which is important to you now or had particular meaning for you in the past. It might be a room, a garden, a street, a lake, an old tower or the like. In doing your drawing be spontaneous. You may want to make important things large but be as fanciful or childlike as you please. Use simple outline where you want to, detail and pattern where you feel like it. Have fun using bright or dark colours, zig-zag lines and so on to convey your feelings. Spend as long as you want to on the drawing and then write about your chosen place with the drawing in front of you as a prompt. You might be surprised by some of its details and as you write it is possible forgotten material will surface. Here is part of a piece by Simon Johnson:

> The open air swimming pool is as blue as the sky above and I am floating on my back, arms and legs spread out. My face is blissful. I am nine years old and I am utterly free in the water, utterly confident. I am there every day in the summer holidays. I believed then that I would be a champion swimmer, that I could do anything . . . Re-living that summer makes me feel both happy and sad.

Exercise 2: A key experience

Choose a key incident in your life and depict this in a drawing, then write or flow-write about it. Possibilities might be a family row, falling in love, a success, an accident, a confrontation, a discovery. Do not rule out using what might outwardly seem like a minor event if it comes into your mind. It may have affected you more than you realize. In a workshop Myra depicted an afternoon in her childhood when her mother pushed her on the floor and smacked her because she had reminded a neighbour with whom they were having tea that she had promised to give her a sweet. As she drew Myra felt a surge of fury about her unjust punishment and put a pool of red rage round the small figure lying on the floor. Here is a short piece written by Tony Field:

> Two great black slabs slant upwards above my head. They almost meet, almost block out the sky. They are the pressures I've been under for months squeezing against my sides. It's hard to breathe. Above them, almost blocking out the sky, are a bunch of open mouths all shouting at me for failing my exams. That's me – a skinny creature looking up at them. I feel failure in every inch of my body, a sense of being totally trapped. This is me at seventeen – if only I'd known there was a way out.

Exercise 3: A time of change

Now focus on a time of change in your life and represent this in a picture or draw a line down the middle of a sheet of paper and do side by side a picture of your life before the change and one of your life after the change. This could be a relationship ending, having a baby, changing your job, moving and so on.

In a workshop Vivienne Fogel drew a picture with a plane on the left going into the twin towers on September 11th 2001, a few days after she had moved house. In the middle of the drawing she showed an ex-lover playing his violin, outside the old home, and on the right in much brighter colours the sun radiating light into the green garden of the new house she had just moved to. Here are extracts from her piece:

> I crossed you out, grey and menacing, your violin case snapped shut, my ears are closed, your music no longer thrills. I have packed my cases and moved away. It was not peaceful, nor easy – and a few days later the towers came down. You could not follow me even though you helped dis-assemble the bed and packed a few boxes. For a while the whole sky turned black – and we turned white with shock at the implications. They were saying NO to the West . . . and in a small way I was doing the same. I would not go along with any more lies – I wanted to knock it all down. Dark clouds hovered, and brokenness – shards, mess, lay scattered. I tried to clear and sort, pick up the pieces, re-order. I tried to carry on as before . . . It's taken time to recover – and now I can see the sun which looms large and strong, its warmth nourishes me.

At the same workshop Yvonne Baker did this drawing which has a number of symbols.

Here is the piece she wrote followed by an explanation:

I'm half woman, half fish. Neither one nor the other . . . wondering how I ended up here. Then a leap from the water reaching for the sun. My tightly constrained life a maze – no escape – suddenly springs open. Pandora's puzzle box can't be closed again – the fireworks that followed – I have listened to the aftermath for years. And the carefully controlled silent mermaid began to sing to shout to fight back. A shock for me let alone everyone else. And another shock. I am tattooed.

It turns out that I'm much more complex than I've been admitting to myself, hiding it. I feel out of control. Eggs crack but instead of fluffy chicks a snake. But what a snake – sleek and glossy. Of course it sleeps now. But I know it's there. There's no road back, although I have drawn a road from the sea to the puzzle box – constantly going back in my mind.

The drawing describes a time when I decided to give up a stressful job. I had come to a point of not just feeling trapped but also feeling I didn't fit comfortably in my life (hence the mermaid). The ambivalent image of the snake seemed more appropriate than a chick as a metaphor for this new life. I remembered a time from years ago when my life had also been overturned by a change I made. There was a cyclical pattern in both experiences of conforming for a long time, deciding to change, and then the change appearing to take on a life of its own.

Exercise 4: Fantasies

This offers you the chance to play with fantasy. Visualize your ideal life. These might include a perfect partner, the surroundings you would like to live in, ambitions you want to achieve, places you want to travel to and so on. Now 'realize' your fantasy pictorially and carry this into your writing.

Exercise 5: Looking at yourself

Try using picture-making to look directly at yourself. Do two pictures side by side. In the first drawing bring out what you see as the negatives in your life and character, in the second bring out the positives. Be impressionistic and exaggerate as much you like. After you have written about each drawing you might want to produce a composite piece about yourself.

Exercise 6: Abstract drawings

This final exercise invites you to leave the representational altogether. Use drawing purely in colour, line and shape to express a state of mind you have experienced. This could be determination, envy, calm, confusion, hope, anger and so on. Be spontaneous. Feel free to use scribble or spiked lines to express anger for example. You could also use this exercise to express a feeling you try to avoid experiencing or to draw an emotion you would like to feel.

Keeping a journal, writing a memoir, shaping work

15

In this chapter we are looking at different ways of extending personal writing: by writing at greater length in a journal or memoir, by giving your work a shape.

Section 1: Keeping a journal

A journal offers the opportunity to record and think about your inner and outer world over a period of time. It can be used to dump and explore feelings, write about key events, people in your life, crises, illuminations, problems, ideas, thought processes and interests. You should not feel tied to making entries every day but you are likely to find your journal more valuable if you write often enough to feel a sense of continuity – perhaps at least once a week.

Quite often journals have a particular focus. Gerard Manley-Hopkins, deeply concerned with nature, frequently used his notebook and journal to write detailed descriptions of the natural world. Some people keep a dream diary, others turn to a journal at a difficult or key time in their lives. In Chapter 6 Myra describes how she used journal writing for a year after she was diagnosed with cancer. The poet Mimi Khalvati has found keeping a journal useful as a way of getting back into writing after a period when she had had no time to write. She also uses it to connect with writing if she is away from her usual surroundings. In Chapter 2 we wrote about Joanna Field's *A Life of One's Own*, a book based on a journal which she kept to observe and analyse her feelings and thoughts. If you are thinking of keeping a journal focused on personal development we suggest you look at this book and also that you read Tristine Rainer's *The New Diary* which offers many ideas.

It is worth remembering that the letters of people such as Keats, Van Gogh and Elizabeth Bishop are the equivalent of journals and this mode can be used in a journal. Indeed, Anne Frank's famous diary is in the form of letters to an imaginary friend whom she treats as a confidante. Alternatively letters can be incorporated into a journal. The following exercises suggest some ways of approaching journal writing.

Exercise 1: At this moment

This is an extension of the 'Here and Now' exercise (Chapter 12) and is useful especially if you are uncertain what you want to write about or how to sort out the material which suggests itself. It makes you focus on what is immediate both externally and internally. Begin by describing your surroundings and focusing on what catches your attention: headlines in the newspaper, a worn out slipper, your child's toy, a spoon stuck in a jar of marmalade and the like. Alternatively begin by describing something that has happened today: reading a letter, listening to music, an irritating phone conversation, being awakened by cats fighting outside and so on. After a few minutes write a sentence about how you are feeling and shift into flow-writing. Here is part of a potent piece by Maggie Bevan in which she interweaves details about the garden and the weather with her own feelings:

> The garden through the summerhouse window. Long grass – needs a haircut – dandelions growing at odd angles, ajar, awry. Why do people have to cut grass? Why be so neat, so tidy and ordered? Follow rules?. . . Behind bare trees the sky is darkening – like a frown. Why is life so difficult?. . . I am sitting at the edge of my chair, the air cold about me – I feel it like a tangible presence. I am so aware of my own body, my awkward pose. No. I'm not happy today . . . My boys' dad is getting married in July . . . More responsibility for me – emotional and physical – just at the point when I had started to see my way more clearly. Suddenly I look up and the sky is blue. White clouds travelling across – the black mood has vanished. Ironic, as I do not feel this. I identify with dandelions. They are just waiting, waiting to have their heads cut off because somebody else other than they will decide to do that. I feel I have little choice or control. The boys will need me more than ever now. Their dad will just disappear . . . Freedom is being able to choose a future and mine disappeared down the wrong end of a telescope quite a few years back. I keep trying to prise the end open, see the light. There are tantalising flickers of it and then – wham! up it clams again. I think I should stop wanting and hoping because it seems to bring the opposite. Pain. It's windy outside now and I still feel the cold like a layer around my arms and legs. I don't want it to get inside my heart and start to freeze it . . .

It can be very productive to try out this exercise in a variety of places: on a train journey, in a waiting room, on a beach and so on.

Exercise 2: Dumping feelings

This simple method for letting go of feelings can be surprisingly powerful in offering a sense of release. It is also a useful way of identifying the different feelings one is experiencing and can be a first step in coming to terms with them. It is particularly helpful in a time of crisis or stress. You 'dump' what is on your mind either by making a list of items in single words, phrases or short sentences or by writing a series of sentences, each in the same pattern, as described in 'Getting Started' (Chapter 12). You can also mix both methods. Myra used dumping several times in her cancer journal and there are two examples in Chapter 6. Here is an excerpt from a piece by Tony Thompson:

I am bored with my job.
I'm bored with the mess in here but I can't be bothered to clear it up.
I'm bored with my parents' aches and pains and hints about my life.
I'm bored with going out for a month or two with someone I've chatted to on
   the internet.
I want something more, something satisfying.

A next step with such a piece could be to take one of the statements and investigate it by using it as a starting point for writing which could include flow-writing or clustering. You may find these two techniques and others in Part 2, especially secret letters, dialoguing and visualizations, are useful in writing your journal.

Exercise 3: Recording

A journal is also a place for recording things that make a powerful impression on you. These may have no direct connection with your life: a film, a mediaeval building you saw in Prague, watching the sun rising over the Alps and the like ... You may also want to make entries about a central interest – music, the environment, space exploration, tennis and so on. Whatever you feel strongly about is an aspect of yourself. Mary MacRae, as her contribution in Chapter 11 shows, cares passionately about nature. Here is her journal entry for 30th December 2007 – what she sees moves her deeply:

Walk at Oare. What would heaven be like if we could choose? It's so very beautiful at Oare – so many different blues and greys melting and merging under grey-purple clouds – mud, river, sea, sky, bright yellow marsh-grass. Every colour – the red of the boat-hull, houses on the opposite shore, all so intense. Silky reeds with long stems and little birds – bearded tits? – swinging on them, tearing the seeds out. I wanted to experience it all for ever – to be the brightness of the colours, the mud on the water's edge, feel the redshank's toes sink in, blow in the wind through the reeds and see it all, feel it all and know what it was like to be it all – a god.

It is also very well worth using a diary to note down comments about books you read. What you read feeds into your thinking and writing. John sometimes copies into his journal a sentence or a paragraph from a book which he finds significant.

Whatever kind of journal you have decided to keep you will probably find you want to write your entries in different ways and within one entry you may find yourself switching from one kind of writing to another. We end this section with a piece by Caroline Carver. In a short space she looks back and forward, thinks about practicalities, considers her journal's prevailing tone and assesses her feelings.

New Year entry for 1997

Most years I find it hard to get used to the new year, 1996 seemed impossible to acclimatise to, I clung to 1995 as if I was about to lose something important. (Subconscious – my 50s?) Whatever, I've rushed into 1997 without a backwards glance. Perhaps it will be a good year. I'm certain it will be a year of change, without any clear feelings of what that may be, although losing a dearest friend will be part of it. 1997 may have been easy to get into, but getting up to drive 100 miles to work, and 100 home again, once a week will continue to seem almost impossible. But I will get up each time, I know, an unpaid-for car and a mortgage being mighty spurs to action.

Looking at this journal I notice how often I refer to being depressed, run down, exhausted etc. I suspect one just doesn't note happy days very often, unless something very special has happened, and the impression given is a distorted one. All this is to note that I've been much happier since back in England. I feel English. But the Canadian years were hugely important, and my heart sometimes lingers in the backwoods and wilderness.

Section 2: Writing a memoir

The word 'memoir' comes from 'memory', and much of the writing quoted or referred to in this book derives from recollection. However, how we organize and present our material can have the effect of enhancing or devaluing the original qualities enshrined in it. Certain significant memories are best given solo space in a poem or short piece of prose. Others can gain from being linked as in a chain (think of a gemstone compared with a necklace). There are poem-sequences and groups of short stories which have this character. These do not possess the scale or ambition of a detailed autobiography but can achieve a perfection all their own.

This section is about continuous narratives of some length which attempt to present a whole life or at least a significant part of one. We exclude from consideration those volumes which crowd our bookshops and which purport to 'spill the beans' about the lives of the famous or notorious. Many of these are 'ghosted' anyway and are either elaborate 'cover-ups' or full of exaggerated revelations. They have nothing to do with works which burrow, unearth, organize and evaluate experience in the real business of 'writing the self'.

There are many ways of putting a memoir together. The most straight-forward is illustrated by James Kirkup in his *A Child of the Tyne* (Chapter 1). He does not indulge in deep analysis of relationships or social and political conditions but recreates the surface of his early life with wonderful precision and in great detail. His account is chronological and this is ideal for his purpose. Mark Doty, on the other hand, adopts a kaleidoscopic approach in his book, *Heaven's Coast*, and since this outstanding work is not discussed in our book it is worth featuring here. This is a partial autobiography, since it covers predominantly a decade in the author's life, though there are sorties into earlier events in order to illuminate certain themes and incidents. It is also a portrait of Wally, Mark Doty's partner during this period, who contracts HIV and dies of AIDS, so the book becomes a memorial to him and a posthumous celebration of their relationship. A binding subtheme is how the surviving partner finds ways of coming to terms with his grief.

Doty finds straightforward storytelling too constricting; he needs something more open-ended and experimental, so he begins with a number of impressions, telescoping the time-element. He then moves into the core of the book made up of more conventional narrative, though interspersed with letters, journal entries and quotations from other writers. The final part is the most discursive of all: short pieces of prose enshrining new insights, or meditating on topics already raised. Miraculously the whole hangs together: by pushing the boundaries, and through his unquenchable passion for life, Doty has created a distinctive work of art.

His comments on the process are always apposite. More than once he voices the fundamental question: 'What does a writer do, when the world collapses, but write?' (Doty 1996, p. 263). He honestly confronts the difficulty of the endeavour:

> To write was to court overwhelming feeling. Not to write was to avoid, but to avoid was a way to survive. Though writing was a way of surviving, too: experience was unbearable, looked at head-on, but *not* to look was also unbearable. And so I'd write, when I could, recording what approached like someone in a slow-moving but unstoppable accident, who must look and look away at once. (Ibid., p. 205)

After short opening chapters about his earlier life and his time in Beirut before he was kidnapped, Brian Keenan focuses his book, *An Evil Cradling* (see Chapter 3) on his six intense years as a hostage. These began with months of solitary confinement. His situation forced him to turn inwards to find moral and spiritual guidance. Joanna Field in *A Life of One's Own* (Chapter 2) and subsequent volumes chose to develop her inner resources by a course of experiential practices, and her books chronicle her progress. Sydney Poitier in *The Measure of Man* (Chapter 11) also gives prominence to this aspect of the human. The spiritual autobiography is a distinct sub-genre of the memoir, though of course many other attempts at personal narrative contain this element to a greater or lesser degree.

In planning a memoir you will first of all need to decide the format you wish to adopt. This will depend upon the aspect(s) of your life you wish to include, and your own predilections. Jamaica Kincaid in *My Brother* (Chapter 3) could have adopted a straightforward prose style but preferred a kind of disjointed, stream-of-consciousness, semi-poetic narrative, and it seems to suit the nature of her imagination. You will have to decide whether you wish to deal with the whole expanse of your life up to the present, or concentrate on one period in detail, or take a series of slices out of it, chosen for the contribution those episodes made to the growth of your sense of identity. And you will also need to decide whether the exploration is for your eyes only or whether you wish to share your insights more widely, in which case issues of confidentiality (even libel) may arise. This could profoundly affect the way you approach the task.

Another aspect you will need to consider is the extent to which you will be able to attain veracity in the telling. The process of accumulating memories of things which happen to us is one of construction which is influenced by our pre-existing beliefs, perspectives and needs. This, of course, influences the issue of whether we can ever claim to be researching 'the truth'. Lauren Slater in her extraordinary book *Spasm*, subtitled *A Memoir with Lies*, proclaims truthtelling but at the same time admits to embroidering events throughout her narrative. She had epilepsy between the ages of thirteen and seventeen, a period covered in great detail in the book, and fantasizing is often a by-product of this condition. By the time she had undergone neurosurgery for the seizures, the habit of invention had become a constant in her psychological makeup. Her book is an extreme example of this phenomenon but a most fascinating one. Slater justifies her practice in the following passage:

> *Spasm* is a book of narrative truth, a book in which I am more interested in using invention to get to the heart of things than I am in documenting actual life. The text I've created uses, in some instances, metaphors, most significantly the metaphor of epilepsy, to express subtleties and horrors and gaps in my past for which I have never been able to find the words. Metaphor is the greatest gift of language, for through it we can propel silence into sound. And even if the sounds are not altogether accurate, they do resonate in some heartfelt place we cannot dismiss. (Slater 2000, pp. 219–20)

For one final reflection we return to Mark Doty. In his acknowledgements at the end of his memoir of his early life, *Firebird*, he makes a similar point to Slater about the nature of memory: 'The allegiance of this book is to memory: this is a past colored, arranged, and choreographed entirely by that transforming, idiosyncratic light' (Doty 1999, p. 199).

In an interview with Michael Klein in 1995 Mark Doty outlined one of the profoundest motivations that can lead a person to write a memoir:

> There was a point when it was very important for me to try to explain myself to myself in a kind of psychological way. I think that we all have that desire to make the story of our lives. Of our artifacts, it's one that's very fluid because you re-tell the story of your life in each new circumstance. As your life changes you need to understand the story from another perspective. I wrote perhaps two books about telling myself the story of my life. It was crucial to me. Beginning to view your history as a story is a work of interpretation, a way to wield some power over the past, gain authority over it. Rather than be controlled by my own history, I could say this, this is how I will understand what memory is, this is how I will understand my life. (Doty 1995, p. 23)

Section 3: Shaping work

Spontaneity, jotting down whatever suggests itself, allowing your imagination to take off, are all-important as you find your way into subject matter. If you try to control and organize what you are writing at this point you may fail to reach the heart of what you really want to explore. A first step in taking writing further, therefore, is very likely to be extending your material – maybe by making more use of the techniques we have described in the previous three chapters or keeping a journal or writing pieces which may be the beginnings of a memoir. When you feel ready to develop a piece of finished work then it is time to think about where it should begin, how it should proceed and where it should end – in other words to consider the structure which will bind it together.

Sometimes there is a straightforward narrative thread which makes shaping comparatively easy but often it is not obvious how to sort out material, how to decide what should or should not be included in a poem, short autobiographical piece or story. What we call the hook technique can be very useful to have in mind as you sort out ideas. Consciously or unconsciously most successful short poems are built round a hook – that is they have a central idea or image which holds the poem together and all the material is in some way hooked onto it. Here is a poem by Gill McEvoy which is a particularly good example of how such linking forms the backbone of a poem and carries its emotional weight:

Scissors

'Scissors', my mother told me when I was five,
was my first real word. That word *real* troubled me:
I had watched her hold her sheet of newsprint
over the mouth of the fire to make it draw,
seen how it singed in the middle, how the words
melted away, no longer real but gone.

The scissors remained, snipping, cutting,
slashing at things. 'Dangerous. Don't touch'.
Always missing when she wanted them,
which made them somehow yet more real
like a person whose absence is keenly felt.

The absence of you, for example, my father,
whose telephone number I still have by heart,
can still count on my fingers the things you kept
in your kitchen drawer: two knives, two forks,
one tablespoon, three teaspoons – the scissors,

that real word that had you, after my mother's death,
paring away your life, snipping at edges,
hacking off frills, shearing it all down to so little:
a handful of cutlery, a pair of scissors.

The scissors are the hook in this poem and the lines of thought which the implement triggers direct what McEvoy writes. The scissors become increasingly metaphorical as the poem proceeds and they are the link as she connects ideas about the meaning of 'real' and 'missing' and then shifts to the loss of her father.

In Vivienne Fogel's poem, 'The Nursing Chair', (Chapter Fourteen) the chair is the hook. Identifying this kind of pivot when you look through pieces of raw writing can help you decide both what to develop and the direction you want it to take. This in turn will tell you what to select from your raw material and how to use it.

The hook method is also valuable in prose writing. The hook in Patricia McFarland's 'Beyond the Pale' (Chapter 2) is her childhood memories of Irish Catholicism. John Fowles' short book, *The Tree*, presents a notable example of the technique. The book is about his passion and relationship with nature. The passion is so strong it is part of his identity. In the opening chapter he focuses on the differences and connections between himself and his father by contrasting their ideas about gardens and wildlife. Using gardening as a hook Fowles gives the reader a graphic picture of his father's personality. It is used too to show how father and son reacted to each other and the hook structure is underpinned by the recurrent image of his father's fruit trees:

> I think I truly horrified him only once in my life, which was when soon after coming into possession, I took him round my present exceedingly unkempt, unmanaged and unmanageable garden . . . He thought it madness to take on such a 'jungle' and did not believe me when I said I saw no need to take it on, only to leave it largely alone, in effect to my co-tenants, its wild birds and beasts, its plants and insects. He would never have conceded that it was my equivalent of his own beautifully disciplined apples and pears, and just as much cultivated, though not in the literal sense. He would not have understood that something I saw down there . . . two tawny owlets fresh out of the nest, sitting on a sycamore branch like a pair of badly knitted Christmas stockings and ogling down at this intruder into *their* garden – means to me exactly what the Horticultural Society cups on his sideboard used to mean to him: a token of order in unjust chaos . . . (Fowles 2000, pp. 26–7)

When you are trying to decide how to develop work there will, of course, be occasions when the amount or complexity of the subject matter makes it impossible to build it round a single hook. Now is the time to start thinking in terms of producing a longer piece of work. One possibility is to write a sequence. This form is useful for putting together connected pieces of subject matter which cannot be satisfactorily combined in a single piece of writing.

The sequence can make a stepping stone to writing at greater length if you have not done so before because once the idea has been conceived and roughly planned it can be built up in separate units. The putting together of poems or sections on the same theme to depict different relationships, events, times, viewpoints and so on can be very potent.

In Chapter 1 Myra described how she read an anthology of sequences when she was a relatively inexperienced poet and saw at once that this was the way to present material about her mother and grandmother. In Chapter 3 Linda Chase examined a long relationship in her sequence, 'Younger Men Have Birthdays Too'. A single, short poem would not have allowed her the space she needed to write about her different feelings.

Short prose pieces can also make effective sequences and sometimes sequences include both poems and pieces of prose. The pieces John quotes in Chapter 1 belong to a prose and poetry sequence about his childhood written over a long period of time. Another example is *In Parenthesis* by David Jones which describes his experiences in the trenches in World War One. Sequences can be put together formally with a title as those named above or be a series of poems or pieces which could be grouped together in a publication. Myra wrote a series of six poems which looked at bodies, in particular her own. They follow one another as a group in her book, *Insisting on Yellow*. Because the poems were very different from each other in approach and language she did not feel they had the unity of a formal sequence.

Finishing work

In this final chapter we examine the writing process in more detail as we consider how to achieve finished work. First of all, though, we want to look at the difference between raw and finished work. Spontaneous writing, whether it is in a journal or on the back of an envelope, in a workshop or a series of notes written at home, has its own validity and it is important to recognize this. The crystallizing of experience and feelings, problems and partly-perceived ideas, the placing of them outside oneself on paper is likely to be a release. It is also a way of clarifying one's responses and coming to terms with them. This self-expression can be energizing and exciting. It may contain unexpected details, extraordinary images and open up new perspectives. Such writing, while being unshaped, is frequently potent. We have quoted several examples in this book. These include the pieces of flow-writing in Chapter 12, the flow-writing by Elke Dutton in Chapter 5, and the image explorations in Chapter 12.

There may well be material in raw writing which could be developed into finished work but no one should feel that they *ought* to go beyond this stage, or the stage of extending raw material with further associations unless they want to. The original piece of writing may be sufficient. Even if there is a strong wish to develop work it is counterproductive to try to do so unless the writer feels emotionally ready to deal with the subject matter and has ideas about how to take it forward.

Finished work developed from personal material is likely to have a deep therapeutic effect but in the first place it must stand in its own right as a work of art. To achieve finished work it is crucial to distance oneself from raw writing in order to transform and shape it into a poem, story or novel. This may mean drastic cutting, focusing on one aspect of it, or presenting it in a completely different form, and all this has to be done without losing the original impetus. How to bring about such a transformation? There is no quick route. In dealing with central personal material it is often helpful to extend your raw material by writing down everything connected with it, everything you feel and think before you start developing it. Once all this is on paper it is easier to work out what is needed for any particular poem, autobiographical story or memoir. Beyond that it is a matter of practice, of learning the craft of writing by reading widely and building up techniques. Good courses and workshops – and these are now widely available – are immensely helpful, as is getting feedback from and giving feedback to other writers.

In the previous chapter we described the 'hook' technique as a useful step when you start thinking about shaping work. We also indicated points that need to be considered before starting a memoir, points to help you decide how you might focus it. In this chapter we are going to examine, with the help of examples, some key aspects of the writing process which we think you might find valuable.

In the first place there needs to be a sense that you are creating something, not simply recording the detail of personal experience. In the creative process there is a take-off point, a moment when the writer finds the image, the focus, the hook which drives the poem, the chapter, the story. Maggie Sawkins describes such a moment in a commentary she wrote on the creative process. She had struggled for weeks to write a poem for a workshop on the theme of noise and in the end she produced one about where noise goes to when it is no longer there. She was not happy with the poem because it seemed forced:

> However, thinking about noise had awakened a memory. I remembered an incident from my childhood when my parents, who were always fighting, suddenly stopped all communication for weeks. The silence was unbearable, but what I remember most was the moment of release: one day I came home from school and found them kissing . . . I attempted to adapt the memory to the theme of noise . . . As I was drying my hair one morning, a line came: 'She got used to the birds flying around the house.' From that moment the poem had been born – the noise of the birds would represent the noise of constant arguing.

After a week, during which words and lines kept suggesting themselves, sometimes at awkward moments, the poem was written. The central bird image is surreal and the piece of work is all the more powerful for being written as a fable in the third person. Here it is:

The Birds

She got used to the birds
flying around the house

except for the days
when their cawing filtered
through the floorboards

and even the dog was afraid.

When friends or relations came
the birds disappeared through the windows
and waited on the roof top
or under the eaves.

One day the cawing stopped.

The birds settled in the silence
like a big black cloud.

In her bedroom she built a cage
and the birds flew in
one by one.

Weeks later she returned from school
found her mother and father
in the kitchen – kissing.

From her room she could hear
the flutter of a million tiny wings.

The door opened and birds
glided through the house

weightless and blue.

Inside the cage were their feathers
heaped like a black slag of tar.

(from *Charcot's Pet*)

A take-off point is essential but there are, of course, many other consi-
derations. Clarifying and focusing are not automatically straightforward
because you have found a central image or hook. You need to be willing to
explore, re-organize material, re-draft, revise in fine detail. This often requires
patience and persistence over a period of time. Yvonne Baker began a poem in
the workshop where she did a dramatic drawing representing a time of change
in her life followed by flow-writing. (See Chapter 14.) Afterwards she wrote
further versions of the poem. These had powerful and haunting images but
because the ideas and the central, symbolic snake metaphor were not fully

worked out the whole was confusing to read and it did not convey the message or the kind of ambivalence she wanted it to. Perhaps because of this the writing was rather wordy. She put the poem aside for a while, then did some research into snakes, clarified the part played by the main image and fined the poem down. The process took about seven months during which time she produced fourteen drafts. Here is the beginning of the untitled draft written in the workshop followed by the final poem:

Under my grey trouser suit, my limbs and torso are tattooed.
Around my neck, disguised as a chiffon scarf,
my snake sleeps. She is quiet now, tightly coiled,
but just watch her when she's hungry.

I still visit the flat above the pet shop,
calling when I know you won't be at home
because someone else sleeps in that big bed now.
Climbing the shadowed stairs to escape
the opaque afternoon light,
I let myself in with the key you lost . . .

Revisiting

I climb the shadowed stairs,
let myself in with your key I haven't returned.

Each time I call the room grows smaller.
Each time I promise myself this visit is the last.

Today I bring ox-blood chrysanthemums,
arrange them in cracked blue water.

The room, silent with light, is in disarray,
snake's skin crumpled on the floor;

Griselda, the python I thought
years ago to tame, consumes

the space, lies across the big bed
where someone else sleeps now.

She ripples over sheets, curves around the pillows;
the gold and olive pattern deepens on her silver body,

smoke-grey eyes glisten, mouth agape
she stretches towards me, teeth shaped like tears.

The points about taking-off and focusing also apply to the writing of prose and we are now going to consider the transformation of personal material to fiction. We looked at Jeanette Winterson's novel, *Oranges are Not the Only Fruit*, in Chapter 2. In a forward to it she commented as to whether or not it was autobiographical: 'No not at all and yes of course.' This apparently contradictory reply is an important statement about writing fiction with an autobiographical base. Miriam Hastings has explored the contradiction in writing about her first novel, *The Minotaur Hunt*, in Chapter 7. She looks at the topic in further detail in the following piece.

The transformation process: Miriam Hastings

I find it helps to keep some distance between myself and my central characters, so that they are presented vividly but they don't take over the novel. Using the third person narrative voice can be helpful in this respect; also the device of having more than one narrator. In my novel, *The Burnings*, there are three central narrators who each see the main events of the story from a different perspective.

This novel feels very personal to me – possibly the most personal of all my novels - although it is set in the north of Scotland during the early years of the nineteenth century, at the time of the Highland Clearances. The narrators, Grace, Lizzie and Charity, are all young women whose lives were irreversibly affected by the brutal clearances in Sutherland.

I've always enjoyed writing fiction; it has been a means of escaping reality and the more imaginative, the more removed from my own life, the better. But life has a habit of creeping up on us unawares. Writing fiction can be similar to the process of dreaming: often when we analyse our dreams, they echo aspects of our lives and facets of ourselves are revealed to us in unexpected ways. I find that my fiction, however remote it may seem from my own experiences in terms of historical period or life events, can always show me something about myself from the patterns that have emerged from my unconscious mind. These are rarely obvious and it is unlikely that another person would notice them, but they gradually appear like a developing photograph, or like clouds taking recognizable shapes: faces, mountains, islands surrounded by water, mirroring the terrestrial world in a strangely transformed manner. When I look at the fiction I have written in the past, I find certain patterns being played out over and over again; patterns of relationships, patterns of survival, which frequently have resonances in my own life. An obvious example is a relationship between two girls or women that recurs again and again in my novels and often mirrors my complex and sometimes difficult relationships with my sisters.

The following extract from Part 10 of *The Burnings*, narrated by Elizabeth, the daughter of the minister at Reay, dramatizes her close but complicated bond with her orphaned cousin Charity:

> "I must stay, Lizzie," Charity said, "I may be able to help Grace and our other friends. Darling Lizzie, I know you will understand." I felt more angry then. Why did she put Grace before me?
>
> "We have refugees in Reay," I argued.
>
> "Not so many, and now there are more and more in Farr. I should stay indeed, Lizzie – there's so much I might do here to help victims of the flittings. Besides," she went on, "Aunt MacKenzie has begged me to stay longer, she says she relies so upon me she'll ail badly if I go."
>
> This made me feel even worse, knowing that our aunt wanted Charity but not me for Aunt hadn't asked me to stay. It seemed no one wanted me. Even my father was more anxious to have Charity home than me, I felt sure.
>
> "You never think of your duty, Charity," I said bitterly, "only what you want to do. Then you twist everything to make yourself look noble, while you just follow your pleasure. It is contemptible. It's all a lie! How can you be so dishonest!"
>
> She turned away from me and began to sob. I was seized by shame, I knew I had been mean and cruel.
>
> "I'm sorry, Charity, forgive me. I know you want to do good. I'm just upset that you won't come home with me."
>
> I put my arms around her and began to cry myself. She kissed me then and we made up, but she still wouldn't change her mind.

Miriam Hastings' account bears out what Myra discovered in writing her book-length narrative poem, *Becoming*, which was based on personal material. In writing about this in Chapter 1 she mentioned that she found the material hard to manage. In fact it was only after six months of false starts when she finally fleshed out the fictional characters, thought out a convincing narrative and separated herself from her own experience that the poem began to work. And it was not until then that she felt she was exploring the central issue from her own experience in the way she wanted to.

We end this chapter and Part 2 of the book with an in-depth look at a writing journey undertaken by John Mackay. From the time he was a teenager he had a skin problem which seriously affected his life. In a residential workshop he began writing about skin with a cluster which is quoted in Chapter 12 and an idea for a fable quoted in Chapter 14. He also wrote a first draft of a poem. Two months later he did some flow-writing (see Chapter 12) and on the same morning he wrote two more skin clusters. In addition he wrote notes about steroid cream and these moving 'Skin Notes':

> Skin, the layer we present to the world. Our protection against the elements, and metaphorically against what life throws at us. Those who are good at rebuffing what life throws at them are said to have thick skin. Or skin like a rhino. What about my skin? What has it been like? I feel like it has let me down from an early age. It wasn't up to the job, like that of many of my friends who had 'normal skin'. Mine was skin that reacted badly to life, that was weak, that embarrassed and humiliated me. That shattered my confidence. Eczema is a disgusting skin condition: it causes the most intense itching, that is almost impossible not to scratch, and then when you scratch, it makes the skin much worse. The skin 'weeps', which is a very appropriate word, and then afterwards causes an incredible soreness, which won't tolerate anything, water or soap.
>
> As a child, I had to contemplate the fact that my skin was not my ally, was not there to protect me, to shield me from life's blows but was in itself life's biggest blow. A skin that fell apart. A skin that could not tolerate soap or shampoo or anything that had the remotest resemblance to perfume. It was a skin that should have been to war, looked like it had been to war. I did not trust my own face. Didn't trust my own face not to let me down. The day my face fell apart.

The poem begun at the writing workshop was revised several times and finished a few months after the second set of notes. John Mackay has written a frank and illuminating commentary on his own process which illustrates that one can only write about a difficult subject when and if one is ready. It shows too that it is not always possible to deal with difficult material entirely through writing and that other kinds of support must be found. Here is his account:

Writing about skin: John Mackay

In a short burst of activity, I produced quite a lot of material in the form of flow writing, notes, clusters and story frames about my skin condition – acute eczema that I suffered from when I was a teenager and a young adult. In my early twenties, the eczema all over my face became badly infected – to the point where most of my skin was an open sore and I was forced to go to casualty. Before this point, I hadn't been able to leave the house for weeks because my face was so unsightly, and I was extremely self-conscious about the way I looked.

Writing the background material was an illuminating experience and acted as an emotional release. However, in the year since I wrote it, I have only produced one short poem about my skin condition and the associated feelings. Why is this? In the most obvious sense, to return to these notes causes much of the emotional and physical pain in the material to re-emerge.

But what I am also aware of is that I have done as much as I can possibly do at the moment with the material. I feel that the skin poem I did write, 'Coming of age', is valuable but that it doesn't get to the heart of what I want to say. This is inevitable given the weight and complexity of feelings associated with my skin condition and its effect on my self-image. Perhaps a sequence of poems will go further towards doing justice to the subject – once I feel able to explore in more detail the raw material.

In essence, writing the background material and the poem 'Coming of age' – although beneficial in a number of ways – brought me into close contact once again with a condition that has caused long-term emotional damage, and I realized that I wasn't ready to deal with it – or at least not before I had explored it through other means, for instance through psychotherapy.

My unwillingness to look at the material appears to reflect an unwillingness, through a lot of my life, to look at my face in the mirror, or to have it looked at by other people. This is interesting because my poetry is in one sense a face that I present to the world, and expose for scrutiny in public places.

Coming of age

At fifteen his skin was taken away
and stared at. They told him
to stay out of the sun; he worried
about dimmed living rooms and girls.

A few months later he clawed his neck
in the night. They scolded him, said
not to scratch, then bound his fingers
with handkerchiefs and string; he worried
about lovebites and wandering hands.

The next week his eyelids wept, fissures
opened up in the soft folds around
his chin. They tutted, took him downstairs
to the TV to see fly-flecked children.
He worried about the ins and outs of sex.

At sixteen he woke, crying, from a dream
about a new-born face. They told him
to toughen up – his skin was too thin.

Conclusion

This book has had a declared practical bias: we have looked at the ways in which a number of individuals have used personal writing to explore and express aspects of themselves, and we have examined a series of techniques which have been found useful by ourselves and others in embarking on such quests.

What we have not done is engage in an enquiry into the nature of selfhood. This is a fascinating and complex subject which deserves a volume of its own, and psychologists and philosophers would need to be consulted in the process. Such a book already exists and it also relates these discoveries to the art of writing. *Writing: Self and Reflexivity* is by Celia Hunt and Fiona Sampson, and we highly recommend it.

We feel, however, that we do need to visit the idea of reflexivity briefly, and this seems the appropriate place to consider it. Expressed in the simplest terms, by the very act of writing we are projecting the self outwards onto the page. But if that was all that we were doing we would be only partly availing ourselves of the opportunity to objectivize our experience. The material would be likely to remain attached as if umbilically to the person, and would probably lack coherence and not communicate to anyone else. For that leap to happen there needs to be an act of creation which brings order and focus to the material.

The shaping process is not an imposing but a gradual realization of the structure inherent in the material. We have illustrated this in Chapter 16 which focuses on finishing work, and it features in varying degrees in the examples quoted in Part 1. There is nothing academic about the process we are describing. There may well be something mysterious, even magical, about it. It is what puts the 'creative' into 'creative writing'. It is what transforms the personal into the universal, allowing readers to recognize similarities in their own lives and in the lives of the rest of mankind.

The final realization for writers is that they perceive in what they have written layers of meaning and applicability of which previously they have been aware only dimly if at all. In this sense a novel or play or poem or auto-biographical work, if the writer is skilled, can start from 'in here' and end up with 'out there' – a truly reflexive achievement.

Our aim has been to be as comprehensive as space will allow in examining a spectrum of self-referential writing, and to offer as much help as possible to those who want to embark on their own voyage of discovery. There are, of course, many cross-references between sections as a particular approach cannot be neatly pigeonholed into one subject-area or confined to one technique.

We should like to take by way of an example of this a remarkable book by Inga Clendinnen, an Australian historian. She was in her mid-sixties when she was diagnosed with active autoimmune hepatitis, a form of acute liver disease. She went into hospital for tests, returned home for a period, then was read-mitted where she underwent a successful liver-transplant. Her book, *Tiger's Eye*, was begun during this period. It is completely different from her previous published work (academic texts about the Incas and the Holocaust) being personal, immediate, and open in form. She describes it as 'a memoir' but it is much more than that. It is made up of a number of strands, which include: an acute portrayal of hospital life; a vivid recreation of childhood; a number of short stories drawn from experience; an in-depth analysis of her parents and their relationship; a journal account of the days of her operation and recupera-tion, including detailed accounts of her hallucinations; reflections upon topics such as memory and personhood; and an essay showing her fresh approach to historical narrative. The whole is held together by Clendinnen's fearless confrontation of experience, and an extraordinary command of the creative possibilities of language. Here she is commenting upon the experience:

> Being ill had taught me how much of ourselves there is in all the stories we tell about the past. I had also begun to see the multiple barriers to understanding between ourselves and enigmatic others, and how fiction invites us to overleap these barriers. And I was beginning to suspect, after my drug-induced thrashings and wallowings, that we are fictions too: not coherent and continuous objects in a changing sea, but half-illusory creatures made out of the light and shadows cast by that sea, articulated by our own flickering imaginations. That the Other begins not at the skin, as had I thought, but within. (Clendinnen 2001, p. 191)

This book refuses to be categorized either in terms of its areas of explora-tion or the writer's craft employed. Most significantly, we are vouchsafed a multitude of insights into the process of self-exploration, which is, of course, our subject too. Clendinnen sums up her life-enhancing conversion to the creative approach in the following passages:

> Illness granted me a set of expressions otherwise unobtainable. It liberated me from the routines which would have delivered me, unchallenged and unchanged, to discreet death. Illness casts you out, but it also cuts you free . . .
>
> Illness also made me a writer. Through all its permutations I used writing to cling to the shreds of the self, and to sustain the fraying strands of memory connecting me to my past self, and to the people I love. (Ibid., p. 288)

We end with a poem which we believe is redolent of possibility. It is mysterious because it is venturing into the unknown. It is unnerving because to accept change is painful. It is hopeful because it envisages new beginnings. The poet herself introduces it:

Notes on 'The Badge': Hilary Llewellyn-Williams

This poem comes from a dream that I had some years ago. At that time I was going through a period of trauma and transition – call it a mid-life crisis! – and was dreaming vividly, night after night, and writing the dreams in a notebook. Several of the dreams involved bodily processes, with different types of dismemberment. In one of them I was lying on an operating table, while the surgeons pulled out my intestines (which were diseased and black), washed them, and replaced them – I watched quite calmly as they squeezed the putrefaction from them. In another, I disturbed midnight intruders in my house, one of whom was a black man. After a short struggle I removed his head and slipped it on over my own head . . . So the dream that became 'The Badge' was very much part of a pattern.

I wrote the poem a few years later, during another time of change, after glancing through one of the old dream notebooks and coming across this one. With the benefit of a new perspective I decided to retell it as a poem. The poem is faithful to the dream's details and events, just as they occurred. I deliberately refrain from comment or interpretation, letting the images speak for themselves; but it seems clearly to describe some process of initiation. I use rhyme that enhances the ritual nature of the experience, but I keep it fluid and irregular to convey the ambiguity of dreams – and the same with the stanza groupings. As a poem, it is a bit of a cheat – it was all there already, the powerful physical details, the horror and the humour. But I hope it succeeds on its own terms. It is in my book, *Greenland*.

The Badge

Finding myself after nights of grief and dread
in a room full of rainy light
knife in my hand, no-one can do this for me,
I prepare for the ceremony

I am about to join the community
of those who have removed and replaced their heads.

Cutting it off is easy, I feel no pain,
what's difficult is finding the thing again
wherever on the carpet it's rolled to.

Headless, but I see with shadow-sight
a fluid shudder of colours, images
which will soon falter and disintegrate
unless I reattach my head quickly

and I must do it quickly, it's not too late
while nerves and flesh are still living.

I'm trembling cold and bright
as a knife-edge, I feel high
and light as you do when shrugging off a pack
you've slogged under for miles. And there

on the floor it lies, I recognise the hair
tumbled and black, the face
turned mercifully aside, a glimpse of cheek and brow

that's mine all right so I take it
lift it like a warm and weighty stone
up to my neck and steady it in place.

I must wait now while vein and bone
and fibres knit together
motionless in case it all untethers
as round me the others gather

praising, giving me space. Thin fluid
oozes from the join – is this normal? They nod
yes, yes, don't worry, it's healing.

My lover wants to hug me, and I say no
not yet, this is still too new

but he leads me to a seat beneath the window
plump with purple cushions, he kisses me
and promises he won't disturb my head

which balances on its stem
like a flower just opened.

As he enters me I touch my neck
very softly and think of the scar I'll have,
the badge of those who've lost their heads and regained them

a fine red necklace, indelible thread.

About the contributors

Linda Chase is an American poet living in Manchester. She is the co-ordinator of the Poetry School in Manchester and founding director of Poets and Players. Her two latest books are published by Carcanet.

June English has three collections of poetry: *Counting the Spots* (Acumen Pamphlets 2000), *The Sorcerer's Arc* (2005) and *Sunflower Equations* (2008), both Hearing Eye. She has set up many poetry initiatives in Kent.

Vicki Feaver has three collections of poetry, *Close Relatives* (Secker 1981), *The Handless Maiden* (Cape 1994), for which she received a Cholmondeley Award, and *The Book of Blood* (Cape 2006). She is an Emeritus Professor at Chichester University.

Kate Foley's fourth collection, *The Silver Rembrandt*, was published by Shoestring Press in 2008. Over time, she has found that writing from personal experience can create a new perspective and depth for both life and work.

Katherine Gallagher is an Australian-born poet and translator, resident in London since 1979. She has four collections of poetry, including most recently, *Circus-Apprentice* (Arc Publications 2006).

Miriam Hastings has published fiction, poetry, and literary criticism; also essays and articles on mental health. She works as a tutor and counsellor, using creative writing as a tool for healing and growth.

Wendy Lawson (Bss, Bsw(Hons) GDip(PsychStud) GDip(Psych)) has an autistic partner, mum, grandmother and friends. Her latest book, *Concepts of Normality* prefers 'diff-ability' to disorder, defines being differently abled in a neuro-diverse world.

Lance Lee is a poet, dramatist, novelist, writer on drama and film, and environmentalist. He lives in California and is active in both the UK and US. His most recent book is *Human/Nature* (poetry).

Grevel Lindop lives in Manchester. His *Selected Poems* and *Playing with Fire* are published by Carcanet. His prose books include *A Literary Guide to the Lake District* and *Travels on the Dance Floor*.

Hilary Llewellyn-Williams has published four collections of poetry, the latest of which is *Greenland* (Seren 2003). Her work is informed by myth, imagination and the natural world. She lives in Gwent, gardens, teaches, and practises psychotherapy.

John Lyons, an award-winning poet and painter, is an experienced public performer of his poetry. He has exhibited nationally and internationally and has paintings in private and public collections. He lives and works in Cambridgeshire.

John Mackay was born in South Yorkshire and now lives in London, where he works as a freelance journalist. His poems have been widely published in magazines.

Mary MacRae lives in London. Her poems have appeared in a number of anthologies. Her first collection, *As Birds Do*, was published by Second Light Publications (2007). She taught English for many years.

Chris McCully was born in Yorkshire in 1958. His sixteen books include *Goodbye, Mr. Wonderful*. In 2009 he is nine years into recovery from alcholism. He lives near the Waddenzee in the north of the Netherlands.

Pascale Petit's last two collections, *The Huntress* and *The Zoo Father* (Seren), were shortlisted for the T. S. Eliot Prize and were Books of the Year in the *TLS*. *The Treekeeper's Tale* appeared in 2008.

Maggie Sawkins lives near Portsmouth where she teaches students with specific learning difficulties. Two Ravens Press published her first full poetry collection, *The Zig Zag Woman*, in 2007. She runs a poetry venue.

Clare Shaw's first poetry collection, *Straight Ahead* was published by Bloodaxe in 2006. She is also widely known for her work and publications around mental health, and is director of harm-ed, a self-harm training organization.

Penelope Shuttle's most recent collection is *Redgrove's Wife* (Bloodaxe Books 2006); it was shortlisted for The Forward Prize For Best Collection, and for the T. S. Eliot Prize. She lives in Cornwall.

Matt Simpson has published six collections of poetry, the most recent is *In Deep* (Shoestring). He has also written poetry for children and several books of literary criticism. He lives in Liverpool.

Duncan Tolmie is a professional calligrapher who lives in Coatbridge in Central Scotland. The passages he quotes are from his first book which he is still working on.

Dilys Wood founded, and is the organizer, of Second Light, a 300 member network of women poets. Publications include *Women Come to a Death* (Katabasis 1997) and *Antarctica* (Greendale 2008). She has co-edited anthologies of women's poetry.

Poetry acknowledgements

The poems, extracts from poems, and pieces of prose in this book are reproduced by permission as required of the publishers, authors, and estates of authors. Thanks are due to all the copyright holders cited below for their kind permission.

Adams, A. 'Dead Letter', *The London Magazine*, December/January 2007.

Bailey, R. V. (2004) 'With You', *Marking Time*. Peterloo Poets.

Baker, Y. 'Revisiting'.

Bellerby, F. (1986) 'Convalescence', *Selected Poems*. Enitharmon Press.

Bennett, D. (2000) 'Black Shells', *American Dresses*. Flarestack Publishing.

Brown, J. (1993) 'Thinking Egg: Poaching', *Thinking Egg*. Littlewood Arc.

Chase, K. (2007) 'Out of the Blue Fell Snow', 'A Magnificent Orange Glare', 'The Duet of Voices', *Land of Stone*. Detroit: Wayne State University Press.

Chase, L. (1995) 'Undressed', *These Goodbyes*. Fatchance Press; (2006) 'Purification', 'Restaurant', 'Scuffing', *Extended Family*. Carcanet Books.

Cluysenaar, A. (2009) 'Seeing that Woman', *Water to Breathe*. Flarestack Publishing.

Darling, J. (2004) 'Nurses', *Apologies for Absence*. Arc Publications. Reprinted by kind permission of Julia Darling's family.

Druce, C. (2006) 'Night Feed', *National Poetry Competition, Winners and Commendations Anthology*. The Poetry Society.

Dutton, E. H. 'Among Strangers'.

English, J. (2004) 'Bunny Girl', 'The Last Kiss', 'The Big C', *The Sorcerer's Arc*. Hearing Eye Books; (2006) 'Thanksgiving', *Images of Women*, (eds Schneider, M. and Wood, D.). Arrowhead Press; (2008) 'Whore Games', *Sunflower Equations*. Hearing Eye Books.

Feaver, V. (1994) 'Women's Blood', *The Handless Maiden*; (2006) 'Girl in Red', 'Hemingway's Hat', *The Book of Blood*. Both books published by Jonathan Cape. Reprinted by permission of the Random House Group.

Feldt, L. D. with Feldt, B., Feldt A. G. and Feldt, D. A., Feldt L. K. (1996) 'Portraits', 'The Unweaving', 'Thirty Nine', *Dying Again*. Ann Arbor: Moon Field Press.

Fogel, V. The Nursing Chair.

Foley, K. (1999) 'Milk', *A Year Without Apricots*. Blackwater Press.

Gallaccio, M. 'Wedding List'.

Gallagher, K. (1989) 'The Affair', 'Lines for an ex', *Fish-Rings on Water*. Forest Books; (2000) '1969', 'Poem for a Shallot', *Tigers on the Silk Road*; (2006) 'On the Pass from Kathmandu', 'At Delphi', *Circus-Apprentice*. Both books, Arc Publications.

Jordan, S. 'Old Friends'.

Khalvati, M. (2007) 'Sundays, Part 1', *The Meanest Flower*. Carcanet Books.

Killick, J. (2008) 'Getting Through 2', *Dementia Diary*. Hawker Publications. 'The Big House', 'Escapist', 'Dreams of my Father', 'In Noirmortier', 'SHORT, SHARP, SHOCKING', 'Women Inside', 'Inside Again', 'Central', 'Last Wish', 'End Note', 'Therapy Circus'.

Latif, T. (1999) 'The Outsider, Section 5', *Skimming the Soul*. Littlewood Press.

Lee, L. (1990) 'Opossum's Death', 'What Happens After', *Wrestling With The Angel*. New York: The Smith; (2001) 'Becoming Human', 'Bats', 'Ravens', 'Totem', *Becoming Human*. Lincoln, USA: Authors Choice Press.

Lindop, G. (2006) 'Night', *Playing With Fire*. Carcanet Books.

Llewellyn-Williams, H. (2003) 'The Badge', *Greenland*. Seren Books.

Loveday, M. (2008) 'Big Mike', *Smiths Knoll*, Issue 43.

Lyons, J. (1989) 'Lure of the Cascadura', 'Tobago Days', 'Carnival', 'Island Muse', *Lure of the Cascadura*. Bogle L'Ouverture; (1994) 'The Game Keeper', 'Livin in Bonne Langue', *Voices From A Silk-Cotton Tree*. Smith/Doorstop Books.

McEvoy, G. (2006) 'Diagnosis', 'Message to the Well-Meaning', *Uncertain Days*. Happenstance Press; (2007) 'Scissors', *Mslexia*, Summer Issue.

McFarland, P. 'Beyond the Pale'.

Mackay, J. 'Coming of Age'.

MacRae, M. (2007) 'Gannet', *I Am Twenty People*, third Poetry School Anthology (eds Khalvati, M. and Knight, S.). Enitharmon Press; (2007) 'Blue Tits', 'By Faversham Creek', *As Birds Do*. Second Light Publications.

Noel-Scott, B. (2000) 'Hansel and Gretel', *Parents* (eds Schneider, M. and Wood, D.). Enitharmon Press.

Petit, P. (2001) 'My Father's Body', 'The Strait Jackets', *The Zoo Father*. Seren Books.

Pizzey, H. 'Sweet Painted Ladies', 'First Love', 'Granny's Party'.

Price, C. (2008) 'The Day My Father Died', *Wishbone*. Shoestring Press.

Redgrove, P. (2006) 'One Wedding, One Funeral', *A Speaker for the Silver Goddess*. Stride Publications. Reprinted by kind permission of the author's estate.

Roper, M. (2008). 'Unbecoming', *Even So: New & Selected Poems*. Dedalus Press.

Rowbotham, C. (2002) 'Christening Gifts', 'Flowers and Thorns', 'Fugue': 'Insanity Rag', 'Blackouts', 'Ward Round', 'Lost', *Lost Connections*. Arnos Press.

Ruth, S. (2003) 'A Crowd', *I Could Become That Woman*. Five Leaves Publications; (2006) 'The Autobiography Class', *My Mother Threw Knives* (eds French, W. Sawkins, M. and Wood, D.). Second Light Publications.

Sawkins, M. (2002) 'Rogue Gene', 'Crossfire', 'The Birds', *Charcot's Pet*. Flarestack Publishing; (2007) 'The Bruise', 'Date Unknown', *The Zig-Zag Woman*. Two Ravens Press.

Schneider, M. (1984) 'Flooring', *Fistful of Yellow Hope*. Littlewood Press; (1998) 'The Panic Bird', 'The Waving Woman', *The Panic Bird*. Enitharmon Press; (2000) 'Belonging', 'Willows', 'Need', *Insisting on Yellow*. Enitharmon Press; (2003) 'Amazon', 'Release', *Writing My Way Through Cancer*. London, Philadelphia: Jessica Kingsley Publishers; (2004) 'Finding My Father, The Old Testament', *Multiplying the Moon*. Enitharmon Press; (2008) 'Bird', *Circling The Core*. Enitharmon Press.

Shaw, C. (2006) 'Poem about Dee Dee', *Straight Ahead*. Bloodaxe Books.

Shuttle, P. (2006) 'Missing You', 'Redgrove's Wife', *Redgrove's Wife*. Bloodaxe Books; (2007) 'The Keening', (2007–8) *The Manhattan Review*, Fall/Winter vol. 13.no. 1.

Simpson, M. (2006) 'Tongues', The River on a Black Day', 'An Autumn Rose', *In Deep*. Shoestring Press.

Stevenson, A. (2005) 'The Victory', *Poems 1955–2005*. Bloodaxe Books.

Sutherland, P. (2008) 'The Waiting Room', *Pendulum, The Poetry of Dreams* (ed. Gaye, D.). Avalanche Books.

Thomas, R. S. (1993) 'The Absence', *Collected Poems 1945–1990*. Dent. By kind permission of the author's estate.

Wilson, V. (2006) 'Denial', *My Mother Threw Knives* (eds French, W., Sawkins, M. and Wood, D.). Second Light Publications.

Wood, D. (2003) 'Veronica', *In the Company of Poets*, (ed. John Rety). Hearing Eye Books. 'Letters to a Dying Friend', 'Lament Based on a Corona of Sonnets'.

Bibliography

Locations of publishers have been included where they are outside the UK.

Introduction

Ruth, S. (eds French, W. and Sawkins, M. and Wood, D.) (2006) *My Mother Threw Knives*. Second Light Publications.

Chapter 1

Angelou, M. (1984) *I Know Why the Caged Bird Sings*. Virago Press.

Cluysenaar, A. (2009) *Water to Breathe*. Flarestack Publishing.

Frame, J. (1987) *To the Is-Land*. Paladin.

Kirkup, J. (1996) *A Child of the Tyne*. Salzburg: University of Salzburg Press.

Rowbotham, C. (2002) *Lost Connections*. Arnos Press, Maggie Hindley, 41 Windermere Avenue, London NW6 6LP.

Schneider, M. (1988) *Crossing Point*. Littlewood Press (Arc Publications).

— (1998) *The Panic Bird*. Enitharmon Press.

— (2000) *Insisting on Yellow*. Enitharmon Press.

— (2004) *Multiplying the Moon*. Enitharmon Press.

— (2007) *Becoming*. Second Light Publications.

Further reading

Dillard, A. (1987) *An American Childhood*. New York: Harper & Row.

Galloway, J. (2008) *This is Not About Me*. Granta Books.

Lee, L. (2006) *Human Nature* ('Late Spring' sequence about relationship with father). Birch Brook Press.

Morrison, B. (2007) *And When Did You Last See Your Father*. Granta Books.

Chapter 2

Bishop, E. (1994) *Collected Prose*. Chatto & Windus.

— (1984) *The Complete Poems 1927–1979*. The Hogarth Press.

Burnside, J. (2006) *A Lie About My Father*. Jonathan Cape.

Dirie, W. (with Miller, C.) (2001) *Desert Flower*. Virago Press.

Doty, M. (2001) *Firebird, A Memoir*. Vintage.

— (1996) *Heaven's Coast*. New York: HarperCollins Publishers.

Feaver, V. (1994) *The Handless Maiden*. Jonathan Cape.

— (2006) *The Book of Blood*. Jonathan Cape.

Field, J. (pseudonym of Milner, M.) (1986) *A Life of One's Own*. Virago Press.

Lee, L. (1990) *Wrestling with the Angel*. New York: The Smith.

— (2001) *Becoming Human*. Lincoln USA: Authors Choice Press.

Roper, M. (2008) *Even So: New & Selected Poems*. Dublin: Dedalus Press.

Stevenson, A. (2005) *Poems 1955–2005*. Bloodaxe Books.

Thomas, R. S. (1993) *Collected Poems 1945–1990*. Dent.

Van Gogh, V. (ed Roskill, M.) (1983) *The Letters of Vincent van Gogh*. Fontana Paperbacks.

Williams, A. (with Brown, R.) (1987) *To Live It is To Know It*. Yorkshire Art Circus.

Winterson, J. (2001) *Oranges are Not the Only Fruit*. Vintage.

Further reading

Cusk, R. (2008) *A Life's Work* (motherhood). Faber and Faber.

Levine, P. (2006) *Stranger to Nothing: Selected Poems* (poverty and work). Bloodaxe Books.

Schneider, M. and Wood, D. (eds) (2006) *Images of Women*. Arrowhead Press.

Chapter 3

Athill, D. (2000) *After a Funeral*. Granta Books.

Bailey, J. (2007) *Can Any Mother Help Me?* Faber and Faber.

Bailey, R. V. (2004) *Marking Time*. Peterloo Poets.

Chase, L. (1995) *These Goodbyes*. Fatchance Press.

— (2006) *Extended Family*. Carcanet.

Gallagher, K. (1989) *Fish-Rings on Water*. Forest Books.

— (2000) *Tigers on the Silk Road*. Arc Publications.

— (2006) *Circus-Apprentice*. Arc Publications.

Ginsberg, D. (2004) *About My Sisters*. New York: HarperCollins Publishers.

Kafka, F. (ed. Haas, W.) (1983) *Letters to Milena*. Penguin.

Keenan, B. (1993) *An Evil Cradling*. Vintage.

Kincaid, J. (1998) *My Brother*. Vintage.

Rety, J. (ed.) (2003) *In the Company of Poets*. Hearing Eye Books.

Rowbotham, R. (2002) *Lost Connections*. Arnos Press, Maggie Hindley, 41 Windermere Avenue, London NW6 6LP.

Ruth, S. (2003) *I Could Become That Woman*. Five Leaves Publications.

Shuttle, P. (2006) *Redgrove's Wife*. Bloodaxe Books.

Simpson, M. (2006) *In Deep*. Shoestring Press.

Further reading

Bass, E. (2007) *A Secret Madness* (marital relationship). Profile Books.

Feinstein, E. (2007) *Talking to the Dead* (marital relationship). Carcanet Press.

Gluck, L. (1998) *Meadowlands* (the end of a marital relationship). Carcanet Press.

Rhys, J. (2000) *Voyage in the Dark*. Penguin Modern Classics.

Van Gogh, V. (ed. Roskill, M.) (1983) *The Letters of Vincent van Gogh*. Fontana Paperbacks.

Chapter 4

Briscoe, C. (2006) *Ugly*. Hodder & Stoughton Ltd.

English, J. (2004) *The Sorcerer's Arc*. Hearing Eye Books.

— (2006) (eds Schneider, M. and Wood, D.) *Images of Women*. Arrowhead Press.

— (2008) *Sunflower Equations*. Hearing Eye Books.

Kirk, P. (ed) (1994) *A Survivor Myself*. Yorkshire Art Circus

Petit, P. (2001) *The Zoo Father*. Seren Books.

Spring, J. (1987) *Cry Hard and Swim*. Virago Press.

Further reading

Pelzer, D. (2004) *My Story*. Orion Books Ltd.

Pennacchia, Y. M. (1994) *Healing the Whole:The Diary of an Incest Survivor*. Continuum International Publishing Group.

Chapter 5

Cheng, N. (1995) *Life and Death in Shanghai*. Flamingo.

Foley, K. (1999) *A Year Without Apricots*. Blackwater Press.

Hoffman, E. (1991) *Lost in Translation*. Minerva.

Keller, H. (1996) *The Story of My Life*. New York: Dover Books.

Latif, T. (1991) *Skimming the Soul*. Littlewood Arc.

Lawson, W. (2000) *Life Behind Glass*. Jessica Kingsley Publishers.

Lyons, J. (1989) *Lure of the Cascadura*. Bogle L'Ouverture.

— (2002) *Voices from a Silk-Cotton Tree*. Smith/Doorstop Books.

Potok, A. (2003) *Ordinary Daylight: Portrait of an Artist Going Blind*. Bantam.

Schneider, M. (2000) *Insisting on Yellow*. Enitharmon Press.

Further reading

Berry, J. (2007) *Windrush Songs* (exile). Bloodaxe Books.

Calderwood, L. (2003) *Cracked: Recovery After Traumatic Brain Injury*. Jessica Kingsley Publishers.

Keenan, D. and Lloyd, R. (eds.) (1990) *Looking for Home: Women Writing about Exile*. Minneapolis: Milkweed Editions.

McConnel, J. (2006) *Life Interrupted: The Memoir of A Nearly Person*, (Tourette's Syndrome). Headline Book Publishing.

Sellin, B. (1995) *In Dark Hours I Find My Way: Messages from an Autistic Mind*. Gollancz.

Chapter 6

Bauby, J.-D. (1998) *The Diving-Bell and the Butterfly*. Fourth Estate.

Bellerby, F. (1986) *Selected Poems*. Enitharmon Press.

McEvoy, G. (2006) *Uncertain Days*. HappenStance.

Sacks, O. (1991) *A Leg to Stand On*. Picador.,

Schneider, M. (2003) *Writing My Way Through Cancer*. Jessica Kingsley Publishers.

Further reading

Bryden, C. (2005) *Dancing with Dementia: My Story of Living Positively with Dementia*. Jessica Kingsley Publishers.

McCrum, R. (1998) *My Year Off*. (Recovering from a stroke). Picador.

Potter, D. (2003) *The Singing Detective* (television filmscript). Faber and Faber.

Chapter 7

Chase, K. (2007) *Land of Stone*. Detroit: Wayne State University Press.

Hastings, M. (1987) *The Minotaur Hunt*. The Harvester Press.

McCully, C. (2004) *Goodbye, Mr. Wonderful*. Jessica Kingsley Publishers.

Murray, L. (1993) *Translations from the Natural World*. Carcanet Press.

— (1997) *Killing the Black Dog*. NSW: The Federation Press.

— (2003) *New Collected Poems*. Carcanet Press.

Rowbotham, C. (2002) *Lost Connections*. Arnos Press, Maggie Hindley, 41 Windermere Avenue, London NW6 6LP.

Schneider, M. (1984) *Fistful of Yellow Hope*. Littlewood Press (Arc Publications).

Shaw, C. (2006) *Straight Ahead*. Bloodaxe Books.

Further reading

Hornbacher, M. (1998) *Wasted, A Memoir of Anorexia and Bulimia*. New York: HarperCollins Publishers.

Jamison, K. R. (1996) *An Unquiet Mind* (manic depression). Picador.

Plath, S. (2005) *The Belljar*. Faber and Faber.

Styron, W. (2004) *Darkness Visible*. Vintage.

Chapter 8

Druce, C. (2006) *National Poetry Competition Winners and Commendations Anthology*. The Poetry Society.

Ginsberg, D. (2003) *Raising Blaze*. New York: HarperCollins Publishers.

Gross, P. (1998) *The Wasting Game*. Bloodaxe Books.

Khalvati, M. (2007) *The Meanest Flower*. Carcanet Press.

Plath, S. (2002) *Collected Poems*. Faber and Faber.

Sawkins, M. (2002) *Charcot's Pet*. Flarestack Publishing.

— (2007) *The Zig-Zag Woman*. Two Ravens Press.

Starkman, E. M. (1993) *Learning to Sit in the Silence*. Watsonville, CA: Papier-Mache Press.

Further reading

Hale, S. (2007) *The Man Who Lost His Language: A Case of Aphasia*. Jessica Kingsley Publishers.

Olds, S. (1996) *The Wellspring* (part 3, caring for children). Jonathan Cape.

Wearing, D. (2005) *Forever Today: A Memoir of Love and Amnesia*. Corgi Books.

Chapter 9

Bennett, D. (2000) *American Dresses*. Flarestack Publishing.

Didion, J. (2005) *The Year of Magical Thinking*. Fourth Estate.

— (2008) *The Year of Magical Thinking Playscript*. Fourth Estate.

Hurndall, J. (2007) *Defy the Stars*. Bloomsbury Publishing.

Lewis, C. S. (1961) *A Grief Observed*. Faber and Faber.

Price, C. (2008) *Wishbone*. Shoestring Press.

Redgrove, P. (2006) *A Speaker for the Silver Goddess*. Stride Publications.

Schneider, M. (2003) *Writing My Way Through Cancer*. Jessica Kingsley Publishers.

— (2004) *Multiplying the Moon*. Enitharmon Press.

Shuttle, P. (2006) *Redgrove's Wife*. Bloodaxe Books.

Further reading

Hall, D. (2003) *The Painted Bed*. New York: Houghton Mifflin Company.

Moffat, M. J. (ed) (1992) *In the Midst of Winter*. Vintage.

Walker, T. (1992) *The Last of England*. Phoenix.

Zeitlin, S. and Harlow, I. (eds) (2001) *Giving Voice to Sorrow: Personal Responses to Death and Mourning*. New York: Perigee Trade.

Chapter 10

Adams, A. *The London Magazine*, December/January 2007.

Athill, D. (2008) *Somewhere Near the End*. Granta Books.

Darling, J. (2004) *Apology for Absence*. Arc Publications.

Feldt, L. D. with Feldt, B., Feldt A. G. and Feldt, D. A., Feldt, L. K. (1996) *Dying Again*. Ann Arbor: Moon Field Press.

Further reading

De Hennezel, M. (1997) *Intimate Death: How the Dying Teach Us to Live*. Little, Brown.

Selzer, R. (2001) *Raising the Dead: A Doctor's Encounter With His Own Mortality*. Michigan State University Press.

Chapter 11

Dillard, A (1984) Teaching a Stone to Talk: Expeditions and Encounters: Picador books.

Killick, J. (2008) *Dementia Diary*. Hawker Publications.

Lindop, G. (2006) *Playing with Fire*. Carcanet Books.

MacRae, M. (eds Khalvati, M and Knight, S) (2007) *I am Twenty People*, third Poetry School Anthology. Enitharmon Press.

— (2007) *As Birds Do*. Second Light Publications.

Poitier, S. (2000) *The Measure of a Man*. San Francisco: Harper.

Schneider, M. (2008) *Circling the Core*. Enitharmon Press.

Further reading

Burnside, J. (2007) *Gift Songs*. Jonathan Cape.

Cousineau, P. (ed) (1995) *Soul: An Archaeology*. Thorsons.

Levertov, D. (2003) *New Selected Poems*. Bloodaxe Books.

Lindbergh, A. M. (1991) *Gift From the Sea*. New York: Pantheon Books.

Roper, M. (2008) *Halcyon*, article in *The North 42*.

Chapter 14

Frame, J. (2000) *Faces in the Water*. The Women's Press Ltd.

Noel-Scott, B. (eds Schneider, M. and Wood, D.) (2000) *Parents*. Enitharmon Press.

Sawkins, M. (2007) *The Zig-Zag Woman*. Two Ravens Press.

Sutherland, P. (ed Gaye, D) (2008) *Pendulum, The Poetry of Dreams*. Avalanche Books.

Wilson, V. (eds French, W., Sawkins, M. and Wood, D.) (2006) *My Mother Threw Knives*. Second Light Publications.

Chapter 15

Doty, M. (1995) *PN Review*, Issue 104.

— (1996) *Heaven's Coast*. New York: HarperCollins Publishers.

Fowles, J. (2000) *The Tree*. Vintage.

Jones, D. (1975) *In Parenthesis*. Faber and Faber.

McEvoy, G. (2007) *Mslexia*, Summer Issue.

Rainer, T (1980) *The New Diary*. Angus & Robertson Publishers.

Schneider, M. (2000) *Insisting on Yellow*. Enitharmon Press.

Slater, L (2000) *Spasm: A Memoir With Lies*. Methuen.

Further reading

Abse, D. (2008) *The Presence* (journal). Vintage.

Chapter 16

Sawkins, M. (2002) *Charcot's Pet*. Flarestack Publishing.

Conclusion

Clendinnen, I. (2001) *Tiger's Eye: A Memoir*. Cape.

Hunt, C. and Sampson, F. (2006) *Writing: Self and Reflexivity*. Palgrave Macmillan.

Llewellyn-Williams, H. (2003) *Greenland*. Seren Books.

Further reading: General list

Bolton, G. (1999) *The Therapeutic Potential of Creative Writing – Writing Myself*. Jessica Kingsley Publishers.

Field, V. and Ansari, Z. (2007) *Prompted to Write*. Fal Publications.

Goldberg, N. (2005) *Writing Down the Bones*. Boston, US: Shambala Publications Inc.

Manjusvara (2005) *Writing Your Way*. Windhorse Publications.

Index

Titles of poetry collections are not included in this index
but they appear with the actual poems.

The index lists key subjects which do not appear in the chapter titles